5

Sex and the Sexual during People's Leisure and Tourism Experiences

Sex and the Sexual during People's Leisure and Tourism Experiences

Edited by

Neil Carr and Yaniv Poria

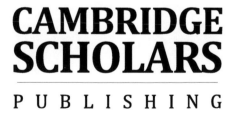

CAMBRIDGE
SCHOLARS

PUBLISHING

Sex and the Sexual during People's Leisure and Tourism Experiences,
Edited by Neil Carr and Yaniv Poria

This book first published 2010

Cambridge Scholars Publishing

12 Back Chapman Street, Newcastle upon Tyne, NE6 2XX, UK

British Library Cataloguing in Publication Data
A catalogue record for this book is available from the British Library

ISBN (10): 1-4438-2229-9, ISBN (13): 978-1-4438-2229-9

TABLE OF CONTENTS

List of Figures vii

List of Tables ix

Chapter One 1
Introduction: Provision, Marketing, and Consumption of Sex
and the Sexual in the Leisure and Tourism Environment
Neil Carr and Yaniv Poria

Part I: Provision of Sex and the Sexual in the Leisure and Tourism Experience

Chapter Two 17
Sex Shops of the 21st Century: Are 'you' being Served?
Neil Carr and Steve Taylor

Chapter Three 35
Parallel Universes: Male Sex Trade in Public Spaces of Veracruz, México
Rosío Córdova Plaza

Chapter Four 57
Flying Tigers in a Dominican Tourist Town
Deirdre Guthrie

Chapter Five 81
Regulatory Space and Child Sex Tourism: The Case of Canada
and Mexico
Linda M. Ambrosie

Part II: Sexual Behaviour and Desires in the Leisure and the Tourism Experience

Chapter Six 105
Casual Sex and the Backpacking Experience: The Case of Israeli Women
Liza Berdychevsky, Yaniv Poria and Natan Uriely

Chapter Seven 119
Sexual Encounters between Men in a Tourist Environment:
A Comparative Study in Seven Mexican Localities
Álvaro López López and Anne Marie Van Broeck

Chapter Eight 143
White Gay Women's Leisure Spaces in Bloemfontein, South Africa
Gustav Visser

Chapter Nine 165
Queering the Pitch: An Exploration of Gay Men's Amateur Football
in the UK
Louisa Jones and Mac McCarthy

Chapter Ten 181
What Have We Done and Where Should We Go?
Yaniv Poria and Neil Carr

Contributors 197

LIST OF FIGURES

2.1   Sex shop website female imagery
3.1   Male prostitution circuit at the historic centre
3.2   Boca del Río area and the historic centre
4.1   Messages and host/guest relations
4.2   The Beach as meeting place
7.1   Main tourist destinations in Mexico, 2005
7.2   Gay places in Mexican towns, as per an international tourism gay
        guide
7.3   Age of the interviewed sex workers
8.1   Gay women's leisure spaces of support and avoidance (2006)
8.2   Gay women's leisure spaces of support and avoidance (2008)
8.3   Gay men's leisure spaces of support and avoidance (2006)

LIST OF TABLES

2.1   Number of sex shop websites studied by country
2.2   Products available in sex shops
8.1   Biographical details of participants

CHAPTER ONE

INTRODUCTION:
PROVISION, MARKETING, AND CONSUMPTION
OF SEX AND THE SEXUAL IN THE LEISURE
AND TOURISM ENVIRONMENT

NEIL CARR AND YANIV PORIA

Introduction

Sex and the sexual, in all its diversity, is a constant feature of contemporary society both within and beyond the boundaries of a leisured context. Sex may be defined as an act that leads to physical sexual stimulation and includes a variety of penetrative and non-penetrative acts. These acts can be undertaken in a variety of locations and with a range of types of partners (either as couples or larger groups) or individually (Gini, 2006). Sexual, whilst obviously related to sex, is not directly a physical act. Rather, sexual refers to everything that, suggests, promises, and/or stimulates sex.

Today, a significant and diverse array of items and experiences designed for sexual purposes are available to the individual. These include, the sex and sexual services and products provided by the sex industry which incorporates brothels, individual prostitutes/sex workers, the sex film industry, sex magazines (including the infamous Playboy magazine and its less well known Playgirl counterpart), sex shops (both on-line and on the urban High Street), pole dancing venues, sex toys (including vibrators and blow-up dolls) and medication (such as Viagra) manufacturers. In addition to deliberately offering sex or overtly sexual products, indirect provision of products and experiences that offer sexual stimulation is widespread. Mainstream television broadcasts, movies, and video games are examples of this where they are not primarily focused on sex and/or the sexual but often include content of a sexual nature. Indeed, a variety of studies have been undertaken that have identified the widespread nature of sex and sexual references in material shown on television (Gunter, 2002). Similarly widespread is the promise or at least suggestion of sex in a wide range of marketing campaigns (Stern, 1991). The diversity of the sex industry and the myriad ways in which sex and the sexual is utilised and portrayed throughout society means, according to Gini (2006: 180) that we live today in a "sex-saturated society." Consequently, it is perhaps not surprising to find that the consumption of and engagement in sex and the sexual has assumed a central place in contemporary societies. This encompasses everything from gazing at sexualized advertisements to the active search by people, individually and/or with partners/groups, for sexual stimulation and intimate contact.

Consumption of sexual items and experiences is commonly, though not necessarily exclusively, undertaken during leisure time. This consumption is enhanced through the common depiction in marketing campaigns of the holiday destination as a sexualised environment. Indeed, the use of sexual innuendo, erotic images, and the sexualized—most commonly female—body to 'promise' sex has been a common and widespread feature of tourism marketing campaigns (Cater & Clift, 2000; Ryan & Hall, 2001). Furthermore, McKercher and Bauer (2003) have noted that a wide variety of tourist destinations have promoted themselves based on associations with love, romance, and sex. Amongst such destinations, Paris is arguably the most famous. Infamous red-light districts such as in Amsterdam and London have also become a feature of these cities tourism and leisure industries and the images they sell (Oppermann, 1998).

The consumption of sex and the sexual in the leisure and tourism environment incorporates everything from the direct consumption and pursuit of sexual encounters in holiday destinations such as Ibiza and Hedonism II and III in Jamaica to the utilization of bars and nightclubs as pick-up joints for the pursuit of casual sexual encounters. The beach is also used in a variety of sexualised ways, including voyeuristic ones, as is the hotel room which can be viewed as a miniature and more intimate version of the liminal space which the entire holiday destination represents. In addition to the consumption of sex and the sexual at sites in the leisure environment designed at least partially for this purpose, a variety of sites have been utilized in sexualized ways that they were never designed for. For example, as early as 1975 Humphreys noted the manner in which public conveniences in parks were used by gay men for casual sexual encounters.

At the point of consumption of leisure and tourism experiences the individual may also sexualize the experience and/or themselves through their own actions and thoughts. This recognizes the personal agency of the individual in becoming a sexual being rather than existing as just a sexual object. Consequently, it is the actions and desires of the individual that drive the sexual nature and direction of the leisure and tourism experience though this may be influenced by the leisure and tourism sectors as well as marketing generated images of the sexual. This means that the sexual nature of the leisure and tourism experiences will always be open to negotiation and hence in a constant state of evolution as the behaviours of the individual influence the sexual images associated with specific environments and experiences. Support for the agency of the individual in the sexualisation of a leisure experience is provided by Collins (2006: 1) who asks the reader to:

> "Consider the large packs of men and women who roam, in circuit drinking mode, the huge number of pubs and bars of Newcastle, England (and of course many other towns and cities around the world). They are not only engaged in socialising and drinking, but are also instinctively aware that opportunities for sexual contact can be acquired through this route."

Despite all the apparent richness and diversity of the topic of sex and the sexual in the leisure and tourism experience there has arguably been a relative dearth of publications on the topic. *Sex and the sexual during people's leisure and tourism experiences* provides an initial response to this critique. As such, the book is designed to highlight emerging work on sex and the sexual in the leisure and tourism experience. Furthermore, the book is a call and potential map for further research that can fully capture and understand the rich diversity and complexity of sex and the sexual in the leisure and tourism experience without being inhibited by a moral straightjacket.

Furthering understandings of sex and the sexual in tourism and leisure potentially offers a range of beneficial outcomes. Beyond the obvious addition to academic knowledge in tourism and leisure developing understandings of sex and the sexual in these fields offers a lens through which the wider social realm can be viewed. This allows links between social constructions of deviance and morality and their link to sex and the sexual to be explored. Such studies also highlight the mundane, and the role leisure and tourism play in it. The research highlighted in this book also has a variety of implications for the leisure and tourism industries both in terms of what they offer potential consumers and how they market their products and services.

The book begins by highlighting why sex and the sexual in the leisure and tourism experience have been relatively understudied to date.

However, before this is examined it is important to briefly identify what is meant by 'leisure' and 'tourism' and the relation between these two phenomena within the context of this book. This is necessary as it is recognised that the material presented in the book may appeal to those outside of the field of leisure and tourism research who, consequently, may not be familiar with the rich debates that have shaped the definitions of these two terms.

The meaning of 'leisure' and 'tourism' and their interrelatedness

Defining 'leisure' has been an ongoing issue since the emergence of it as an academic field of study in the modern era. A common thread of most attempts to define leisure has been the establishment of commonalities between contemporary leisure and leisure as defined by philosophers in the Ancient Greek civilization such as Socrates, Aristotle, and Plato. The product of debates about the meaning of leisure has been the conceptualisation of it as a time, activity, and state of mind that is differentiated from 'work' in that it entails an activity that is relatively freely undertaken primarily for purposes of pleasure that is internally rewarding to the individual. This is not to say that pleasure can only be found in the leisure environment but that leisure is different, if not distinct, from non-leisure (i.e., 'work') experiences. In the latter we recognise that individual freedom is overtly curtailed by the employer and/or other agencies external to the individual. In contrast, in leisure whilst absolute freedom is impossible given the continued presence of socio-cultural norms and values that constrain behaviour and desires there exists a perception of freedom that is bolstered by the absence of overt externally imposed rules. This identifies the leisure environment, where leisure experiences are consumed and performed, as a liminal space where any rules that govern this environment are distinct from and less constraining than the rules associated with the non-leisure/work environment.

Consequently, the cornerstones of contemporary definitions of leisure are the concepts of perceived and relative freedom (Iso-Ahola, 1999; Neulinger, 1974; Roberts, 1978). Indeed, Godbey (2003: 5) has stated that "the important thing in defining an experience as leisure is that individuals believe that they are free or that they are controlling events rather than being controlled by events." This measure of freedom allows people to behave during their leisure experiences in a manner that would not necessarily be socially acceptable outside of a leisure setting. Within the context of sex and the sexual the implications of perceived, relative freedom are, of course, significant as it suggests that during leisure people are more able to engage in sex and sexually related behaviours as well as different types and forms of sex than outside of leisure.

Tourism and leisure academics have often worked in isolation from one another with the result that concepts derived from work in one field of study have not always been utilised in the other (Harris, et al., 1987; Smith & Godbey, 1991). Despite this, it has been argued that there is a strong link between tourism and leisure (Mannell & Iso-Ahola, 1987; Ryan & Glendon, 1998). A variety of links between tourism and leisure have been identified, including the suggestion that the socio-cultural influences that govern the nature of individual behaviour and desires cut across both leisure and tourism experiences even when individual observable behaviour may differ across the two (Carr, 2002a).

Based on the recognition of a link between tourism and leisure the former has been defined as leisure on the move (Shaw & Williams, 2002). Yet not all moments of a tourism experience may entail leisure. Rather, tourism experiences include timeframes in which leisure may occur. The duration of these timeframes is dependent on the nature of the individual tourism experience engaged in. Therefore, a 'tourist' may be someone who travels away from their home for at least one night, but not permanently, at least partially for leisure (i.e., non-work) purposes. One of the primary motivations for taking a holiday has been identified as 'escape'; the chance to break free of the socio-cultural bounds that govern their behaviour in their home environment. As such, the perception of freedom is central to both leisure and tourism experiences.

Within the framework of these definitions of leisure and tourism place becomes the feature that distinguishes these two social phenomena. Leisure is associated with the home environment (i.e., the locale in which the individual lives) and tourism with the holiday environment (i.e., a place located away from the home). The physical and socio-cultural distance between the home and holiday environments is potentially important as it may provide the opportunity for the loosening of social restraint and an associated increase in perceive personal freedom for the tourist compared to in the leisure environment (Carr, 2002b).

So where does sex and the sexual fit in

Despite the key role of sex and the sexual in the history of humanity there has, arguably been a dearth of publications on the topic. Indeed, Hawkes (2004: 1) has argued that sociology in particular has, "until relatively recently, ignored the two most fundamental aspects for humankind – sex and death." This situation has arguably been mirrored in other social science/humanities disciplines. Sex and the sexual in the public arena appear to have been an especially taboo subject for general debate and academic study (Hubbard, 2002). Indeed, Tuan (1998: 50) has stated that "Sex is the ultimate private act. Ethnographers who do not hesitate to intrude upon the most intimate behaviours in the name of their science hesitate to observe and record the sex act." The relative lack of analysis of sex may be related to a traditional tendency to avoid talk of sex in general society as it is deemed a socially inappropriate topic for open discussion and by academics due to concerns about the ethical sensitivities of studies of sex and the sexual. Furthermore, academics may have avoided analysis of sex and the sexual due to problems associated with collecting accurate data on the subject. For example, Earle and Sharp (2007: 1) have stated that "men who pay for sex are less readily located and it has been difficult for researchers to find men willing to participate in social research." Additionally, the study of sex behaviour has been labelled a 'mundane' activity and as such it has been identified as being less prestigious and important for academic research (Cohen & Avieli, 2004; Larsen, 2008).

With particular reference to leisure and tourism studies relatively little material has been published that has focused on issues of sex and/or the sexual[1]. This is problematic given the statement by Gini (2006: 173) that people have sex because "It feels good. It's fun. We like it, a lot! And so, we pursue it and do it, as often as possible. Sex is, arguably, humankind's most common and immediate form of pleasure and entertainment." While this clearly places sex within the remit of leisure it is important to recognise that this is not necessarily the case for all sex or everyone engaged in anything sexual. Whilst not disputing the fact that pleasure can be a significant component of sex, at least for those voluntarily engaged in it, and leisure Szasz (1968: 116) provides a suggestion of how socially constructed moral values may have split the two when stating that "When the Catholic Church invented the dogma of the Original Sin, the idea was to brand sexual pleasure as something shameful, filthy, abominable, so that anyone indulging in it should feel guilty and afraid of punishment."

Beyond the general avoidance of sex as a research topic within academic circles the dearth of such work in leisure studies may be related to a tendency within the discipline to focus on the central ground of 'conventional morality' (Rojek, 1999; Veal & Lynch, 2001); either

---

[1] Sexuality being a distinct issue concerned with sexual-orientation which has, in recent years, been extensively studied within leisure and tourism studies

avoiding discussion of morally questionable leisure activities or analysing them from a 'moral' perspective. A similar argument may be made to explain the relative lack of analysis of sex and the sexual in the tourism experience. As a consequence of the tendency in tourism and leisure studies to remain within the bounds of conventional morality there appears to have been a lack of transfer of potentially relevant research on sex and the sexual outside of leisure and tourism studies into the disciplines. For example, some work has been conducted on the use of sex in marketing that arguably has relevance for understanding the leisure and tourism experiences but this material has yet to be utilised within the fields of leisure and tourism studies.

Given the general conformity to conventional morality it is not surprising that the main foci of the limited amount of work that has been undertaken on sex within the leisure and tourism experience has dealt with the issue of morality. For example, some work has been undertaken looking at the sex trade in general and child sex tourism in particular from a conventional morality perspective within the context of tourism (e.g., Beddoe, et al, 2001). Although this moral perspective on sex is a worthy area of study it is only a small segment of the wide arena of sex in leisure and tourism. This view is reinforced by McKercher & Bauer (2003: 4), who have stated that whilst the focus on studies of sex tourism and child sex tourism has "helped raise awareness of legitimate issues, the commercialization of sex and tourism represents only a small portion of the total spectrum of tourism and human sexual relationships." Yet whilst a moral perspective may be of value it also potentially results in colonial style moralising and cultural blindness (Ryan & Hall, 2001). Outside of the conventional morality perspective sex, the sexual, and the sensual have been identified as motivators for travel but there are almost no studies that have focused exclusively on this subject. Indeed, even amongst studies of tourist motivation sex has often been disregarded.

Whatever the reason, the result of a lack of analysis of sex and the sexual in the leisure and tourist experience has been a limited and rather biased understanding of the complexity of the role sex and the sexual plays in the construction and nature of both leisure and tourism experiences and how this is influenced by and feeds back into the general society and non-leisure environments. This is particularly important as tourism and leisure (as well as sex and the sexual) play a significant role in our daily lives. This critique recognises the need for the boundaries of research on sex in the leisure and tourism environments to move beyond morally defined analyse to fully understand the place and nature of sex in leisure and tourism.

A general global trend towards social liberalisation may be responsible for a toning down of the established taboo on discussions and public displays of sex and the sexual. This trend has arguably led to previously hidden sexual desires and experiences being displayed more publicly than in the past (Ryder, 2006). As part of this process Cameron (2006: 17) has stated that "The Internet is helping to create an image where it is seen as a more everyday thing to express sexual fetishes, buy sexual 'toys', hire escorts, look at pornography, etc." Reducing taboos associated with sex and the sexual may have driven and been driven by social acceptance of sexual displays. An example of this process arguably includes the legalisation of prostitution in New Zealand in 2003. In addition, it is now becoming common to see sexually related products including edible body paints, condoms, and vibrators on the shelves of mainstream retailers such as Wal-Mart (Heinecken, 2007). There has also been a growth in the presence of adult entertainment shops on urban high streets that indicates an increasing social acceptance of expressions of sex and the sexual (Pattinson, 2004). The liberalisation of displays and discussion of sex and the sexual indicate the timely nature of investigations into sex in the tourism and leisure experiences. A reduction in taboos associated with displays and discussions of sex and the sexual may also have an effect on the role of sex in tourism and leisure experiences. This increases the need for research into sex and the sexual in the leisure and tourism environments. Another reason for looking at sex and the sexual in the leisure and tourism experience is a growing recognition that analysis of the mundane is not only important to developing understandings of tourism and leisure, but that everyday activities play an important role in leisure and tourism experiences (Cohen & Avieli, 2004; Larsen, 2008).

Given its focus and cross-disciplinary nature this book should appeal to researchers and students across the humanities and social sciences both for the value of the research in its own right and the ability of it to be used as a lens through which to view the position of sex and the sexual in society in general as well as within the tourism and leisure experiences in particular. The material presented in the book should also be of interest to health scholars and psychologists concerned with sexual behaviour and health, with a particular focus on sexually transmitted diseases

Book Structure

The work displayed in this book cuts across a variety of academic disciplines bringing a diverse range of viewpoints and conceptualisations to the debate about sex in the leisure and tourism experience. This diversity reflects the cross-disciplinary nature of analysis of leisure and tourism. The diversity of disciplinary viewpoints presented in the chapters of this book provides the foundation for the development of understandings of sex and the sexual in the leisure and tourism experience that are uninhibited by artificial disciplinary boundaries. The chapters are broadly divided into two sections; the first of which examines the provision of and for sex in leisure and tourism experiences. The second section focuses on the experience of sex and the sexual in the leisure and tourism environment. These research based chapters encompass a wide range of leisure and tourism experiences and geographical locales.

The first section of the book begins with a look at contemporary physical sex shops via the content of their websites. As the authors, Carr and Taylor, argue these outlets have traditionally been defined as a space dominated by the heterosexual male. This chapter shows how the research that has been undertaken on women-focused sex shops speaks from the perspective of the morally acceptable empowerment of women; conforming to the tendency of research on sex and the sexual to be situated within socially constructed conventional morality. Carr and Taylor's findings suggest that the sex shops of today are attempting to cater to a diverse range of sexualities and both genders, though the heterosexual male tends to be the primary focus of the majority of sex shops and relatively few women or homosexual focused shops exist. The next chapter, by Córdova-Plaza, talks about the gay sex trade and how it is negotiated within public. This negotiation requires the camouflaging of the trade whilst simultaneously advertising its products. As such this chapter is related to the work of Humphreys in 1975 on the 'tea room' trade that examined the casual gay sex experiences of men in public conveniences. The chapter also shows how socio-cultural norms and values govern the positioning of sex within the tourism experience. Discussion of this issue is continued in chapter 4, entitled 'Flying Tigers in a Dominican Tourist Town,' where the representation and positioning of women hosts in the tourist destination is studied. The chapter examines the sexualisation of the female body, the policing of it by socio-cultural norms and values, and the role of the individual women in these processes. Chapter 5 discusses the morally sensitive issue of child sex tourism and the problematic issue of law enforcement authorities' efforts to combat this phenomenon. It recognises how definitions of acceptability and deviance are constantly evolving and space specific which can be problematic when dealing with international tourists who transcend national legal boundaries. Interestingly, the chapter notes how regulations are "more often than not negotiated by and for adult men;" an issue that is clearly potentially problematic when it is recognised that adult males are the main participants in child sex tourism.

The second section of the book, which focuses on experience of sex and the sexual in the leisure and tourism environment, begins by examining the sexual behaviour of women in the holiday experience. As such, chapter 6 marks a recognition of the sexual empowerment of women. The authors, Berdychevsky, et al., examine both the quantity and quality of sexual experiences from the perspective of their female participants and illustrate the diversity of these experiences. Chapter 7 focuses on the sexual encounters of gay men and identifies how the nature of the encounter is influenced by the space in which it occurs. Drawing on work based in Mexico the material presented in this chapter whilst distinct from that studied in chapter 3 complements, and is complemented by, the work highlighted in the latter. In contrast to chapters 6 and 7 the material presented in chapter 8 is clearly focused in the leisure environment rather than the tourism one. It also focuses on the sexual experiences of a group not previously studied in this section of the book; namely the lesbian population. The need for the work focused on lesbians is based not only on the significance of this population but also the relative neglect of lesbians to date by tourism and leisure academics compared to the gay male population (Hughes, 2006). The chapter maps, both temporally and spatially, the seeking of sexual experiences of lesbians across the urban landscape of Bloemfontein, South Africa. The final chapter in this section is based on the recognition of the growing significance of openly gay competitors and participants in sports. In particular, the chapter focuses on the gay football scene in the UK and the experiences and motivations of its participants. The chapter offers a lens to see how leisure and non-leisure experiences are interrelated and how identities developed in one can be utilised in the other.

The final chapter of the book provides a discussion of the main contributions to tourism and leisure research by the material presented in *Sex and the sexual during people's leisure and tourism experiences*. Following this discussion an attempt is made to provide a theoretical framework that conceptualises the roles sex and sexual desire play in tourism and leisure. Finally, the chapter examines potential new directions for research on sex in the tourism and leisure experience and methodological approaches to such studies. This includes recognition of ethical issues concerning research on sex that stress the need to avoid harming potential research participants whilst at the same time warning against the dangers of not undertaking research based on the perceived morality of the material to be studied.

References

Beddoe, C., Hall, C. M. and Ryan, C. 2001. *The incidence of sexual exploitation of children in tourism.* Madrid: World Tourism Organization

Cameron, S. 2006. Space, risk and opportunity: The evolution of paid sex markets. A. Collins (ed). *Cities of pleasure: Sex and the urban socialscape.* Routledge: London. pp. 13 - 27

Carr, N. 2002a. The tourism-leisure behavioural continuum. *Annals of Tourism Research.* 29 (4): 972 - 986

—. 2002b. Going with the flow: An assessment of the relationship between young people's leisure and holiday behaviour. *Tourism Geographies.* 4 (2): 115 - 134

Cater, S. and Clift, S. 2000. Tourism, international travel and sex: Themes and research. S. Clift and S. Carter (eds). *Tourism and sex: Culture, commerce and coercion.* London: Pinter. pp. 1 – 19

Cohen. E. and Avieli, N. 2004. Food in tourism: Attraction and impediment. *Annals of Tourism Research.* 31 (4): 755-778.

Collins, A. 2006. Sexuality and sexual services in the urban economy and socialscape: An overview. A. Collins (ed). *Cities of pleasure: Sex and the urban socialscape.* Routledge: London. pp 1 - 11

Earle, S. and Sharp, K. 2007. *Sex in cyberspace: Men who pay for sex.* Aldershot: Ashgate

Gini, A. 2006. *Why it's hard to be good.* New York: Routledge

Godbey, G. 2003. *Leisure in your life: An exploration* (6th ed). State College: Venture Publishing

Gunter, B. 2002. *Media sex: What are the issues?* London: Lawrence Erlbaum Associates

Harris, C. C., McLaughlin, W. J. and Ham, S. H. 1987. Integration of recreation and tourism in Idaho. *Annals of Tourism Research.* 14: 405 - 419

Hawkes, G. 2004. *Sex & pleasure in Western culture.* Cambridge: Polity Press

Heinecken, D. 2007. Toys are us: Contemporary feminisms and the consumption of sexuality. A. Hall and M. Bishop (eds). *Pop porn: Pornography in American culture.* Westport: Praeger. pp. 121 – 136

Hubbard, P. 2002. Maintaining family values? Cleansing the streets of sex advertising. *Area.* 34 (4): 353 - 360

Hughes, H. 2006. Lesbians as tourists: Poor relations of a poor relation. *Tourism and Hospitality Research.* 7 (1): 17 - 26

Humphreys, L. 1975. *Tearoom trade: Impersonal sex in public places. Enlarged edition with a retrospect on ethical issues.* Chicago: Aldine Publishing Company

Iso-Ahola, S. E. 1999. Motivational foundations of leisure. E. Jackson and T. Burton (eds). *Leisure studies for the twenty-first century.* State College, PA: Venture Publishing, Inc. pp. 35 - 51

Larsen, J. 2008. De-exoticizing tourist travel: Everyday life and sociality on the move. *Leisure Studies.* 27(1): 21-34.

Mannell, R. C. and Iso-Ahola, S. E. 1987. Psychological nature of leisure and tourism experience. *Annals of Tourism Research.* 14: 314 - 331

McKercher, B. and Bauer, T. 2003. Conceptual framework of the nexus between tourism, romance, and sex. T. Bauer and B. McKercher (eds). *Sex and tourism: Journeys of romance, love and lust.* New York: The Haworth Hospitality Press. pp. 3 - 17

Neulinger, J. 1974. *The Psychology of leisure.* Springfield: C. C. Thomas

Oppermann, M. 1998. Introduction. M. Oppermann (ed). *Sex tourism and prostitution: Aspects of leisure, recreation, and work.* New York: Cognizant Communication Corporation. pp. 1 – 19

Pattinson, G. 2004. Selling sex on the high street. *BBC News.* http://news.bbc.co.uk/2/hi/uk_news/magazine/3998481.stm. 30/3/09

Roberts, K. 1978. *Contemporary society and the growth of leisure.* London: Longman

Rojek, C. 1999. Deviant leisure: The dark side of free-time activity. E. Jackson and T. Burton (eds). *Leisure Studies: Prospects for the twenty-first century.* State College, PA: Venture Publishing, Inc. pp. 81 - 95

Ryan, C. and Glendon, I. 1998. Application of leisure motivation scale to tourism. *Annals of Tourism Research.* 25 (1):169 - 184

Ryan, C. and Hall, C. M. 2001. *Sex tourism: Marginal people and liminalities.* London: Routledge

Ryder, A. 2006. The changing nature of adult entertainment districts: Between a rock and a hard place or going from strength to strength. A. Collins (ed). *Cities of pleasure: Sex and the urban socialscape.* London: Routledge. pp 29 - 56

Shaw, G. and Williams, A. 2002. *Critical issues in tourism: A geographical perspective* (2nd ed). Oxford: Blackwell Publishers Ltd

Smith, L. J. and Godbey, G. C. 1991. Leisure, recreation and tourism. *Annals of Tourism Research.* 18 (1): 85 - 100

Stern, B. 1991. Two pornographies: A feminist view of sex in advertising. *Advances in Consumer Research.* 18: 384 – 391

Szasz, K. 1968. *Petishism: Pet cults of the western world.* London: Hutchinson & Co

Tuan, Y-F. 1998. *Escapism.* Baltimore: The Johns Hopkins University
    Press
Veal, A. and Lynch, R. 2001. *Australian leisure* (2nd ed). Frenchs Forest:
    Longman

PART I:

PROVISION OF SEX AND THE SEXUAL
IN THE LEISURE AND TOURISM EXPERIENCE

CHAPTER TWO

SEX SHOPS OF THE 21ST CENTURY: ARE 'YOU' BEING SERVED?

NEIL CARR AND STEVE TAYLOR

Introduction

A sex shop, for the purpose of this chapter has been defined as a shop with a physical location as opposed to one that exists exclusively on the Internet or as a mail-order entity. It stocks products that are mainly, though not necessarily exclusively, of a sexual nature. These products may include videos/DVD's, magazines/books, sex toys, lingerie, and sex pills/potions. Such shops may, but do not necessarily have to describe themselves as a sex/adult entertainment/erotica shop or give themselves a similar title. The definition of sex shops utilised in this chapter does not include establishments where sexual acts may be purchased or live acts of a sexual nature are on offer.

The sex industry has been widely labelled as deviant. Indeed, in polite society simply talking about sex has long been viewed as a taboo subject (Gini, 2006). Furthermore, within an academic context Ryder (2004: 1661) has claimed that "despite abandoning the view that adult entertainment is 'vice', recent work has continued to describe adult entertainment districts as part of a range of activities whose marginalisation in spaces reflects marginalisation in society." However, given the extent and scale of the sex industry it is not surprising to find that it has been extensively studied though the relatively recent nature of these studies contrasts with the age of the industry. In particular, sex industry research has been focused on prostitution and sex clubs (e.g., Hubbard, et al., 2008) and primarily concerned with urban zoning and regulation (e.g., Harcourt & Donovan, 2005; Papayanis, 2000; Tucker, 1997; West & Orr, 2007) and women's rights (e.g., Dworkin, 1985; Kempadoo, 1998; Strossen, 2000). In contrast, despite being a component of the global multi-billion sex industry, the sex

shop is a relatively under-researched topic. For example, as Malina and
Schmidt (1997: 352) note "the emergence of the sex shop industry in
Britain is largely undocumented in academic literature." Consequently, it
is not surprising to find that there has been a dearth of research that has
assessed the nature of the sex shop industry to determine the types of
market it is catering to in contemporary society.

Despite this dearth it may be argued that, traditionally, sex shops have
predominantly been a heterosexual male domain, especially outside of
mega-urban centres. Such a view is supported by Heinecken (2007: 136)
who stated "most local sex shops outside of centres like New York, Seattle
or San Francisco still cater to mainly male clientele." Similarly, Malina
and Schmidt (1997: 352-3) have defined sex shops as "businesses run by
men for men, sex shops rarely consider women." Yet against this historic
backdrop in recent years we have witnessed an increasing social
acceptance of women, gays and lesbians in public leisure spaces and
formerly hetero-male dominated leisure experiences and the provision for
them in such spaces and experiences (Cohen & Taylor, 1992; Loftus, 2001;
Mowlabocus, 2007). This changing pattern has, at least partially, been
driven by a general liberalisation of societal views; particularly in western
countries. In addition, these changes may be linked to the increasing
economic power and independence of women (Nikunen, 2007) and
recognition of the significance of the value of the gay community and its
size which, for example, has been estimated at 10% of the overall
population of the USA (Pritchard, et al., 1998). Indeed, Pritchard et al
(1998: 275) have identified the gay population has having become the
"latest target of mainstream marketers." In addition, the gay and lesbian
population has been identified as a 'dream market' due to its higher than
average disposable incomes and whilst it is seen as a relatively small
market the increasing social acceptance of open displays of homosexuality
may arguably be increasing the viability of businesses seeking to focus on
it (Wardlow, 1996).

In addition, there is an increasing recognition of the sexuality of
women in their own right rather than just as sexual objects for the
heterosexual male gaze and social acceptance of their sexual needs and
desires. This has arguably been at least partially driven by the women's
liberation movement of the 1960s and influential magazines such as
Cosmo and its sexual, female focused content. Indeed, as Nikunen (2007:
74) states, "the Cosmo brand has developed in tandem with cultural
transformations in the rights, employment and education of women that
have contributed to their increased independence, as well as increased
interest toward their sexual power." This recognition of the sexuality of

women is epitomised by Cohen and Taylor's (1992: 124-5) claim that masturbation has:

> "lost its traditional masculine image. Just at [as] the yachting and golfing clubs have opened their doors to women members, so there are now books, magazines and apparatus available to female masturbators. To the list of technological aids available to hobbyists – the power drill, the electric lawn mower, the rotary cultivator – must now be added the vibrator. Everyone can now become a masturbator and most of us happily do."

This view has, of course, been popularised via the television sitcom Sex and the City and the highlighting of the vibrator known as the Rabbit on the show which arguably contributed to making it the most popular vibrator on the market (Attwood, 2005). Consequently, it has been suggested that "according to sexual critic and author Laura Kipnis, women have discovered the secret that men have known for a long time. Secret sex (sex outside the rules, risky sex) is alive, an adventure, and deliciously dangerous" (Gini, 2006: 174). All of these trends in the liberalisation of the leisure experience and society in general, and the recognition of the economic significance and sexuality of non-heterosexual male populations suggest the potential broadening of the target markets for sex shops.

Indeed, work has begun to emerge that has focused on the position of women as potential clients of sex shops, the creation of sex shops and sex-toy parties for women, and the use of the Internet by women for sexual stimulation (Leiblum, 2001; McCaughey & French, 2001). The sex industry has apparently recognised the sexual liberation of women and consequently begun to cater to this population. As a result we have seen the creation of products for the female market including warming lubricants, edible body paints, and condoms with vibrating rings by companies such as Durex who had traditionally focused on the male market (Heinecken, 2007). Similarly, the traditionally heterosexually focused pornographic film industry has begun to cater to women and non-heterosexual markets to the extent that female directors are now beginning to produce sexually explicit movies (Davies, 2008). It is not therefore surprising that "a number of women-oriented sex shops have also emerged in recent years, selling everything from vibrators and strap-on harnesses to floggers and anal beads" (Heinecken, 2007: 121).

Despite the emerging focus on the role of women as clients in sex shops little work has been undertaken that examines the provision for homosexuals in the sex shop environment despite claims about the increasing openness of modern societies that recognise the rights of the needs and desires of all groups, irrespective of sexual orientation.

Furthermore, the limited research to date focused on women as sex shop consumers has dealt exclusively with sex shops designed by women for women, ignoring traditional sex shops. Consequently, the aim of this chapter is to assess the nature of the contemporary sex shop and the extent to which it provides for heterosexuals and non-heterosexuals of both genders.

Method

In order to meet the aims of this research a content analysis of the websites of sex shops that have a physical outlet in New Zealand, Australia, Canada, the UK, or the USA was undertaken. The decision to conduct the research via websites was based on practicality; it being unfeasible to visit the physical location of each sex shop and/or conduct a content analysis of material portrayed in a shop when physically visiting it. The research did not encompass sex shops that only exist within cyberspace as it was felt these would potentially be more specialised (i.e., focused on specific market segments) than their physical space counterparts. This, of course, would not allow full analysis of the extent to which sex shops cater to all sexualities and both genders. Furthermore, the lack of a physical entity means that web based sex shops are not subject to the same social and cultural influences as their physically based counterparts, at least not to the same extent, and hence may be identified as a separate segment of the sex industry. The focus on shops with a physical outlet also heightened the likelihood that these outlets would be legal in contrast to shops that only exist on the Internet whose legality may be questionable. This was important as it guaranteed researchers were not visiting websites that may break laws and/or university rules. Whilst the benefits of analysing the content of sex shop websites are significant it is important to recognise that these are online shops and a form of advertising and may not therefore fully represent the reality present in the physical shops with which they are associated. Despite this, the websites do clearly play a role in the impression management of the physical shops.

Initially, sex shops were identified in each country via a search of the Yellow Pages web site. The search terms utilised were: "sex shop," "adult entertainment shop/store" and "adult novelty shop/store." Concerns about the reliability of the Yellow Pages websites to identify sex shops meant that Google was also employed as a search engine, as was Yelp (a site where members of the public write reviews of a wide range of establishments) in the case of the USA. As Google routinely delivers hits numbering in the millions for each search, in order to ensure the research remained practicable the first 200 returns were assessed for relevant web sites. A web site for a chain of sex shops was assessed only once and counted as a single return. A note was made of the number of hits returned for each search term, regardless of whether the hit related to a sex shop (it transpired that in each country studied all of the search media utilised, invariably provided hits for many other, irrelevant, types of shop under each search heading including, for example, cake shops and baby clothing stores). Each listing for a sex shop was assessed to ensure that the web site was complemented by a physical shop. Those web sites that pertained to only an online store were discounted from the study. In addition, those web sites that displayed only the basic details of a physical sex shop such as address and contact number, without advertising any of their products for sale, were discarded. In total 125 sex shops were selected and analysed through this process. Details of the number of shops analysed in each country are highlighted in Table 2.1. The numbers highlighted in Table 2.1 reflect the fact that an upper limit of 30 shops per country was set to provide a viable sample size for analysis and that in New Zealand the UK it was not possible to attain this figure.

Table 2.1: Number of sex shop websites studied by country	
New Zealand	19
Australia	30
Canada	30
The UK	16
The USA	30

A content analysis of each website of the 125 shops was undertaken that entailed an exhaustive search of each product menu on the site. Products were situated in groupings that were devised as a result of a pilot exercise. The nature of these groupings is highlighted in Table 2.2. The pilot exercise entailed accessing five sex shop websites in New Zealand that met the project parameters in terms of representing a physical shop or chain of shops. The product categories that were devised were based initially on those used by the websites to classify the products that they were selling. In order to facilitate the content analysis process it was acknowledged that a number of the sexual products advertised on web sites could attract both male and female heterosexual and homosexual prospective buyers. In order to facilitate the practical collection of data it was agreed that all products would be classified according to the likely predominant user group. Synthesis of the categories from each site resulted in the development of 20 representative product categories. The product categories were discussed between the authors and refined, where necessary, to ensure that they would fulfil the research objectives.

As part of the content analysis the nature of any models shown on the sites and any interaction between models and their relative dominance and submissiveness was recorded. This task was undertaken to assess the representation of men's, women's, heterosexual's and other sexualities bodies and their empowerment/dominance on the site. This material was utilised to help determine the nature of a shops' target market. Gathering data on representations of the body on sex shop websites entailed searching sites for pictorial portrayal of bodies, usually but not exclusively in connection with the advertisement of male and female clothing and bondage or fetish related products. Many of the web sites in four of the five countries studied displayed no images of either men or women; approximately one quarter in New Zealand, Australia and Canada and 17% in the United States. No such sites were found in the case of the UK.

The non-heterosexual male market

Analysis of the material collected for the study on which this chapter is based identified shops that stated they were aimed exclusively at gay men in three of the five countries studied. There were 2 shops for gay men in New Zealand and 2 in the USA. In the UK one site was targeted specifically at gay men and a sister site specifically at lesbians. This result clearly suggests that very few sex shops exist in the countries studied that focus exclusively on the homosexual market. Furthermore, it shows a strong bias towards the gay male market as opposed to the lesbian one within homosexually focused shops. The low number of shops focused on the homosexual population may be a direct consequence of the suggested relatively low numbers associated with this demographic group in comparison to the heterosexual population (Bancroft, 2009; Pritchard, et al., 1998).

Table 2.2: Products available in sex shops		
	Number	Percentage
Bondage	104	82
Sex Toys – Female	117	93
Sex Toys – Male	96	76
Gay Toys	11	9
Male Enhancers	111	88
Books and/or Magazines for Heterosexual M & F	73	59
Books and/or Magazines for Gay Men	23	19
Books and/or Magazines for Lesbians	20	17
DVDs for Heterosexual Males & Females	81	63
DVDs for Gay Men	40	30
DVDs for Lesbians	44	33
Lingerie and Clothing – Women	97	78
Clothing – Men	62	50
Jewellery and Body Adornments – Women	38	32
Jewellery and Body Adornments – Men	3	2
Pills, Potions and Lotions – Erotic	113	91
Potions and Lotions – Massage	95	75
Safe Sex	72	59
Games	81	64
Rude Food	58	46

Table 2.2 reinforces the view that relatively few shops are marketing products directly at the homosexual population. For example, results in Table 2.2 show that far fewer shops provide books and/or magazines for the gay and lesbian markets than the heterosexual one. It is, however, interesting to note that whilst the number of stores overtly providing materials for the homosexual market is relatively low it is greater than the number of stores that were exclusively aimed at this market. This suggests at least some shops are attempting to cater to a range of sexualities. It is also important to note that the extent to which the gay and lesbian market is catered to by sex shops may actually be relatively high when set alongside the percentage of the population generally identified as homosexual (Bancroft, 2009; Pritchard, et al., 1998). Furthermore, the extent to which gay and lesbian consumers are catered to across all the shops studied is, according to the material highlighted in Table 2.2, very similar. This contrasts with the bias in the number of exclusively gay and lesbian stores identified.

In addition, whilst a higher number of sex shops were found that were aimed primarily or exclusively at a female audience than a homosexual one these shops still only represent a small proportion of the overall sample. The content analysis study found a total of 17 sex shops aimed directly at the female audience. One shop in each of New Zealand and Australia, and another two in Canada were targeted at a heterosexual female audience while two others in Australia appeared to be rather ambiguous in terms of the sexual orientation of their intended female market. Six UK shops were aimed specifically at women, although they were also relatively ambiguous in identification of the sexuality of the intended audience. Of these shops, one was also present in the US market which recorded 5 shops aimed at the female market. These results support the claim by Malina and Schmidt (1997: 352) that "sex shops exclusively targeted at women are a new and ground-breaking phenomenon, challenging the traditional notion of sex shops as male domains."

As well as finding sex shops focused primarily on female customers, the results of the content analysis of the 125 sex shop websites sampled for this research suggests shops that do not at least partially cater to females, or at least provide products intended for women, are a rarity. Indeed, Table 2.2 shows that female sex toys were sold in 117 of the 125 shops studied. Similarly, 97 of the stores stocked female lingerie and/or clothing. This finding confirms the claim by Attwood (2005: 396) that "the marketing of sex products for women focuses strongly on toys and clothing." The ambiguity identified concerning whether some of the sex shops for women were aimed at heterosexual or homosexual groups reinforces the point about the difficulty of differentiating between stores based on potential markets and could suggest that the number of stores targeting lesbians is actually higher than that catering to the gay male market. However, the ambiguity is important as it suggests that these shops whilst focusing on women are not focusing exclusively on a single market but instead are seeking to cater to both the heterosexual and homosexual female populations.

The dominant target market: the heterosexual male

Whilst the vast majority of web sites were aimed predominantly at the heterosexual market it was not possible to distinguish any that openly marketed themselves primarily or exclusively to heterosexual males. This may be surprising given the suggestion that sex shops have been designed by heterosexual men for heterosexual men (Heinecken, 2007; Malina & Schmidt, 1997). However, the very fact that sex shops have long been assumed to be frequented by heterosexual males may be the very reason why they feel no need to identify themselves with this population. Similarly, whilst Table 2.2 clearly shows that the heterosexual male is widely catered to by the sex shops studied it is often difficult to identify which, if any, products are designed and marketed exclusively for this population.

The manner in which men and women's bodies are portrayed and the way sites are generally constructed suggests most are aimed primarily at heterosexual men. In total, 100 of the 125 sex shops studied utilised depictions of the body, or parts of the body, on their websites. Only 2 of these websites did not use pictures of women whilst 52 did not show men in their pictures. Furthermore, 17 of the 48 web sites that displayed pictures of men mostly used images of just the relevant area of the body. These pictures mainly consisted of clothing covering the genitalia. In comparison, female imagery frequently portrayed the whole body irrespective of the items being marketed. One potential explanation for this is that web sites cater mainly to heterosexual male purchasers who wish to look at the female body. However, it is impossible to single out portrayal of the female body for a predominantly heterosexual male clientele as the reason. Instead, the explanation may be rather more prosaic. For example, it may be argued that the nature of women's clothing means that more of the female body needs to be displayed than in the case of male clothing. However, this argument is undermined by the sexual poses often utilised by female models and the overtly sexual way in which the female form is utilised on many sex shop websites, as shown in Figure 2.1. The poses and female clothing depicted in Figure 2.1 may all be said to conform to classical western views of female sexuality designed to appeal to the heterosexual male making the women in the pictures the "object" of the heterosexual male gaze. Indeed, Paasonen, et al (2007: 1) have identified "women's open, moist and lipstick-red lips, half-closed eyelids or hands suggestively placed on a bare bosom or stomach are staple elements in pornography." It is interesting to note that this objectification of the female body for the titillation of the heterosexual male is a feature that is not just restricted to general sex shops but also appears in some of the ones the market themselves primarily at women such as Joanna G, as featured in Figure 2.1, and Ann Summers (http://www.annsummers.com).

The data highlighted in Table 2.2 also shows how the majority of the sex shops studied in this chapter stock products that are aimed at the male market and particularly the heterosexual one. For example, the data shows that 81 and 73 of the shops stocked videos/DVDs and books/magazines, respectively, aimed to appeal to the heterosexual male. Furthermore, 96 of the sex shops advertised that they sold sex toys designed specifically for men. An interesting point about these findings is that the number of sex shops selling sex toys for men is greater than the number providing visual material for this market. This suggests that contrary to popular belief sex shops are not primarily focused on pornography; even those who are mainly targeted at the heterosexual male market. This result compares with the claim by Joanna G (2008), a sex shop focused on female consumers and couples, that "Joanna G is proud to be a pornography-free Company. Joanna G does not stock R18 classified products." There would, therefore, appear to be a degree of similarity between some of the sex shops oriented towards the female market and those focused on the heterosexual male market.

Figure 2.1: Sex shop website female imagery

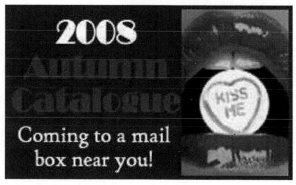

Source of pictures from top to bottom right: Strictly Adult (2008), The Pleasure Chest (2008), and Joanna G (2008)

Diversity and inclusiveness in the Sex Shop environment

Further to the suggestion that there are similarities between a number of sex shops focused on the female market and those oriented towards the heterosexual male there is evidence to suggest that a significant number of sex shops are, if not exclusively seeking to target people other than the heterosexual male, interested in providing for people outside of this population; as evidenced in Table 2.2. The subjective impression, particularly of the sites studied in Canada, The USA, and the UK not catering specifically for the gay, lesbian or heterosexual female markets was that there was a tendency to utilise pastel colours which suggests a less overtly heterosexual masculine web design. In addition, the advertising of male-targeted DVDs was, in relative terms, unobtrusive. Relatively few scantily clad females were also represented on homepages.

It is not only those sex shops not openly marketed towards a specific population that appear to be attempting to reach out to more than one type of customer. Rather, several of the sex shops marketed primarily to women emphasised on the introduction pages of their websites their commitment to such concepts as "couples" and "relationships." For example, Joanna G (2008) states on its website that "romance, love & intimacy are 3 key ingredients for a healthy relationship. We hand pick and test our products to ensure they meet our quality & relationship enhancing standards. Take time to grow and enhance your relationship and above all have fun." Similarly, the Good Vibrations, another store originally set up to cater primarily to women, (2008) website states "She [Joani Blank, the company founder] set out to make Good Vibrations a friendly, "clean, well-lighted" alternative to conventional "adult" bookstores. Her efforts met with immediate enthusiasm and appreciation from women and men alike." The championing of this type of terminology by the women focused sex shops is clearly an attempt to broaden the appeal of sex shops and change their image from one of questionable morality to one focused on more wholesome ideals such as personal and relationship health and wellbeing. It is also a clear example of sex shops seeking to appeal to both men and women.

Conclusion

The results highlighted in this chapter have shown that relatively few sex shops exist in the countries where data was collected that cater specifically to either the homosexual or female markets. However, the small number of shops focused on the homosexual market may be related to the relatively small size of this population. Furthermore, it is clear that both homosexuals and women are widely catered to by sex shops that are not specifically targeted at them. However, the results of the analysis of portrayals of the body suggest that the heterosexual male market is the primary focus of the majority of sex shops.

The relative paucity of sex shops aimed specifically at homosexuals and women and the dominant focus on the heterosexual male in other sex shops appears problematic given the recognition that both women and homosexuals are as aware of their sexualities as the heterosexual male and just as eager to explore it. The paucity may of course simply be due to a lag effect between the growing desire for sex shops amongst homosexual and female populations and the creation of such shops and the re-orientation/design of existing ones. If this is the case then the question is where are homosexuals and women going in the meantime to find sex products. The Internet is of course a viable option that provides anonymity and accessibility in a way physical shops cannot compete with though at the expense of the ability to fully see products and potentially talk to knowledgeable staff before making a purchase. The existence and popularity of sex shops on the Internet targeted to women and homosexuals may also of course inhibit the development of physical sex shops catering to these markets.

Whilst homosexuals and women may already be being catered to by sex shops not targeted specifically at them the extent to which this is a viable option is potentially limited. Sex shops are clearly operating in a sensitive area of society and their ability to provide for, especially within their physical shop, the needs and comfort of men and women of disparate sexualities all at the same time is questionable. For example, whilst we live in a relatively socially liberated world at the current time that potentially enables more enlightened heterosexual couples to visit sex shops, particularly those marketing themselves as aids to healthy relationships rather than sources of pornography, hand in hand it is questionable to what extent single men and women would be comfortable with the presence of members of the opposite sex in a sex shop they were visiting. Sh!, a sex shop designed primarily for women, in recognition of the potential for a level of discomfort amongst its female clients if males were to frequent the shop offers the following advice to male partners:

> "Guys ... You're more than welcome to visit our London store ... and certainly many of you appreciate our relaxed, non-judgmental atmosphere, collection of good quality sex toys, hot cuppa [tea] and sound advice as much as the women Sh! was created for. All we ask is that you come along to the store accompanied by a female friend" (Sh!, 2008).

This of course immediately restricts access by single males, be they homosexual or heterosexual, to this type of sex shop unless they can find a female friend willing to accompany them. Furthermore, whilst the majority of sex shops not targeted primarily at women are now selling products aimed at the female consumer they exude an image that suggests these spaces are heterosexual male domains and are therefore unlikely to appeal to the majority of potential female customers. This, of course, begs the question of who therefore is buying the female-oriented products on sale in these stores. The aura of heterosexual masculinity in these shops also appears to be a barrier to the homosexual market despite the fact that many such shops are now stocking items aimed at this population which raises the same question as in the case of the female-oriented products. However, attempting to operate a sex shop that overtly caters to and does not disenfranchise homosexuals may alienate the heterosexual male market.

The nature of the sex shops studied in this chapter, both in terms of their overt market orientations and content and displays may be said to provide a valid representation of the wider social reality regarding acceptance of women and homosexuals in the public gaze. Within this context it is not surprising to see the continued dominance of the heterosexual male in the sex shop market followed by women, then gay men with lesbians as the least empowered social group bringing up the rear in terms of being overtly catered for in sex shops. These findings reinforce the notion that gays, lesbians (Hubbard, 2001), and women (Paasonen, et al., 2007) are subservient, in terms of their accessibility, to the hetero-male in public space in general and the sex shop in particular. Changes in the nature of the sex shop industry in the future may therefore be used as a barometer of public social acceptance of groups other than the heterosexual male. The creation of non-heterosexual male focused sex shops may also be a catalyst to an increase in the acceptance of women and diverse sexualities in the public space. This is supported by Paasonen, et al's (2007: 14) claim that "making sex public, pornography [and sex shops] confronts tendencies to silence or demonize sexualities – and queer sexualities in particular."

There is clearly a need for significant further research to be undertaken to fully understand the nature of sex shops and fully answer the questions raised in this chapter. As part of a research agenda for sex shops an assessment of whether physical sex shops can really appeal to multiple markets needs to be undertaken. This will of course require significant discussion with diverse population segments about the potential of them visiting such shops. Further research with the public is also needed to examine how marketing by sex shops is interpreted by the intended and unintended audiences. Whilst clearly trying to distance themselves from the heterosexual male focused sex shops it is interesting to see a number of the women-oriented sex shops utilizing female imagery that has traditionally been used to entice and titillate the heterosexual male. Further research is clearly required to see why such material is being used by these shops and how it is experienced by the female population in general and female sex shop consumers in particular. Research is also needed to expand the work presented in this chapter to include sex shops located in other countries, particularly outside of the western context. In addition, work needs to be undertaken that considers the nature of the Internet-only sex shops and the comparison between these and their physical counterparts. Arguably all of these research ideas would benefit from being situated in a temporal context which of course necessitates longitudinal research.

References

Attwood, F. 2005. Fashion and passion: Marketing sex to women. *Sexualities*. 8 (4): 392 - 406

Bancroft, J. 2009. *Human sexuality and its problems* (3rd ed). Edinburgh: Churchill Livingstone

Cohen, S. and Taylor, L. 1992. *Escape attempts: The theory and practice of resistance to everyday life* (2nd ed). London: Routledge

Davies, L. 2008. Paris intellectuals make case for porn. *The Guardian*. http://www.guardian.co.uk/film/2008/oct/12/france-festivals. 12/10/08

Dworkin, A. 1985. Against the male flood: Censorship, pornography, and equality. *Harvard Women's Law Journal*. 8: 1-29

Gini, A. 2006. *Why it's hard to be good*. New York: Routledge

Good Vibrations. 2008. *Who we are*. http://www.goodvibes.com/content.jhtml?id=1787. 30/10/08

Harcourt. C. and Donovan, B. 2005. The many faces of sex work. *Sexually Transmitted Infections*. 81: 201-206

Heinecken, D. 2007. Toys are us: Contemporary feminisms and the consumption of sexuality. A. Hall and M. Bishop (eds). *Pop porn: Pornography in American culture*. Westport: Praeger. pp. 121 – 136

Hubbard , P. 2001. Sex zones: Intimacy, citizenship and public space. *Sexualities*. 4 (1): 51 - 71

Hubbard, P., Matthews, R., Scoular, J. and Agustin, L. 2008. Away from prying eyes? The urban geographies of 'adult entertainment'. *Progress in Human Geography*. 32 (3): 363–381

Joanna G. 2008. *Welcome*. http://www.joannag.com. 11/7/08

Kempadoo, K. 1998. Introduction: Globalizing sex workers rights. K. Kempadoo and Doezema, J. (eds). *Global sex workers: Rights, resistance and redefinition*. London: Routledge. pp. 1 – 28

Leiblum, S. 2001. Women, sex and the internet. Sex*ual and Relationship Therapy*. 16 (4): 389 - 405

Loftus, J. 2001. America's liberalization in attitudes toward homosexuality, 1973 to 1998. *American Sociological Review*. 66 (5): 762-782

McCaughey, M. and French, C. 2001. Women's sex-toy parties: Technology, orgasm, and commodification. *Sexuality & Culture*. 5 (3): 77-96

Malina, D. and Schmidt, R. 1997. It's business doing pleasure with you: Sh! A women's sex shop case. *Marketing Intelligence & Planning*. 15 (7): 352–360

Mowlabocus, S. 2007. Gay men and the pornification of everyday life. S. Paasonen, K. Nikunen and L. Saarenmaa (eds). *Pornification*. Oxford: Berg. pp. 61 – 71

Nikunen, K. 2007. Cosmo girls talk: Blurring boundaries of porn and sex. S. Paasonen, K. Nikunen and L. Saarenmaa (eds). *Pornification*. Oxford: Berg. pp. 73 - 85

Paasonen, S., Nikunen, K. and Saarenmaa, L. 2007. Pornification and the education of desire. S. Paasonen, K. Nikunen and L. Saarenmaa (eds). *Pornification*. Oxford: Berg. pp. 1 – 20

Papayanis, M. A. 2000. Sex and the revanchist city: Zoning out pornography in New York. *Environment and Planning D*. 18: 341–353

Pritchard, A., Morgan, N., Sedgely, D. and Jenkins, A. 1998. Reaching out to the gay tourist: Opportunities and threats in an emerging market segment. *Tourism Management*. 19 (3): 273 – 282

Ryder, A. 2004. The changing nature of adult entertainment districts: Between a rock and a hard place or going from strength to strength? *Urban Studies*. 41 (9): 1659–1686

Sh! 2008. *Home*. http://www.sh-womenstore.com/ 30/10/08

Strictly Adult. 2008. *Welcome to strictly adult*. http://www.strictlyadult.co.nz. 28/10/08

Strossen, N. 2000. *Defending pornography: Free speech, sex, and the fight for women's rights*. New York: New York University Press

The Pleasure Chest. 2008. *Home*. http://www.pleasurechest.co.nz. 28/10/08

Tucker, D. 1997. Preventing the secondary effects of adult entertainment establishments: Is zoning the solution? *Journal of Land Use and Environmental Law*. 12 (2): 383 – 431

Wardlow, D. 1996. Introduction. D. Wardlow (ed). *Gays, lesbians and consumer behavior: Theory, practice, and research issues in marketing.* Binghamton: Haworth Press. pp. 1 - 8

West, D. and Orr, M. 2007. Morality and economics: Public assessments of the adult entertainment industry. *Economic Development Quarterly.* 21 (4): 315-324

CHAPTER THREE

PARALLEL UNIVERSES: MALE SEX TRADE IN PUBLIC SPACES OF VERACRUZ, MÉXICO

ROSÍO CÓRDOVA PLAZA

Introduction

This chapter presents the results of six months of research with male street sex workers who have sex with men but identify themselves as heterosexuals, working in one of the most famous (and visited) parks of the port of Veracruz, México, a coastal, mainly domestic touristic destination located at the Gulf of Mexico. The main objectives of this chapter are a) to analyse the differences between "traditional" sexual and gender identities, and "gay," globalised identities (defined by recognised homosexual desire and practices) among male sex workers; b) to examine how the differentiation between traditional-heterosexual/"*mayate*" identities and modern-gay identities operates at several aspects: socioeconomic status, territorial distribution, ways of solicitation and clientele; and c) examine how, as male prostitution implies different transgressions to heteronormativity, both workers and clients must preserve the secrecy of sex negotiations in the public sphere by developing an esoteric code to recognize each other.

In contrast to female and transgender sex work, which is easily identifiable in the public sphere,[1] the male sex industry exists in a kind of "parallel universe." This is a concept imported from Physics that refers to multiple realities that coexist relatively independently from one another. The idea of parallel universes coexisting in the same space and time but

---

[1] According to Kandel '... [u]nder the current regime, since [women] prostitutes have no legal way of notifying clients of their whereabouts, high visibility in public places is the easiest way to meet clients' (Kandel, 1992: 338).

that are not mixed-up, permits further reflection on how the male prostitution industry is publicly developed but not acknowledgeable by those who are not related to it. The need of an esoteric code for understanding who buys and who sells sex protects the anonymity of workers and clients (Córdova, forthcoming), due to its strongly negative character in the hetero-normative order (Altman, 1996; 2001; Butler, 1999).

Prostitution is a human activity that reveals the complexities of the dichotomy between public/private modern societies. On one side of the debate are the issues of regulation and public health, on the other, the reality of the intimate relationships between individual participants. In this way prostitution, marginalised, criminalised and degrading as it may be held by a society, is also believed to be indispensable for the protection of the society, the family and the moral integrity of group members (Kandel, 1992; Szasz, 2007).

Although throughout history there have existed different ways of categorising and normalising sexual practices in the context of sexual commerce, it was not until the beginnings of the 19th century, in what Foucault (1991) described as the "dispositive of sexuality," that the medicalisation of sex placed prostitution at the heart of public hygiene concerns. This vision holds prostitution as a dirty and dangerous occupation, disposed to medical and social pathologies, always undertaken by women from classes considered "dangerous," and associated with different vices and crimes, such as alcohol, violence, drugs use, theft, and scandal. Male prostitution is even more morally condemned as it implies transgressions on "normalized" gender, sexual desire and sexual practice imperatives.

However, male sex work is becoming more visible as it has emerged as an important focus of research on HIV transmission (Parker, 1999; Zuilhof, 1999). Also, it is becoming more evident that there is a sizeable increase in men dedicated to sex work throughout the world. This has generally been associated with the deterioration of conditions in the global workplace where large sections of the population are permanently excluded from society (de Moya & García, 1999). This instability in the labour market has converted sexual commerce into an attractive and easily accessible option for many un- and underemployed youths, who find in this activity a relatively lucrative, non-qualified job to make some extra money (Córdova, 2005). To explain how workers can deal with the stigmatisation and marginalisation that sex work implies for men, it is important to learn the cultural protocols that allow having sex with men and preserve a heterosexual identity.

Methodology

Following an anthropological approach that could provide the necessary introspection of a thick description (Geertz, 1994) of cultural meanings, the research on which this chapter is centred is based on nineteen in-depth interviews. In the course of the research, I conducted field observation as well as numerous non-recorded conversations and fifteen in-depth recorded, semi-structured interviews with male sex workers, one with a stripper, one with an escort and massage agency manager, and two with clients. The main topics of the interviews referred to the following issues: family, former jobs, socioeconomic conditions, entry into sex work, contact with clients, negotiation, rates and payment, sexual practices, sexual and gender identities, emotional relationships, drug use, police harassment, and perceptions of risks and danger. The duration of each interview varied from twenty minutes to two and a half hours depending on the willingness of the respondents. All the data was processed with *Ethnograph* software and the interview fragments presented were selected. It is important to point out that these narratives are not used as examples of my statements, but are a central part of the argument itself. Here I subscribe Ricoeur's (1981: 145) idea of inscription, which means that narrative "refers to a world that it claims to describe, to express, or to represent."

Due to the stigmatisation of both workers and consumers of sex services, none of the men involved wanted to be acknowledged as worker or consumer of these services, and the sample had to be patiently constructed by using the snowball technique; that is, the first worker successfully approached facilitated the contact with others. Generally, those that could be identified as consumers, local or tourist, refused to be interviewed, and just two clients accepted to be interviewed on a non-recorded basis. Ethnographic data was gathered during several periods of 2007 and 2008 during different moments of Mexican holidays (Carnival, Holy Week and Christmas Holidays). The names of the interviewees have been changed to protect their anonymity, and only the age is kept to show the age range.

Dimensions of male prostitution

Veracruz, as the main Mexican port, exhibits great economic dynamics. With diversified industrial and commercial activities, it is also an important domestic touristic destination. These circumstances make the port an attraction for the workforce throughout the country that is employed in formal activities, temporary jobs, or in the informal sector. But, as a result of the concentration of population and the lack of enough jobs, this also means an increasing unemployed people, as official sources state,[2] that could explain the rise of male prostitution. Besides, places with long-standing and intense human traffic, like Veracruz, have usually observed the constant presence of sexual commerce between natives and outsiders. Furthermore, recent conditions are linked to the appearance of a general change in recreational habits during leisure times (Corrales, 1993). In this sense, it is common to find frequent comments in the literature regarding sexual tourism and its emergence within the context of globalisation (Cantú, 2002; Clift & Forrest, 1999); namely the speed and volume of transportation (Ford, 2003), the development of communications and the internet (Chow-White, 2006) which permit mobility and intercultural exchanges on a scale previously unknown, and the creation of specific consumer niches.

In contrast to other urban areas in México (Sánchez & López, 2000) and elsewhere like San Francisco (Sinclair, 2004) or Madrid (Urgel, 2008), Veracruz does not have a "gay zone," per se, nor are the places offering homoerotic services located in typical tourist sites, though certain points of intersection do exist. As such, it is noticeable that sex work in Veracruz exists through two relatively exclusive environments, which makes it possible to link the junction of the geo-historical port conformation and its economic activities. On one side is the old Spanish centre, which attracts visitors due to its historic significance and Caribbean festival culture, and, on the other side, the newer leisure and tourist infrastructure developed in Boca del Río, which has created a cosmopolitan area with modern hotels and entertainment centres. Within these two main areas, where we can find men-to-men offerings and solicitation, the following aspects will be analyzed:

- Territorial dimension
- Socioeconomic conditions of both clients and sex workers
- Tourist place of origin: domestic or international
- Different forms of solicitation
- Sex worker identities

---

[2] Instituto Nacional de Estadística, Geografía e Informática (National Institute for Statistics, Geography and Informatics) reports the highest open unemployment levels for Veracruz, at 5.2 percent in 2004 (http://www.inegi.gob.mx).

Prostitution and Sex Workers in Veracruz

During the first years of the 20th century, Veracruz attempted to provide a better urban infrastructure in order to attract domestic tourists seeking the benefits of the sea air (García, 1996). Towards this end, dance halls and bathing facilities were constructed (Gallegos, 2006). In 1925, Veracruz began the annual celebration of Carnival, which initiated the cyclical arrival of tourists during holiday periods that continue today. Nevertheless, between the 1970's and 1980's, the port suffered a touristic shortcoming mainly due to the great efforts and resources channelled into the construction of five new touristic projects elsewhere in México (López, 2001). As a consequence of the lack of governmental interest, Veracruz remained outside the sphere of the international tourist circuit and subsequently dedicated itself to attracting a tourism trade of a more local character, mainly geared towards the middle and lower socio-economic classes from the greater Gulf region and the centre of México (Gallegos, 2006). In a recent study, Propin and Sánchez (2007) pointed out that in 1991 Veracruz had the 6th place among the ten main domestic tourist destinations in México, reaching 836,985 visitors. However, by 2005, Veracruz occupied the 4th place with 1,576,595 domestic tourists. This tourism is concentrated primarily in the city centre and constitutes the main clientele for the street-walker prostitutes. It is interesting to notice that the male prostitutes' route corresponds almost perfectly to the ancient city walls, where, according to historic records, the prostitution circuit took place (Alberro, 1989; Gil, 2002).

Offering and buying sex services on the street:
the historic centre

In the historic city centre it is now possible to find a greater presence of male sex workers, who spread out in the centuries-old prostitution areas, with the Zamora Park as its centre of operations. Surprisingly, the territorial dimension of sex workers corresponds almost perfectly with the old walled city, the Paseo de la Alameda, and the former train station, which today houses a market. The workers interviewed for this project range between 18 and 32 years old, and their services are aimed at so-called "*tapados*" (meaning males identifying as heterosexual, often married and with children, who wish to hide their same-sex desires), both regional and national tourists and local clients. The workers often understand the need to have sex with men and be penetrated as a sort of "disease," as one of the interviewed refers:

Well there're two men who talk to me occasionally, no one else. And we think it's an illness. It's like they like it [sex with men], they have a wife, kids, and they say 'well, it's not as if anyone has died from doing this, right?' (Jose, 22)

There are also foreign consumers, who for so long have appeared in the Veracruzan imagination as users of erotic services provided by male and female natives, and are called *"embarcados"* (embarkers). *"Embarcados"* are generally associated with port activities: sailors, cabin boys, and other maritime personnel grouped in the port, and whose stay may vary between a few hours and several days. Among both female and male sex workers, some specialize in servicing this clientele, for which they are termed *"gabacheras/gabacheros"* (Female/male. *"Gabacho"* is a colloquial Mexican term for the United States) (Flores Martos, 2004).

While there appears to be a standard fee of 200 pesos for the full package (including penetration) there also appears to be a marked preference for tourist clients over locals, in that those interviewed agreed that visitors pay more, offer gifts and invitations, and less effort is involved in servicing them.

Usually I go for outsiders, tourists. Because the people from here, they don't give you what you ask, and they ask a lot of you. The tourists leave me more money, they give it to me better. They call me Kaliman [a comic hero]. That's the way it is. Someone from outside, you can treat him better; you have more expressions or words you can use to talk to him than someone from here. If you really go for it, you can make some $12,000 pesos a month. When I go out to sell, when I dedicate my time, I go for it for sometimes 3 or 4 days in a row (Kaliman, 24).

Well really the difference is they [foreign visitors] give you a little more. [The best ones] are the Columbians. Sometimes they give you up to $1,000 for a service, you let them give you head, you spend some time with them, you're having some beers for maybe 3 hours. You waste more time drinking than in the service (Hector, 21).

In the same way, even though many of the workers who were interviewed are from the port itself, inhabitants of the nearby old barrio of La Huaca or the port's suburbs, there are also many workers who have come to the city to offer sex services in order to supplement other incomes. As such, it is common to see workers with diverse vocations and abilities, such as construction workers, ranchers, itinerant sales people, farmers, or students, also working as prostitutes.

I don't come very much to the park, it's quite rare. I still take care of some cows, and we just got done milking at the ranch. We get up very early every day, at 3 in the morning, and at 7 we deliver the milk. Afterwards we don't do much of anything, and if I don't have anything else to do, I come here once or twice a week (Abraham, 22).

I've worked in construction, as a painter, in engineering, cutting sugar cane, in the fields, picking watermelons, cantaloupes, all that (Manuel, 23).

The ease with which one can work in the sex industry intermittently makes it a more attractive economic activity, in that it allows one to work part-time, sporadically or seasonally, especially when there is more tourist activity to increase demand.

Really I do it out of necessity, to have a little extra money. If I charge 1,000 pesos for a week of construction work, and they charge me 1,500 pesos in rent, obviously I have to do something else, because I'm not going to go around stealing either. That's not for me (Jorge, 22).

A minority of interviewees reside in other cities or states, and come to the port only during heavy touristic times. Some of them follow the tourist circuit, depending on the vacation calendar:

I'm from Matamoros, Tamulipas. I came here just passing through, to do sex work, and I've only been here a month. I started when I was 16, in Quintana Roo, in a park, like Zamora here. There's a park in Quintana Roo called Las Palapas. I went to see it, and work. I left there and went to Playa del Carmen, also to work. And Cancun as well, since I had never been there. And it's like here now. I didn't know the port [of Veracruz], and now I do and I'm working like before (Pedro, 21).

The initial recruitment of sex workers often happens by chance. Sometimes they are solicited by clients themselves when they happen to be in places where services are offered, often without even knowing what goes on there, and they get propositioned by someone who assumes they are available.

A guy paid me 120 pesos once, he came to me. He found me sitting in Zamora Park and asked me what I was doing. I told him I was just hanging out. He said I could make love to him and he would give me 120 pesos. Well, I didn't refuse, and I did it, and he gave me the money. After that it just became a pastime, and since then I began to have money. If not, I wouldn't be doing it (Carlos, 26).

But sometimes recruitment happens through a third person, someone already involved in sex work:

> A friend brought me here to the park. He started to explain to me how it works and what goes on, and I started getting the hang of it (Jaime, 18).

In Veracruz, male prostitution areas have expanded (Aldán, 2009) to include the Plaza de la República, Zamora Park, around the Hidalgo market, the avenues of Diaz Mirón and Gomez Farías, as well as certain stretches of the beach. Sex services are offered 24 hours a day, seven days a week, creating a vast infrastructure of cheap hotels that rent by the hour or day, bars, pharmacies, as well as the old public bathhouse located near Zamora Park. The interior of the park is the main centre of male sex services, though on nearby street corners women compete for the clientele circling the area. Although this centrally located park is not in itself a tourist attraction, it is located in the heart of a commercial zone with a variety of shops. It is well-trafficked throughout the day by groups of students, families with children, and older people who relax in the shade. The park includes street vendors, shoe shiners, newspaper stands, two cafeterias, and a small police station. The map in Figure 3.1 shows the location of the male prostitution circuit at the historic centre. The Zamora Park stands as headquarters where sex workers wait for clients. If they have no luck in getting clients, they walk back and forth in the streets between the Plaza de la República and the Park. Eventually, they go to the beach near the centre.

Figure 3.1: Male prostitution circuit at the historic centre

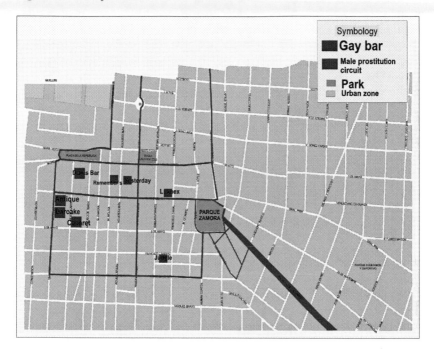

This heavily-trafficked area allows both workers and clients to pass unnoticed by the majority of visitors, but the slightest gesture can open the way for what is a regimented code of understanding for establishing contact. For example, sex workers remain seated, changing places from time to time in order to watch and be watched, while waiting to be casually approached:

> Where you go sit, they're already looking at your fly, or making excuses to talk to you, or offering you a cigarette, something to drink. You know? (Andrés, 21).

> Well you notice here that the people... For example, I'm sitting here, and these other people have been sitting here for awhile too. So you start to distinguish who's really offering something and who's looking for something. Really it's the person who's looking for something that approaches and starts the talking, because the ones offering, they're sitting there waiting for someone to talk to them (Client).

Some clients stay seated, making subtle gestures with their legs spread apart, caressing themselves or touching themselves discretely on the genitals as a way of announcing that they are looking for a sexual encounter and are prepared to pay for it. The most important aspect is that the different signs should be subtle and be accompanied by a certain way of looking at the other person, since, as a client suggested "the look, that's really what makes the connection." The subtlety of the contact between worker and client is necessary for several reasons. First, because it avoids potential misunderstandings and errors, in case the client is attempting to attract someone who is not a prostitute. Second, because it demonstrates both parties' availability to undertake negotiations for the kind and price of service out of the public's eye. Lastly, because it constitutes an esoteric code unrecognized by non-participants.

Protecting heterosexual identities

The argument for considering sex work as a parallel universe leads to an analysis of the identities exhibited by street sex workers, known commonly as "*mayates*". This term is used in reference to dung beetles, a clear allusion to anal sex, sometimes used as a verb, *mayatear*. The *mayate* is a male who is neither recognized by society as nor considers himself to be a homosexual, although he might admit to being bisexual, as long as he maintains the "active" position (i.e., the one who penetrates, or the receiver of fellatio). This means that homosexual practices are not conceived as part of *mayate* sex workers' identities but merely as economic transactions with no sexual meanings (Altman, 1999).

> I'm active only. Passive is the one who gets penetrated. We sex workers, or mayates, as we're called, work in the park. We don't have those crazy cross-dressers here. Sometimes you'll see guys around here that look normal, but they're trannies (Jorge, 22).

All of the interviewees, except one, stated that their physical relations with women were a key part of their identities. Making their sexual preferences, emotional connections, or even marriages to women explicit reinforces the masculinity of these men, which could be doubted if they admitted that they constantly worked as male prostitutes or that doing so gave them some enjoyment.

> I mainly pimp girls; don't think that I just do that other thing [gay sex]. I'm not committed to prostitution. But I respect the ass sex. I go after the girls in the bars and clubs, and they pay me and everything, since they say I

have a good body and…. I'd better not tell you things you already know. That's what they say women like. But I almost don't do it [gay sex], except when I feel really in need, sometimes I do it with a gay, with a man. But I go after women more, in the bars and places like that (Kaliman, 24).

These kind of statements, nonetheless, sometimes contradict the real tales of these workers, such as in the case of Kaliman, who claims to be heterosexual while working as a gay male prostitute four or five times a week. Part of the success of the mayates depends on their macho image, being "very male," which comes up constantly in their insistence that they never take the "passive" position, which they would see as equivalent to their clients.

Yes, the 'actives' play the role of the man. The 'passives' do everything like a woman, they get penetrated, they suck you off, all of that. The 'actives', no. We just penetrate, nothing else. The attitude of the 'passives' is that of a woman, because they like it like that, they like the 'passive' part. I've noticed that (Julio, 24).

The identity construction of *mayates* is based upon the denial of access to the gluteus like an antechamber to the anus, which the social imagination associates with passivity and femininity (List, 2007). The insistence in taking on the role of "active" seems to be a key common theme in the narratives of this kind of sex worker, according to hegemonic cultural norms for males that claim that male sexuality should be aggressive and subjugating (see Schifter & Aggleton, 1999; Parker, 1999). This manner of confronting the symbolic domination of the male principle over the female reveals itself, at least in speech, as the dichotomous assignment of sexual roles within homoerotic relations and a phallo-centric reduction of erogenous zones.

No! What? Sure sometimes they've wanted me to grab their asses. I say, 'no, just put yourself right there.' Because that's the only thing I like, and I let them suck me, it's true. I'm 100% 'active'. 'Passive', no; 100% 'active'. For whatever reason, I'm dark, black, Latin roots, hotter. I can make love until…. When I had my girlfriend, and I always have a girlfriend, sometimes I make love to her 7 times, or I make them come 9 times in one session. I fuck 6, 5 times a day when I can, when I'm feeling horning, when I feel that sensation (Kaliman, 24).

It is also worth noting the racialized content of the conversations that reproduce the stereotypes of some ethnic groups as more sexual and potent. If one considers that Veracruz is a state with a large historic presence of the so-called third race in México (i.e., coloured people), the imagined hyper-sexuality of Afro-mestizos justifies entering the sex work trade as a way to guarantee sexual encounters to satisfy some hungry and indiscriminate desire towards the sex object. Given that these male sex workers claim their virile masculinity through their female partners and in the constant insistence of their overflowing heterosexuality they justify their sexual relations with other men as due to unsatisfied erotic urges.

> '*Cotorreo*' [male sex acts] is fun, no? Disgustingly, yes. Sometimes I go look for it because, like in my house, my wife is young, and I don't know what…what's so fucked up that I want to be with her all the time, and she doesn't want to. She just wants it once, or twice, and not any more. And sometimes she goes to take the kid to school and I'm sitting here like a dumbass watching TV. And seeing all those women undressed, and already feeling stupid, I turn that shit off and masturbate by myself (Javi, 32).

The protection of masculinity in a context where homoerotic acts are demonized allows one to understand the reasons for this artifice between sex workers and their clients. The emphasis made by the workers in occupying the "active" position, their insistence in continuous physical relationships with women and their heterosexual urges, and the reiteration of the economic aspects of their work and intermittent involvement therein, allows them to defend their masculine identity and declared heterosexual orientation. On the other hand, the position of the clients can vary when manifesting certain erotic desires in a safe and anonymous fashion (in the case of the "*tapados*"). But this defensive heterosexuality (Malcolm, 2000) also recreates a series of social imagery. That is, the "obvious" desire to be possessed by a "macho"; the adult enjoying the youth; or the rich dominating the poor (Perlongher, 1999).

Indoors prostitution: The Area of Boca del Río

In recent years, serious efforts have been made by government institutions in Veracruz to reactivate the tourism industry through aggressive advertising campaigns and the improvement and extension of the infrastructure (Estrada in Gallegos, 2006). More than anything, they have emphasized specific niches, such as ecotourism, adventure tourism, and archaeological tourism, besides utilizing more diffuse promotion of Carnival. In that vein, since 1990 several national and international chains have built hotels, increasing the availability of four and five-star lodging, primarily in the suburb of Boca del Rio (Gallegos, 2006). In this same area several restaurants, bars, and nightlife centres, along with the World Trade

Centre, have opened, allowing Veracruz to be the site of large academic and business events in recent years. The growing occupancy rate of five-star hotels in Boca del Rio reveals the higher proportion of upper and middle class tourists, with their subsequent greater purchasing possibilities. Likewise, although its use is still mainly domestic, the World Trade Centre continually offers large business and academic forums that attract people from all over the world. Figure 3.2 shows the location of some of the largest hotels and gay night clubs in the Boca del Río district, where sex work is carried on indoors. It also shows the distance between those hotels and the historic centre.

Figure 3.2: Boca del Río area and the historic centre

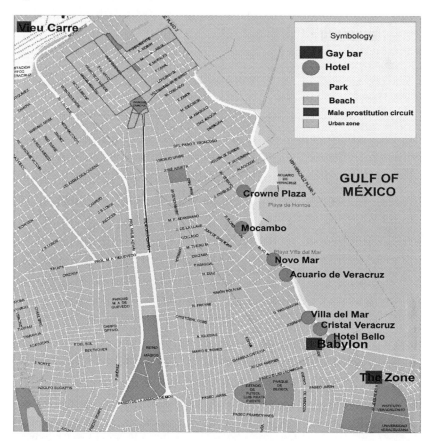

The improvement of infrastructure has contributed to an increase in the offer of gastronomic and amusement services: bars, restaurants, dance clubs, casinos, and coffee shops, to entertain clients. Three of the four gay dance clubs that exist in the Veracruz area are found here. Prostitution is also found here, inside a variety of establishments, or through escort or massage agencies advertised in special tourist guides found in hotel lobbies, at nightclub entrances, or even in the newspaper. These services are directed to consumers with large disposable incomes, both domestic and foreign, and adhere, privately or publicly, to the ruling models of western gay subculture (Altman, 1996). The amounts charged vary between 800 and 2,500 pesos

> Well, it depends on the quality of the guy, but sometimes it costs 800, 1000, 1500 [pesos]. Also, when the services lasts more than an hour but an hour and a half, we add 100 or 200 per hour. So it's convenient for us, for the boy that went to provide the service, for the client. Just so the client pays, so it's not too expensive, but not too cheap, you don't give it away to annoy the guy. So, we agree to a price (Ernesto, 33, massage agency manager).

For a good part of the year, the clients and the workers alike are locals, but in times of greater tourist activity, there is a large contingent of people from other parts of the country, or abroad. In such times, clients and workers congregate in other social areas with intense fluxes of visitors:

> High season is for everybody. Now that it's Carnival, it's the season for everyone, even for those in the sex work, because foreigners come, people from outside who come to consume. The boys [also come from outside]. I have one that comes from Orizaba, I have a Joe that comes from Cancun, I have an Angelo and a Charlie that come from Mexico City (Ernesto, 33, escort and massage agency manager).

Using an agency that attends to a higher class clientele provides the sex workers with less risk, better pay, and greater discretion. It also diversifies the possibilities for the construction (and assumption) of the workers' sexual identities: homo and bisexual, but passive and active too, and even the so-called "internationals" who with the same or different clients can be either active or passive.

> We put an ad in the paper saying, 'Looking for young man, nice appearance, wide experience, interviews in such-and-such a place'. When they show up, 'what's the job?' 'Look, it's like this, you have to have a cell phone, time available, here we practically just give you sex with the client.

He wants to go out with you, go to the bar, when he calls, you go.' We choose. Active, passive, bi, there's guys that do both, which is very attractive for us. Everyone came to us! You have to know what you're going to sell, so we need a gay guy to know what another gay guy likes. But you have to have all kinds: some like cute guys, others the animals, some the whites, I like the blacks. You have to have everything, small, big, medium, thick, everything. Passive, active, bisexual (Ernesto, 33, escort and massage agency manager).

All of these things, the kind of client, the means of contact, business through third parties, service parlours, the diversity of acts and types solicited, subscribe to the globalised gay subculture logic. As Altman (1996: 77-78) suggests, the expansion of an existing Western category points "to the emergence of the global gay," that is, "the apparent internationalisation of a certain form of social and cultural identity based upon homosexuality."

The Port of Veracruz, as the largest and most cosmopolitan city in the state of Veracruz, (though not necessarily the most tolerant towards the public demonstration of homosexuality) offers a variety of venue environments, including strip clubs. These clubs offer strip shows or Chippendales, as well as transgender, and virile go-go dancers, who dance on elevated platforms located throughout the floor, accompanying the main dancer or animating the dancing of the rest of the crowd. In some clubs there are showers with glass walls in which the dancer simulates bathing while moving to the music. Likewise, there is one nightclub located in the port zone that sometimes presents live gay sex shows.

Self image of indoor sex workers

While nude dancers in nightclubs are not strictly sex workers, the milieu in which they work makes it possible to combine dancing and commercial sex satisfactorily. In contrast to streetwalkers, who relate to a greater variety of social classes due to the public aspect of their service spaces, the clientele of dancers is composed of the patrons of these establishments, guaranteeing a certain income level. Some of the indispensable characteristics for gaining entry to work in such places are youth, physical beauty, and a very masculine appearance. It is almost an indispensable requirement to build a nice figure, sculpted in gyms, and to possess the corresponding identifiable aesthetic elements: short hair, tattoos, piercings, and a stereotypical, symbolic masculine outfit (e.g., police, cowboy, or soldier). (Hernandez-Cabrera, 2006)

> I think 26, 27 years old is the cusp [of being attractive], no? At least it goes
> better for you then, because you're on the right track. Passing 29, 30, it's
> not so easy to get picked up, they say, 'that guy's old' (Giovanni, 21).

For these performers, along with a muscular figure, it is also necessary
to maintain a semi-erection throughout the ten or fifteen minutes that each
dance routine lasts. This is achieved by previous stimulation, the
application of creams and sprays, or the use of a tight ring placed at the
base of the penis to avoid the rapid draining of the blood vessels:

> You use xilocaine. It's an anaesthetic that football players use when they
> get hit. You put it on and it gets rid of the pain. That's what they use on
> their penises and it lasts 3, 4 hours (Joe, 21).

Even though nude dancers are obliged to exhibit a hyper-masculinised
appearance, this stereotype is accompanied by doubts of their virility,
since it is assumed that undertaking this activity itself requires a certain
amount of exhibitionism and narcissism that in the collective imagination
are related to homosexuality. In this direction, two aspects that appeared
constantly throughout the interviews were of particular interest. The first
was to find that upon being interviewed all of the respondents, without
exception, placed a great deal of emphasis on defining themselves as
"100% heterosexual," "totally straight," and "a well-defined heterosexual."
Thus, youth, beauty, manliness and a hyper-sexualised body are necessary
to be successful in the sex show business:

> A 'stripper' isn't going to tell you, 'I'm gay', because it has more to do
> with manliness. Like you have to keep an image of strength, of man, of
> masculinity. So obviously if a guy goes out and acts feminine, nobody
> likes that. Of course gay people like that super-macho image, and girls too.
> So you have to take care of that image…the muscles, the body, you take
> care of yourself, you take care of your health, you take care of your body
> and try to have a good-looking image. I think all of us like good-looking
> faces and bodies (Victor, 28).

An apparent contradiction can be observed in the recurrent insistence
on the complete heterosexuality of the dancers. They constantly deny that
they allow the audience members to touch them, but through my
observation during the performances, the clients did touch them with
frequency. Upon being further interviewed, all of the dancers declared that
they were sure to avoid being touched:

You saw right now that I danced, and I didn't go close to the men. I mean, I dance in front of them but I don't get close because it makes me feel uncomfortable, and I don't want to be mean. I mean, if the guy gets close to me and tries to touch me, I'm not going to be rude. That's what I expose myself to, and I try to avoid it by not getting close (Christopher, 22).

I don't like them to touch me, because if they touch my member, they grab it, the gays, as if it was plastic, and it hurts. In my case, I consider myself real uptight, very arrogant. When I go out there erect, I just go out there and get into the groove and let them see me (Charlie, 23).

During the observation period, however, it seemed clear that the dancers did approach the patrons, and interacted with them, letting them touch their bodies. All of this indicates that this kind of worker sees himself as subjected to two types of demands, with his body as the focal point of each. On the one side, his success in the business lies in the exacerbation of his masculinity. On the other side, the dancer must allow the physical proximity on the part of the audience to whom the performance is directed. This proximity may or may not respond to his desires, but at any rate can be accepted as part of the tacit contract between the worker and his male clientele. This contradiction could be explained by the concept of sexual scripts developed by Simon and Gagnon (1999: 33), "the concept of scripting can take on a literal meaning: not the creation and performance of a role, by the creation and staging of a drama" by allowing coherence out of sometimes incongruous materials.

Conclusion

The Western and the westernised worlds have experienced important transformations during recent decades that have placed sex and the sexual at the core of social debates. New requirements of self-identification about the body, sexuality and the way individuals live their pleasures are almost political imperatives (Weeks, 1998). Based on some regularities shown in sex workers' narratives, this work has tried to analyse some aspects relating to, on the one hand cultural protocols and social conventions and on the other hand, the construction of individual identities. These regularities are evaluated through the lens of social values. This means that the elaboration of individual identities is intertwined with collective rules.

The traditional andro-centric sexual conceptions, in which male sexuality must be predatory, insatiable and needing of urgent fulfilment, favours the difference between active-masculine and passive-feminine roles. It also contributes in establishing a hierarchy between dominants and dominated. Erotic desires, practices, and the sexual use of the body are symbolic markers of what everyone is and is not: a full man or a sissy. Activeness, relationship with women, the capability of giving pleasure, and the denial of certain erogenous areas of the boy are essential components of *mayate* street workers identities. So is the insistence of economic motivations in entering prostitution, undertaken by young men from the lower or upper-lower classes, some dedicated to the profession full time, or combining it with other low income economic activities or temporary jobs. In the same way, their clientele consists of locals or regional or national tourists with a generally lower disposable income. This economic argument allows the sex workers to claim their adherence to a hetero or bi-sexual identity, determined by uses of the body.

Male sex services – in contrast to female prostitution that requires a high degree of visibility in public places, appealing to street solicitation to attract the attention of clients (Kandel, 1992), or the trans-gender variety which is impossible to hide or is confused with female prostitution – are offered in a hidden manner, closed to the public eye. In this context, where homoeroticism is devalued and stigmatised, offering or providing homosexual services in the public domain would tend to provoke prejudice. The stigmatisation requires the development of abilities sufficiently subtle to pass unnoticed by others, but explicit enough to announce that sex services are being offered or sought.

On the other hand, as the city has developed an infrastructure aimed at providing modern services directed at specific cosmopolitan markets with greater purchasing power, soliciting and selling services have taken another modality. Because prostitution takes place inside, anonymity and protection are relatively secure. Likewise, the clients as well as the workers tend to fit the mould of western gay subculture, which revolves around desires, orientations and homosexual practices. This allows the assumption of more varied identities among the participants. As Altman (2001: 94) argues, "it is precisely the constant dissemination of images and ways of being moving disproportionately from north to south, which leads some to savagely criticize the spread of sexual identities as a new step in neocolonialism."

The world of male prostitution has, without doubt, multiple edges that demand an interdisciplinary focus. This chapter has tried to shed light on some anthropological aspects in order to explain the possibility of continuities and transformations in its practice in a specific territory, such as the port of Veracruz. There remain, however, many areas to explore in which homoerotic sex work is highly stigmatised, where sexual and gender hierarchies are inverted, where ambiguous and changing relations exist, and where desire, secrecy, fantasy, prohibition, and enjoyment all play a part (Córdova, 2003). In short, it is an intensifying locus of what Foucault (1991) called "the device of sexuality."

References

Aldán, C. 2009. México, tercer lugar en prostitución masculina. *Imagen de Veracruz*. México, 6 October

Alberro, S. 1989. Templando destemplanzas: hechicerías veracruzanas ante el Santo Oficio de la Inquisición. Siglos XVI-XVII', in Seminario de Historia de las Mentalidades, *Del dicho al hecho... Transgresiones y pautas culturales en la Nueva España*, México, Instituto Nacional de Antropología e Historia

Altman, D. 1996. Rupture or continuity? The internalization of gay identities. *Social Text.* 48: 77 - 94

—. 1999. Foreword. P. Aggleton (ed). *Men who sell sex: International perspectives on male prostitution and HIV/AIDS*. Philadelphia: Temple University Press. pp. xiii - xix

—. 2001. *Global sex*. Chicago: The University of Chicago Press

Butler, J. 1999. *Gender trouble: Feminism and the subversion of identity*, New York: Routledge

Cantú, L. 2002. De ambiente. Queer tourism and the shifting boundaries of Mexican male sexualities. *GLQ.* 8 (1/2): 139 - 166

Clift, S. and Forrest, S. 1999. Gay men and tourist: destination and holiday motivations. *Tourism Management.* 20: 615 - 625

Chow-White, P. 2006. Race, gender and sex on the net: semantic networks of selling and storytelling sex tourism. *Media, Culture & Society.* 28 (6): 883 - 905

Córdova, R. Forthcoming. De arrabal extramuros a zócalo de placer: continuidades y cambios en territorios e identidades del turismo homoerótico en el puerto de Veracruz. Á. López and A. Van-Broeck (eds.). *Dimensión territorial del turismo sexual en México*. México: Universidad Nacional Autónoma de México/Consejo Nacional de Ciencia y Tecnología

—. 2005. Vida en los márgenes: La experiencia corporal como anclaje identitario entre sexoservidores de la ciudad de Xalapa, Veracruz. *Cuicuilco.* 12 (34): 217 - 238

—. 2003. 'Mayates', 'chichifos' y 'chacales': trabajo sexual masculino en la ciudad de Xalapa, Veracruz. M. Miano (ed). *Caminos inciertos de las masculinidades*. México: Instituto Nacional de Antropología e Historia/ Consejo Nacional de Ciencia y Tecnología. pp. 141-161

Corrales, L. 1993. *Apuntes para la definición y concepto de turismo rural.*
    España: Fundación Cultural Santa Teresa
de Moya, A. and R. García. 1999. Three decades of male sex work in
    Santo Domingo. P. Aggleton (ed). *Men who sell sex: International
    perspectives on male prostitution and HIV/AIDS.* Philadelphia: Temple
    University Press. pp. 127 - 140
Flores Martos, J. 2004. *Portales de múcara. Una etnografía del puerto de
    Veracruz.* México: Universidad Veracruzana
Ford, N. 2003. Book review: Tourism and sex: Culture, commerce and
    coercion. *Tourism Management.* 24: 228-231
Foucault, M. 1991. *Historia de la Sexualidad I. La voluntad de saber.*
    México : Siglo XXI
Gallegos, O. 2006. Estructura territorial del corredor turístico Veracruz-
    Boca del Río, México, al inicio del siglo XXI. M.A thesis, México,
    UNAM
García, B. 1996. Dinámica y porvenir del Puerto de Veracruz: crecimiento
    y transformaciones en el siglo XX, en *Primer puerto del continente.*
    ICA/Fundación Miguel Alemán, Singapur
Geertz, C. 1994. *The Interpretation of cultures: Selected essays.* España:
    Gedisa.
Gil, A. 2002. Vida cotidiana en Veracruz a fines del siglo XVIII. B. García
    and S. Guerra (eds). *La Habana/Veracruz. Veracruz/La Habana.*
    México : Universidad Veracruzana/Universidad de la Habana
Hernández-Cabrera, P. 2006. El *performance* de las masculinidades de los
    strippers, go-go dancers y teiboleros de los antros 'exclusivos para
    hombres' de la ciudad de México. Paper presented at the Seminario
    Permanente de Género, Sexualidad y Performance, Mérida, Yucatán,
    CINEY/ESAY/PUEG-UNAM, Escuela Superior de Artes de Yucatán.
    8 - 10 November
Kandel, M. 1992. Whores in court: Judicial processing of prostitutes in the
    Boston municipal court in 1990. *Yale Journal of Law and Feminism.* 4:
    329 - 352
List, M. 2007. El que no brinque es buga! Masculinidad e identidad gay,
    Ph.D. dissertation, México, Escuela Nacional de Antropología e
    Historia
López. A. 2001. Análisis de la organización territorial del turismo de playa
    en México, 1970-1996. El caso de Los Cabos, BCS. Ph.D. dissertation,
    Facultad de Filosofía y Letras, Universidad Nacional Autónoma de
    México, México
Malcolm, J. 2000. Sexual identity development in behaviourally bisexual
    married men. *Psychology, Evolution & Gender.* 2 (3): 263 - 299

Parker, R. 1999. Within four walls: Brazilian sexual culture and HIV/AIDS. R. Parker and P. Aggleton (eds). *Culture, society and sexuality: A reader.* London: UCL Press. pp. 253 - 265

Perlongher, N. 1999. *El negocio del deseo. La prostitución masculina en San Pablo.* Argentina: Paidós

Propin, E. and A. Sánchez, 2007. Tipología de los destinos turísticos preferenciales en México. *Cuadernos de Turismo* 19, España, Universidad de Murcia: 147-166.

Ricoeur, P. 1981. *Hermeneutics and the human sciences: Essays on language, action and interpretation.* J. P Thompson (editor & translator). Cambridge: Cambridge University Press

Sánchez, A. and A. López. 2000. Visión geográfica de los lugares gay de la ciudad de México. *Cuicuilco* 7(18), México, Escuela Nacional de Antropología e Historia: 1 - 17

Schifter, J. and P. Aggleton. 1999. Cacherismo in a San José brothel: Aspects of male sex work in Costa Rica. P. Aggleton (ed). *Men who sell sex: International perspectives on male prostitution and HIV/AIDS.* Philadelphia: Temple University Press. pp. 141 - 158

Simon, W. and Gagnon, J. 1999. Sexual scripts. R. Parker and P. Aggleton (eds). *Culture, society and sexuality: A reader.* London: UCL Press. pp. 29 - 38

Sinclair, M. 2004. *San Francisco: A cultural and literary history.* Northampton: Interlink books

Szasz, I. 2007. Sins, abnormalities, and rights: Gender and sexuality in Mexican penal codes. H. Baitenmann, V. Chenaut and A. Varley (eds). *Decoding gender: Law and practice in contemporary Mexico.* Piscataway: Rutgers University Press. pp. 59 - 74

Urgel, J. 2008. 'Chuecadrid': la meca homosexual de Europa. *Epoca.* 1206, Madrid, DINPESA, July 11th

Weeks, J. 1998. *Sexualidad.* México: PUEG/UNAM y Miguel Ángel Porrúa

Zuilhof, W. 1999. Sex for money between men and boys in the Netherlands: Implications for HIV prevention. P. Aggleton (ed). *Men who sell sex: International perspectives on male prostitution and HIV/AIDS.* Philadelphia: Temple University Press. pp. 23 - 39

CHAPTER FOUR

FLYING TIGERS IN A DOMINICAN TOURIST TOWN

DEIRDRE GUTHRIE

Derrida (2000) has observed that receiving someone in your home always rests awkwardly on the border between hospitality and hostility and thus is a fraught situation in which a hostage crisis is always imminent and mitigated by constant negotiation. The (post)colonial encounter is one in which the guest takes the host hostage and tourism is born of such an encounter in which hosts often act as servants in their own homeland, speaking the language of guests, performing various roles that meet guest expectations, but also creating "backstages" of resistance and counter-narratives to challenge guest representations.

This chapter focuses on Euro-American men (French, German, Italian and more recently, North American and Eastern European) and Dominican women engaged in a range of intimate relations in *Las Ballenas* (a pseudonym), a pueblo on the north-eastern coast of the Dominican Republic. "(Re)discovered" by bohemian Europeans in the 1970's, the (formerly) pristine area has recently undergone tremendous development at a furious pace, and Dominican elites, in partnership with foreigners, are now seeking to capitalize on its increased real estate value. For the rest of this chapter I will refer to non-Dominican (or non Dominican-Haitian or non-Haitian) foreigners as "guests" and to Dominican and Dominican-Haitian migrants as "hosts." Both hosts and guests form commodified, symbiotic, contingent relationships in tourist space, in which coercive practices are often disguised through performances and practices based on fantasy and desire. I will highlight the class anxiety that undergirds this emerging dialectic of coercion and desire, and describe its clashing narratives and contentious views, such as those that surround host/guest price negotiations and the use of concubine law.

My findings are based on 24 months of anthropological fieldwork and research conducted between 2005-2009 using the ethnographic methods of participant observation, extended, open-ended interviews, and discourse/ content analysis. In theorizing intersecting identities, I build on post-structural feminist theories that acknowledge difference and have revealed how subjects negotiate multiple roles and positions, though not all carry the same privileges and risks (Butler, 1990; hooks, 1981; Rich, 1986). My analysis also builds on the broader tenets of symbolic interactionism in which the self is reproduced through interactions with others and through staged practices (Bourdieu, 1990; Goffman, 1959). My focus on identity construction in tourist markets through what is termed "sex work" in academia, that is, the engagement of sexual acts for money, also builds on similar work conducted in the Caribbean (Brennan 2004, Kempadoo 2004, Ryan & Hall 2001, Sheller 2003).

Young, resource-poor, uneducated Dominican, Haitian, and Dominican-Haitian men and women who migrate to Las Ballenas and engage in a full spectrum of labour offered within the informal economy (not just sex work) occupy unique social roles in tourist space, challenging middle class values of "respectability" while simultaneously, for those who succeed in social advancement, arousing envy among other hosts for their modern, mobile lifestyles. Hardly passive, they are strategically positioned as cultural brokers to translate and distort local mundane reality into the stuff that gringo's desire. B*uscones (buscar* means literally to "look for"), for example, often seamlessly combine positions such as sex worker, motorcycle taxi driver, handyman, etc., and connect foreigners to their subjects/objects of fantasy, whatever their incarnation (drug, child, male, female, beachfront property with a view of Jurassic park). These individuals also prove adept at absorbing and indigenizing a deluge of foreign images, ideas, and consumer items and, as consumers, refashion themselves as part of a dynamic process of becoming that is continually being rediscovered and defined relationally. However, for the majority of youth who have lost access to land and its provisions of subsistence agriculture, and find themselves trapped in insecure cycles of debt and dependency on foreign capital and remittances, informal labour operates on the level of survival strategy rather than as a viable means of securing socio-economic advancement.

Because of this context, a useful method to confront Dominican subjectivity in tourist space is to locate the strategies people use to create continuity in the face of disruption, such as *"tigueraje"* (tiger) tactics which often involve cultivating strategic, sexual relationships with gringos as a vehicle towards attaining power. The term *tiguere* has been historically used in the DR with admiration when associated with men who, using their bodily assets, virility and charm, excel in their role as trickster or con-man. The Dictator Trujillo was described as the consummate *tiguere*, infamous for his seductions and violence (though he powdered his face to lighten his skin and allegedly had a squeaky voice (Derby, 2000). But the more recent usage, in reference to mobile, moneyed women in an increasingly competitive environment dependent on foreign currency, is more ambivalent. Dominican men now complain that women are more *tiguere* than they are; that is, empowered by their cleverness.

Because of its flexible nature, sex work can evolve into domains that defy clear categorization such as long-term relationships in which one party provides domestic labour and/or companionship as well as sexual services in exchange for a range of benefits that can be hard to distinguish from conventional legal marriage contracts. In the DR, red light districts, pimps, and cash payment upfront for sex work is rare. Host women may be "pimped" by their boyfriends or even family members who receive some kind of "finder's fee" but they are not pimps in the sense of offering protection in exchange for brokering sexual transactions for profit. In the DR, delayed payment is the norm in all commodified transactions and sexual relations are not stigmatized, but rather, when initiated by men, sexual overtures signify robust health. So sometimes it is hard to isolate an act as prostitution, per se. Daniella, 17, who found that she could not work formally in Las Ballenas, being underage and without a *cedula* (ID card), described sexual relationships with senior, foreign "friends" who ranged from those who never asked her name to those who became like surrogate fathers. Women do not identify as prostitutes even as they readily admit accepting monetary gifts for sex, for they may fluctuate in and out of a variety of service sector jobs, and may only occasionally have to go "to the street," or hold a variety of positions simultaneously: hostess, animation director, dancer, waitress, maid, cook, nanny, secretary. In any case there is no social shame attached to sex work practices among a rural-based society which has for centuries been functioning under polygamous social contracts and concubinage designed to reap benefits in terms of material gain and survival.

Instead moral judgment and condemnation comes from members of host and guest middle and upper class society seeking to reify their class position, particularly women (and not men, given the widespread custom among Dominican men to maintain mistresses or *queridas*) and, at least rhetorically, from Evangelicals. In Las Ballenas the protest against prostitution, discussed among the upper classes and in newspaper columns or on local radio, is ideologically defined and discussed in terms of protecting public health and morality. Foreigners or Haitian rather than

Dominican sex workers, who occupy the most marginal position within the social hierarchy, are accused of spreading AIDS in the pueblo. Academic writing (e.g., Brennan, 2004) as well as local newspaper editorials ("La Columna de Raquel" LT-7.com) representing the upper, educated classes in the DR, tend to frame the prostitution debate within the subjective experience of the social actors involved and the bureaucratic need for law and reform; a shift that reflects the broader move from industrial society to the world information economy that values individualization. Yet both lenses (the more conventionally ideological and the apparently more sympathetic subjective critique) can distort our understanding of social practices based on communal networks and structures. Long before postmodernism, working class Caribbean creole society maintained a fluid relationship to sexuality, personhood (the "I" is not autonomous but collective), and spirit (during possession the line blurs between life and death when subjects are mounted by the *lwa* spirits.)

However, while guests tend to project their repressed desire upon host sexuality and read it as emancipatory, hosts recognize how sexual desire can flare into greed and guests can *"come demasiado"* (eat too much). The concept *comer* (to eat) is regarded by Dominicans as a positive, masculine attribute of satisfying one's lustful appetites. Seafood, tonics, and powders are sold locally to ensure the maintenance of this vital function of stoking the male fire. But they also ensure its incessant anxiety in needing to be proven or displayed. Gringos have their own potions, readily sold at the pharmacy in bulk: Viagra and Cialis, known locally as *La Pela*. The translation of *"dar una pela"* (to give a beating) reveals the link between guest masculinity and violence. (NGOS estimate rates of domestic violence are as high as 40% in the DR). One sign along the dusty road to the pueblo reads: *Viagra con pollo* (Viagra with chicken) as if one might sprinkle such potency over ones' lunch. But eating can go awry. A fishermen vendor describes one of his gringo clients (a sex tourist) as sometimes "eating" two or three women in one day. "It is good to eat," he says, "but this is too much." When I ask a New York expat what circumstances keep him in the pueblo he rolls up his sleeve and shows me his tattoo of the Hungry Ghost with its swollen belly and tiny mouth, a Buddhist metaphor for those addicted to satiating their bottomless physical desires. Peddling fantasy and managing desire is a risky business, because of the combustibility of lust, and the ever-present threat of violence which undergirds the post-colonial encounter.

Guests desire "heat" and hosts desire the "freedom to choose"

At 3pm, Peter, my neighbour, a retired 65 year old German architect, pulls Nanci, his 37 year old live-in Dominican girlfriend, into the hammock. You could set a clock to his daily rituals. Espresso at 7:30am, breakfast at eight, Lia, Nanci's granddaughter, is taken to school by 9am, then Nanci tends to household chores; pruning the palms and cutting fresh orchids from the sculpted, tropical garden, amidst aggressive, honking geese and screeching peacocks, followed by lunch at noon, a steaming *sancocho* or *habichuela con pollo,* with Mozart or Wagner playing in the background. *Comida* (lunch) is the most significant meal of the day, digested slowly as the day's heat thickens. And inevitably, after the coffee and dessert, around 3pm, the pair retire to the large hammock. Their bodies entwine, two pairs of light and dark bare feet lolling playfully over the edge, and voices soften into murmurs, babbles of laughter, and Nanci's sweet, tone-deaf lullaby, then eventually Peter's rolling snore.

Nanci and Peter are a remarkable couple in Las Ballenas in that they recognized and respected their vast differences and corresponding needs and yet still found a way to establish intimate connection in a hostile environment teeming with fantasy. "Yes, for this place, we are fortunate to have found something that works," says Peter, who originally came to Las Ballenas with a German companion who decided to return to Europe alone. "She missed the museums, the libraries," he shrugs. "So I found myself, alone in paradise." And he had his share of (mis)adventures before he met Nanci.

When Peter leaves on errands, Nanci puts away Peter's gifts for Lia, the motorized pink car and white dolls with long-lashed blue eyes. She then begins to transition into her own world, playing *reggaeton, bachata,* and *merengue.* She wraps her head in a white scarf, spreads cornmeal on the floor under the sink, where it won't offend Peter's atheism, sprinkles it with rum, and lights the candles to call in the voudou spirits or *lwa* (loa). Nanci is from *San Francisco de Macoris*, a town flourishing from drug money known as the Dominican Republic's "Little Sicily." She acknowledges plainly that she came to this town full of aging European foreigners to look for a gringo to secure her future. Like many women from outside pueblos who live with gringos, Nanci says she has no friends here. The women are envious, and the men who now complement her on her new weave and boutique clothes "just smell money." One day I see her scolding a group of Dominican men, who are laughing nervously as she revs her Quad closer to them, pulling a wide-eyed Lia in behind her. She is a force to behold, her braids dancing around her ears, as she flings curses at them. "*Cabrone,* don't speak to me of my daughter!"

Her daughter (22), Nanci complains, conspicuously within earshot of Peter, does not want to work. She only cares to *disfruta la vida dulce* (enjoy the sweet life) and goes every night to the disco, looking for *una bola* (a free ride) from a gringo. But when Peter goes inside, her expression softens and she describes with a smile how her daughter has successfully seduced a Swiss man who says he will send her money each month.

"La Bola" is a coveted concept among Dominicans. A Dominican professor recounted how a maid lost her job in a free trade zone just to pick up *una bola* from a campaigning politician, which consisted of merely a 200 peso ($6) bag of rice and beans. "It's a holdover mentality from era of dictators and patrons," she explained. Nanci heard Peter complain more than once about the Dominican tendency to "milk the gringo cow." But, she says, although she may have migrated to Las Ballenas to find a gringo, she has always worked, in free trade zone factories (where she made $150/month), as a maid and cook in a hotel ($100/month), and now she tends to Peter and his house. She attributes no moral value to participating in such menial labour. Given the options, sex work or what locals call *buscando para un gringo* (looking for a gringo) is a viable alternative under limited options.

Naturally, Nanci says, her daughters are seduced by the life of leisure the gringos enjoy. They see an easier path in selling themselves at the disco, making in one hour what would take one week in a factory. Enjoying, if only for the evening, the lifestyle of the gringo, dressed in flashy clothes and heels, eating in an ocean-side restaurant or café, kite-surfing, salsa dancing, perhaps even attaining the upper class markers of mobility: a Quad, a jeep, a passport. And they know what the gringo seeks in return. Slogans bearing messages like those in Figure 4.1 speak to the overt nature of host/guest relations in town. Gringos can purchase T-shirts bearing the words: "Kiss me, I'm a pirate"

Figure 4.1: Messages and host/guest relations

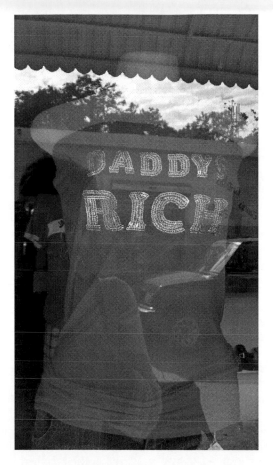

"They want our heat," Nanci says. "They know the Dominican is *caliente* (sexually hot but can also refer to warm qualities such as a personable manner or open generosity (*amable*) associated with uncorrupted peoples who are perceived as having escaped the jaws of modernity), and life, where they are, their people, are cold." But she also understands the risks and costs of fostering intimate relations with guests. She mentions Juanita, who wandered the pueblo dishevelled and half-mad after her husband sent her home from a German suburb without a peso, having replaced her with another Dominican woman. Juanita's experience demonstrates the fragility of *progressando* (social advancement). Given the high probability of such rejection and the resilience most Dominican women demonstrate, Juanita would have recovered. It was only after her former husband came to visit their son and take him to the States on holiday where both were killed in a car crash that she became undone. "What we want from you gringos is your freedom to choose," she says.

Economic Uncertainty and the Dominican Dream: Aspiring to be Another

In a recent National Human Development Report (Ceara-Hatton, ed., et al 2005) promoting the "human development model" of the United Nations Development Program (UNDP), an organization that emphasizes developing human resources over "the neo-liberal notion according to which economic growth is the sole source of welfare in our societies," Dominican national identity is described as forming through and against foreign processes ("externality"). The authors of the report suggest that the,

> ...*solution to the dilemmas of externality is to aspire to be 'another' or at least to 'seem to be another,' [italics mine].* Certain currents of globalization contribute to these aspirations by generalizing consumption patterns and lifestyles around the notion of 'being developed.'

Aspiring to be another is serious business. The pressure to project success, to live como *Dios manda* (as God intends) is intense, and contributes to aggressive borrowing/debt-incurring practices and competitive strategies. Appearing as developed, which means appearing as consumers, wearing fake name-brand clothing, for example, Izod logos blown up ten times on a polo shirt, is not just symbolic of social position but constitutes identity. When Nanci takes her twilight promenade in her four wheel drive vehicle dressed in her white linen dress and two-tone weave, with her grand-daughter similarly coiffed at her side, this is a display of genuine "cargo" and ritual status derived from the social gaze and the marketplace, and hence a source of her power and status. The practice of subjectivity-making, or becoming who you identify as, occurs through the accumulation of signs of otherness. Those migrants (both male and female) who come to tourist zones *buscando para un gringo* and fail in this unprecedented dream of accumulating the other's signs and thereby transcending class barriers, often disappear beyond this critical social gaze: abandoned sex workers return to their mother's houses in the countryside; Haitian labourers are deported across the border; and those suffering with SIDA (AIDS) return to the capital's slums to die.

Nanci's work history is representative of the opportunities available for uneducated migrants in the DR in free trade zone manufacturing and tourism. Over 171,000 workers are employed in zona francas (free trade zones), 70% in textile manufacturing (Human Rights Watch, 2004). These zones, combined with tourism, make up the fastest growing export sector in the Dominican economy bringing in $1.3 billion in annual earnings. Travel and tourism alone employ 14.4% of the population providing 550,000 jobs, roughly 1 in every 7 job (World Travel & Tourism Council 2010). However, formal jobs (e.g., animation director, hotel reception, management) in tourism go to educated Dominicans, from the larger cities of Santiago and the state capital of Santo Domingo. Uneducated migrants access lower tier jobs such as maid, bartender, janitor, and handyman.

Migrants who cannot access the formal economy or only qualify for lower-paying positions perceived as exploitive, diversify their sources of income, a historical pattern that is a common risk-aversion strategy stemming from peasant practices under precarious conditions, and pursue opportunities within the informal sector, such as those found in construction, narcotic distribution, prostitution, out-of-home micro enterprise, vending, taxi service, and security. In addition to an official unemployment rate of 16.4%, over 50% of Dominicans are employed in the informal sector (Jimenez & Santaolalla, 2008) which provides half of the household income for two-thirds of Dominican households (Deere, et al, 1990; Espinal, 1997). The recent economic shift from goods to services production in the DR economy has been cited as negatively affecting Dominican *identity*, in the recent National Human Development Report (Ceara-Hatton, 2005). The authors of the report describe how national identity before 1990 formed around agriculture. But with the shift to a service economy based on goods manufactured in free trade zones, tourist demand, and remittances, two forces emerged to challenge modern Dominican identity: externalization and forced cosmopolitanism. This shift...

> "has strengthened the perception that Dominican society has of itself and which is marked by uncertainty, instability and externality (the perception that the behavior of the people, and the events that occur to them, are determined by external elements)" (Ceara-Hatton, 2005: 6-7).

The report says that despite the growth of free zones and tourism, the collective perception remains that these are risky sectors and remittances are unreliable. In fact, this is an accurate perception. With regard to remittances, in the current global recession the amount of money sent home by Latin/Caribbean expatriates is expected to decline 11% in 2009,

according to a recent study by the Inter-American Development Bank
(Jordan, 2009). Also, a recent report noted that tourist arrivals have fallen
8.6% (from 304,747 in 2008 to 278,620 in 2009) and exports to the US
have fallen 20.8% (from US$585 million in 2008 to US$464 million in
2009) (Anonymous, 2009).

Javier, 27, who was born in the pueblo, thinks one of the persistent
corrupting effects of the tourist economy is the breaking down of
confianza, the trust and unity among the people, particularly between men
and women, in Las Ballenas. He explains how, as subsistence farmers and
fishermen became more dependent on foreign exchange, migrants poured
in from other areas or across the border from Haiti, and women began to
dominate the local economy—in both its formal and informal sectors.

> Javier: There exists a problem in this country with the women who
> work…First the man and the woman are together, and they are poor. Then
> the man finds work and everything is good. He brings money to the house.
> Later the woman finds good work and possibly earns the same as the man
> or even more, because always women earn more money than the man here,
> always they have better jobs, in offices, in houses, while the man has to
> work with his hands or on the mountain, [clearing fields, doing hard labour,
> agricultural work]. …then starts the difficulties because she can do with
> the money what she wants, go to the beauty salon, spend it…because
> already she is taking money for herself…this is different…before only the
> man brought money into the house.
> Author: It's not possible to earn money together?
> Javier: Well, it's the best thing to be united, but it's the money that comes
> between people in a couple. Look, if he [points to Luis, a successful fish
> vendor] is earning money, and I'm not, he is going to separate from me
> because I am poor. He is not going to want to speak with me because he
> thinks I'm going to always ask him for money. The money comes between
> friends, the people. And this is the reason men don't like women to
> work…because the women always buy the cellular, the car. The man
> leaves for here, the woman leaves for there …the best is to work and save
> together, united, but this is not how it is anymore.

Indeed the DR is experiencing the global effects of the feminization of
labour across the island and in the Dominican diaspora, though researchers
differ in their assessment of how this is effecting gender relations on the
island. Women make up 70% of the labourers in free trade zones (FTZ)
which did not exist 30 years ago. In the late 1980's the rate of employment
for women in FTZs more than doubled that of males. This gender shift
accompanied the displacement of male dominated agricultural labour
which had employed 73% of the Dominican labour pool in 1950 and only
35% by the end of the 1980's, replaced by Industry (20%) and Services

(45%) (Malik, 1989). In 1950 women in the labour force represented 17.9% of the population. By 2000 women represented 27.5% of the labour force. However, women are often chosen because of their second class status and perceived gendered qualities (dexterity, patience, docility) and are paid inferior wages because it is assumed they supplement a male "breadwinner," so these patterns do not necessarily translate into less patriarchal gender relations (Fernandez-Kelly, 2005; Grasmuck & Espinal, 2000; Safa, 1995). In fact, machismo can be reinforced in these exploitive patterns of feminized labour. For example, within sex work in Las Ballenas, I was struck by how often host women gave a substantial percentage of their earnings to their boyfriends.

Even so, as women have invaded the male spaces of the streets and become mobile with cell phones and jeeps, they are described by both hosts and guests as ruthless in securing their futures. Lacking pimps and not confined to red light districts, female sex workers are particularly visible and quite free to structure their time and movements among Las Ballenas' open-air cafes, disco, and the local Codatel office. The offices of Codatel, a subsidiary of the American company GTE, are a key site where women eagerly await faxes, phone calls, or money wires from their overseas "boyfriends" in the hopes that an island encounter might extend to a long-term financially viable relationship. Uncontrolled, the needs of young host women become, as one older Dominican woman, critical of the *tiguere* women in the pueblo, put it, "like the river in a flood, it never stops." Like an airplane (*avion* literally means airplane but also can refer to a sexy woman*)* she will fly higher and higher, super-mobile, uncontained. La *tiguere* as *avion* is therefore a troubling subject who must be disciplined by many sectors of society, including local machos, state police, "respectable" upper class Dominican families from the capital buying up vacation property, and newly converted Evangelists.

The Mirage of Las Ballenas as a Space of Transgression: Desire masking coercion

"*What* do these men see in them" says Lucille, a French woman in her late 50's. Lucille's husband, like many married, foreign men in town, left her for the maid after Lucille had already given up her flat in Paris to join him in Las Ballenas. The position of maid is often used to gain intimate access to foreign men and women. Veteran expat women and men know this and only hire domestic help who are old or unattractive. Otherwise they learn the hard way. For example, a missionary's wife was shocked to come home early and find her maid wrapped in a bath towel standing outside the bathroom door where her alleged oblivious husband was taking a shower.

For Lucille, the insult of being cast aside was a shock and she reacted by asserting her class privilege and emphasizing host vulgarity. "They have a sense of fashion, it's true. But have you seen them eat?" Lucille protests, "…hunched over, their hands dripping with meat. *That's* when the charade falls." Lucille could accept adultery, but in the French context. She described how famous French royal mistresses, noted for their beauty and sophistication, highly educated in both arts and sciences, acted as muses, political advisors, and confidantes to their powerful kings. "In France, we understand mistresses can contribute to a secure marriage," she assured me. "But you don't leave your wife." Lucille's second husband was an artist and had been vacationing in Las Ballenas for some time before she decided to join him and discovered signs of impropriety. At first he appeared to be helping women perpetually in need of milk for the baby or medicine for an ailing grandparent. But eventually he declared he was in love and wanted out. "Democracy and women's liberation," Lucille sighed. "I suppose this place represents the backlash. At least when there were rules, there was some pleasure to be had in breaking them. But this?" What disturbs Lucille and many other expats who found themselves initially seduced by the tropical beauty of Las Ballenas and its "natives" as presented through the tourist scrim, and then shocked by the social transgressions, was the "crude vulgarity" of the host-guest transaction, and the way it undermines a basic level of decorum, or class consciousness. The exploitation by the guests is so overtly obvious; the manipulations by the hosts so crude, the exchange of sex for the possibility of attaining a passport so overt, that it offends members used to a society in which power dynamics are more obscured by mystifying and often contradictory discourses, forms of subjectivity, and social practices.

Expat men are not always so bothered by the lack of romantic ritual in the encounter. Giorgio, an Italian felon (he claimed he tried to work "legitimately" as a salesman before he robbed a bank but could not sustain such a career which he sums up by making the gesture of putting on a tie and then pulls it up as if it were a noose, sticking his tongue out, and rolling up his eyes). "I told you before, it is very simple here. *Basico, basico, basico*. And this is why we can achieve a certain level of happiness …like dogs." Giorgio, like many other expat men in Las Ballenas, revelled in the kind of "outlaw" life available in a state-less zone like Las Ballenas which many compared to the "wild west," a kind of mythic frontier playground. He described his dealings with women as "basic" or "primitive" and therefore authentic. One day I found a dog-eared copy of Phillip Roth's novel, *The Dying Animal*, on the beach, with this passage underlined, that echoed this common sentiment expressed by guest men.

> "The French art of flirtatiousness if of no interest to me. The savage urge is. No this is not seduction. This is comedy. It is the comedy of creating a connection that is not the connection... created un-artificially by lust...don't confuse the veiling with the business at hand" (2001: 16).

What is the "business at hand" in Las Ballenas? What fuels guest desire? It is not French artifice, or a Greek idealized beauty, that is evoked by expats in their descriptions of attraction to Dominican and Haitian men and women. Do "we" become "savage" through "them," that is, is it the lack of "complication" in the encounter—the removal of the anxiety that "empowered" women represent with their access to education, mobility, and resources—that sparks a primitive "lust" and is read as "more authentic" because it affirms an uncompromised masculinity? Meanwhile "they" are assumed to be "naturally" lustful, rather than performing a prescribed role which holds the (oftentimes only) possibility for social advancement? "These people—it's their culture—they have sex on the brain 24-7!" said one married Spaniard computer programmer on holiday, grinning widely. "It's we, the Puritans, that have the hang-ups. We are so repressed that we've forgotten to enjoy sensual pleasure!" This attitude was also expressed by homosexual guests, who tended to emphasize host sexuality in terms of embodying a kind of bisexual freedom. "What is the difference between a gay Dominican and a straight Dominican?" a Canadian guest quipped. "About three beers."

Jeffrey, a former Peace Corps worker turned real-estate agent from New Jersey, used an evolutionary biological explanation to explain his desire. "It's all about gaining access to as many fertile females as possible—how many eggs do *you* have left?" Another American, rumoured to be a drug trafficker but also a popular English teacher to many teenage girls, explained that compared to their Western counterparts, host women were grateful and satisfied for the efforts and attentions of Euro-American men.

> "These girls are happy if you buy them a little plastic jewellery, you don't need to put diamonds on their fingers. And they have an expression I like, that describes relationships. You say 'he or she is my *media de naranja* (half of orange). I can handle that, being someone's half-piece of fruit. But back home they want a soul-mate; that's asking for a lot."

The pattern that emerged in the backstories of guest males was a feeling of compromised masculinity. Their sense of emasculation was associated with present-day global socioeconomic conditions, such as divorce, feeling placed in exploitive work environments in which they had little control, or among Western women whom they saw as in a powerful position to limit or deny a vital resource (their bodies). One French man claimed he felt that rising homosexuality in Euro-America was directly connected to the castrating woman's liberation movement in these countries (that is, men turn gay through socioeconomic competition with females). Aging was another reason cited for a sense of compromised masculine identity, untenable in its inability to deal with vulnerability. "In Europe," Peter remarks. "the people are all old. And when I walked the streets of Germany, those who were young, did not see me. I felt invisible. Here, dozens of young, pretty ladies smile and call out to me every day."

Yet Peter also tells me how his new visibility made him susceptible to the *tiguere* tactics of host women. "We are all fools when we first come here," he says, shrugging, and reciting a long list of names of others who felt the sting of Cupid's arrow. He explains how before he moved in with Nanci, he fell in love with the queen of tigers, Estonia, and supported her four children while she was cheating on him with other gringos, in addition to her Dominican boyfriend (introduced as a "cousin" when he slept over). When Peter finally broke things off with her, Estonia flew into a rage and smashed all the windows of his truck. *"El amor 'ta ciego"* (Love is blind), he shrugs.

Flying Tigers

Lucille shows me a painting her husband made of the woman he left her for. "She was in her 30's but he painted her as if she were a girl, in school uniform." She rolls her eyes. "The *picture* of innocence." When her husband informed Lucille that he was in love she thought this woman must have put "crack" in his beer at the local disco, which might explain his "bulging eyes." The belief that various kinds of "date rape" drugs were put into gringos' drinks at bars to seduce them was not uncommon (and in some cases, perhaps plausible, through the various sedatives and/or stimulants used in magical herbal tinctures concocted to bewitch, stimulate, or "zombify" guests, or even through drugs trafficked through motorcycle taxi drivers who were often the relatives or boyfriends of sex workers). But even sober, the disco-bar scene in Las Ballenas is a stimulating, heady experience, for even the most grounded of individuals. In this performance arena, scantily clad, young male/female migrants engage in fierce competition, positioning themselves within arm's reach of seated, world-weary gringos, gyrating and swivelling their hips in rapid-fire figure eights, pumping their buttocks, or simulating fellatio with male friends, dancing *peera* or "doggie style" to the aggressive rap beat of *reggaeton.*

Its visceral appeal to those existential exiles from a bureaucratized, alienating, cold Euro-America is significant. As Lingis writes, "In the embrace of a stranger one is no longer... a virile and self-determined agent...the craving to lose oneself in orgasmic exultation is a repetition compulsion" (2004: 198). As the night wears on, and the bartender pours an endless fountain of *cuba libres*, the disco ball sprays rainbows upon exposed, glistening male and female bodies, moving together, dressed in shimmering beads of metallic-gold and orange fabric hugging every curve and voluptuous bulge, revealing faces with smiling, open lips and glimpses of smoky eyes accented by electric eye shadow. What aging Swiss banker, German computer technician, or American manager would not react to the bold gesture of the unabashed girl who grabs his fingers and inserts them in her mouth, or the Haitian siren who squirms and giggles on his lap, steaming up their bifocals? Or what French divorcee would not feel slightly flush as her dance partner presses his hand against the small of her back and gyrates his groin into her pelvis? But one of my informants, Enrique, 25, who accompanies me to the disco one night, is quick to explain the sexual performance and display before him as *tigueraje,* not as an essentialized, sexual primitivism. "These girls have the snake eyes," he laughs, "Look at that one, [he motions to a girl who is edging her way over to an obese Italian with bifocals] she has found her next victim!"

"Watch this," says Daniella, adjusting her tasselled brassiere as she strides toward a gringo with her long legs in a tight skirt, a counterfeit thousand peso bill in her hand. She asks for change, which the gringo gives her promptly, appearing slightly stunned by her presence and attention. Five minutes later she turns with a wink and strides back toward our table. Lari laughs as she accepts Daniella's repayment of a debt using the gringo's cash, and continues to shell the *gandules* (lentils) spilled out on the table before them. She shares her latest scam: how she enjoyed a nice meal of beer and grilled shrimp on a beachfront chaise lounge next to a sleeping German. When the waiter arrived with the check, she explained that the sleeping German was her *novio* (boyfriend). The German, awakened and puzzled, protested. Then, on cue, a policeman (and Clari's lover) arrived to demand that the feckless gringo pay his due or else risk dishonouring both this woman and the *Republica Dominicana* itself, of which, need he be reminded, he was only a temporary guest.

Fraught Negotiations

Figure 4.2: The Beach as meeting place

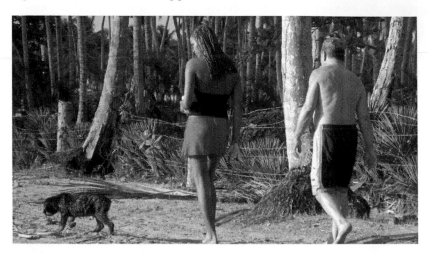

Many host women complained to me of the amount of time that guests desired to spend with them at the beach, which they shunned because of the drying effects of the sea water on their hair, and the sun's darkening of their skin.

Recognizing the fragility of guest masculinity, sex workers acknowledge the trickiness of the negotiation, the need to mask its commercial motivation in order to preserve male fantasy. But the need to disguise a request for payment for services rendered underscores the irony embedded in sex work in which "women are allowed to give free sex but not to negotiate for payment without breaking the law" (Zelizer, 2005: 107). Lari explains,

> "Sometimes it's best not to say it (the price) …but others ask you and I don't like it because the reality is I don't know how much money they have in their pocket. If you ask too much they say forget it, or if you ask too little, they say 'Ah, so easy!' and take your number but don't call. Or there are others—Dominicans too—who say 'if you had not asked I would have given you double or more!' Sometimes I think about that…because it's so stupid that they don't give it to you. But if you ask you are 'of the street' and hateful. So I don't ask. I spend the night and what they give me, they give me from the heart."

Hosts contextualize their intimate relations within their cultural economy which traditionally relies on informal networks and barter, practices that tend to blur lines between commodity and gift. Once a connection is made "there are gringos that give you something because you explain to them your life situation, that your parents work, that you are not rich, and then they pay for your house and they say they want to help you...it's like a little gift," not merely renumeration for sex. And indeed the kinds of intimate economies being brokered involve a range of exchanges, so "gifting" (pampers for the baby, cement for the house) makes the transaction more palatable. "It's awkward and demeaning to ask 'how much?'" says one guest. "So after awhile you say, 'what do you need this week?' and they tell you. And we both feel better about it." But other men are fully conscious of the commodified, *tigueraje* nature of the transaction, as well as the staged nature of the performance. On internet forums guest men also inform each other of how to best manipulate the situation and avoid being conned.

> Like I say, half of them aren't going to work. But the other half will. The trick is knowing who's who before you shut the hotel room door. It's not easy. They will often do a 180--flirt, dance, touch, sweet talk you beforehand and then totally bitch out on you behind closed doors: complain, rush you, try to get more money, tell you that you can't do this or that. Take your time. See how far you can get before you have to pay them (I often pay after the fact). Ask them if they like to go to the beach? Which one? Are they free tomorrow? They think they're practically married at that point. Tell 'em all about yourself. Make friends with them. That goes a long way. Take them out of one club and bring them to another--like a date. Totally throw them off.

As this man's post reveals, the adversarial goal is to "see how far you can get before you have to pay them," in other words, exploit the performance (flirting, dancing, touching, sweet talk) and deny a woman compensation for as long as possible.

Concubine Law

I know I am too mean to be your queen
And yet too good to be your concubine.
(Shakespeare 2001 - Lady Grey to King Edward IV, Part III, Act III, Scene II of *King Henry VI*)

In the DR, the majority of resource-poor women who perform all the duties of wives live as concubines in a kind of common law marriage.

Most men across class are polygamous and if they can afford it have mistresses ("kept women" or *amantes, queridas*) who live elsewhere, in separate households. Within the distorted bubble of tourist space, migrating women seek to reproduce this familiar structure and attain the role of concubine or mistress, which is more secure than living short-term as a prostitute in a cheap hotel with a tourist on holiday. While *tigueraje* tactics allow for individual modes of resistance and class mobility, sex work in the DR usually involves little recourse in terms of legal, contractual, or institutional definitions of protection. But recently state concubine laws have been enforced, albeit unevenly, to host women's advantage.

Penelope complains to her neighbours that a host she is temporarily living with has the nerve to think he "maintains her" because he has bought everything in their shared apartment. She rolls her eyes. "He doesn't understand that here, when the woman lives with the man, everything goes to the woman," she says. "The woman takes the bed, TV... and the man is left with nothing but the radio." The possibility that host women might be attaining some leverage in these unequal transactions instils a great deal of anxiety among guest males. On a newspaper internet forum (Guzman, 2008) one expat asks for specific legal advice around this issue of concubine entitlement to household property.

> I have heard horror stories, he writes, of guys that live with a girl for a 6 months to a year, and then they split up and when the girl leaves, up comes the truck and they take almost everything, including many assets that were purchased long before they were together, like computers, TVs, stereos, and most of the furniture, etc.

Dominican attorney Fabio Guzman assures him that the host woman has no legal rights over the gringo's property but underscores, "you cannot guarantee that courts will not adopt in the future a doctrine allowing division of "companionship" assets...or that Congress will not pass new legislation providing for division of assets." Until 2001 even legal Dominican wives were not allowed to dispose of even their own property, let alone communal assets, without the husband's consent. This situation changed with the passing of Law 189-01 of 22 November 2001, which amended several articles of the Civil Code, granting both spouses the joint administration of common property (Pellerano & Herrera, 2005). Concubines or live-in girlfriends are now well aware of ways to gain materially by living with foreigner. Several guests admitted arriving to Las Ballenas naïve, not speaking the language and enamoured by some *tiguere*-hustler who, after the "break-up," garnered witnesses to testify they were living with said guest male as a legitimate concubine and therefore were accorded property rights (the wooden house and its furnishings and appliances). A similar process works, depending on one's alliances and clout, with regard to land title around squatter's rights.

Guzman (2008) clarifies that the law is currently ambiguous:

> "Living together with a woman is never equivalent to a normal marriage. However, certain provisions in the Labor Code, the Minors Code and the Criminal Code acknowledge that living together has legal consequences. For example, a worker has the right to a few days off work if his concubine gives birth to his child; domestic violence to a concubine is treated the same as domestic violence to a wife. Recently, on October 17, 2001 a Supreme Court decision gave a surviving concubine the right to sue for the wrongful death of her companion in an automobile accident under very restricted conditions: a) the couple must have lived as if they were husband and wife, in a public relationship, not hidden or secret; b) the relationship must be stable and long-lasting; c) the relationship must be monogamous and non-adulterous since its origins; and d) the couple should be of different sexes. The ruling goes on to say expressly that 'marriage and extra matrimonial companionship are not…equivalent realities'."

Attaining communal witness testimony requires substantial local contacts and often the promise of compensation, which many female migrants, particularly Haitians, lack. Also, guest men are becoming more savvy. As one concerned expat writes on a public newspaper forum in response to Guzman's legal advice above.

> Although our resident lawyer is right, I would recommend to our junkies to be wary of long term concubine relationships, specially longer than 3 years. Although it isn't a law, the recent case by the Supreme court raised many eyebrows and with the legal profession beginning to get smart about presenting new challenging cases to the Supreme Court, no one is safe anymore. Yours could be the next test case. With the feminists getting a foothold in politics and government I predict the concubine law is not very far away and in my opinion they will put a three year limit. That means that if you were not married with another woman and you live happily ever after for 3 years or more with a live-in girlfriend in a monogamous relationship and in addition commit the mortal sin of having children, be prepared. Might as well get married. (TW, 2002)

Conclusion

In this chapter I have listed some of the constraints which limit the reality of Las Ballenas as a place of celebratory transgression. I have demonstrated how negotiation tactics around pricing sexual transactions are disguised to make the mutually symbiotic and exploitive encounter more palatable, as well as how hosts resist being "eaten as the other" (hooks, 1991) through asserting rights to property through concubine law. I have thus sought to highlight power dynamics embedded within this *tigueraje* game of intimate relations, rather than critique the commodified nature of host/guest relations through a social justice lens. The field of anthropology itself was born through the reaction to industrialization where "pure" society was defined against commodities. In the West we tend to assume commodification will be resisted by intimate relations that can be defined against it such as love and marriage. But in the DR these areas adapt rather easily to commodification. Hosts contextualize their intimate relations within their cultural economy which traditionally relies on informal networks and barter, practices that tend to blur lines between commodity and gift.

But even though the Dominican historical/cultural context allows for a broad range of commodified sexual relations, this current moment of globalised democracy, is unique and places the transgressive strategies of both upward-mobility seeking hosts and masculinity reaffirming guests at odds. Hosts strive to enter development and modernity as consumers while guests are seeking an imagined authenticity (a "roots" woman who has not been corrupted by feminism) to reaffirm their own compromised masculine privileges. Due to the gap in expectations, both parties revel in the performance of *tigueraje*, displaying a good deal of self-consciousness. In the spirit of Serbian philosopher Slavoj Zizek's observation of modern "cynical reason," "[hosts/guests] know very well how things are, but still they are doing it as if they don't know" (1994: 316). Zizek continues, "For example, they know that their idea of freedom is masking a particular kind of exploitation, but they still continue to follow this idea of freedom" (1994: 316).

Guests in tourist space still dream of abandoning their repressed, bureaucratized "first world" selves and responsibilities, inspired by what they perceive as a naturally sexually open and permissive Caribbean culture. "We long to be a beach bum," writes ecstatic philosopher, Alphonso Lingis. "…an animal making love with them on the night sands" (2000: 154). It is this promise of transgression that marks the tourist zone as special, and assigns young host migrants the role of performing this fantasized other who will guide foreign subjects into their hedonistic dream. Yet because intimacy also involves unsettling exposure of "interpersonal rituals, bodily information, awareness of personal vulnerability, shared memory of embarrassing situations and attentions such as terms of endearment, bodily services, or emotional support" (Zelizer, 2005: 14), the travel encounter can just as easily degenerate into a narcissistic drive to render the strange familiar.

When narratives inevitably clash during intimate relations (i.e., when male guests see that host women do not see them as essential men, but as vehicles from which to gain upward mobility through their pension or passport) the destabilization to masculine identity that such intimacy fosters may provoke a kind of defensive, retracted response, especially since the travel encounter is motivated by a kind of colonial nostalgia, a desire to reassert a fading, imperial privilege. This desire to reaffirm a threatened identity can result in violence. Denise Brennan (2004) has documented the rise in violence in *Sosua,* another Dominican tourist town that has accompanied its reputation as an "international sex destination."

In Las Ballenas the attempt to freeze representation of the other is evidenced in the fairly recent development of internet sex tourism whose explorers have introduced a particularly disassociated kind of intimacy confined to the deterritorialised world of cyberspace. This new type of tourist and his (he is male) strategies/practices represents a research area that deserves more attention. Dominican women who routinely post provocative photos of themselves online for an unknown foreign, male audience speak, mystified, of these recent arrivals who remark that host women compare unfavourably in real life to their cyber counterparts. One afternoon as I pass an internet café (these cafes mushroomed in 2008-9) I note a curious sight: a German tourist is staring at a woman's body on a computer screen, placing his mouse upon her throat to magnify her image. *Hours later* upon my return I see he is still inside, moving his mouse over *the same image*, now enlarging her thigh. What are the implications of this new fragmented subject, the cyborg prostitute and this new form of the male gaze? In what ways is his control of digitized fragments onscreen more satisfying than the prospect of relating with live, whole-bodied women outside the café doors? And what are its implications? Cultural, feminist theorist Margrit Shildrick writes on how we might conceptualize a new "mode of intercorporeality" within intimate relations, beyond this kind of regressive defence that fears the dissolution of personal autonomy. "In place of... the masculinist economy that reduces difference to a property relationship, our selves could form in the dynamic contact with others, not according to a fixed ideal but in a transformatory encounter in

which neither self nor other is a predictable, calculable identity with
inviolable boundaries" (2002: 118).

In the meantime, however, a different kind of borderwork is at play.
The Dominican state in Las Ballenas, with its new police force, now seeks
to clean tourist space for national elite consumption, and rid it of both
socioculturally transgressive (lawbreaking) hosts *and* guests. In this light,
we may look tentatively at the concubine law in its recent evolution to
define rights (on a ad-hoc basis) and transfer assets to sex workers and
away from foreigners as providing rationale for state intervention to re-
establish order, moral purity, and the viability of the nation. As one
Dominican hotel developer from the capital said, "Tell the French, the
Germans, the Spanish and their Haitian (not Dominican) whores, we
Dominicans are coming back to reclaim our land," (parenthesis mine).

References

Anonymous. 2009. Exports to the US fall 20.8%. *DRI Daily News*.
    http://dr1.com/news/2009/dnews050109.shtml
Bourdieu, P. 1990. *The logic of practice*. Stanford: Stanford University
    Press
Brennan, D. 2004. *What's love got to do with it? Transnational desires
    and sex tourism in the Dominican Republic*. Durham: Duke University
    Press
Butler, J. 1990. *Gender trouble: Feminism and the subversion of identity*.
    New York: Routledge
Ceara-Hatton, M. (ed). 2005. *National human development report:
    Dominican Republic*. New York: United Nations Development
    Program
Deere, C. D., Antrobus, P., Bolles, L., Melendez, E., Phillips, P. and
    Rivera M. 1990. *In the shadows of the sun: Caribbean development
    alternatives and US policy*. Boulder: Westview Press
Derby, L. 2000. The dictator's seduction: Gender and state spectacle
    during the Trujillo regime. *Callaloo*. 23 (3): 1112 - 1146
Derrida, J. 2000. *Of hospitality*, trans. by Rachel Bowlby, Stanford:
    Stanford University Press
Espinal, R. 1997. Gender, households, and informal entrepreneurship in
    the Dominican Republic. *Journal of Comparative Family Studies*. 28:
    103 - 126
Fernandez-Kelly, P. 2005. The future of gender in Mexico and the United
    States: Economic transformation and changing definitions. D. Bills

(ed). *The shape of social inequality: Stratification and ethnicity in comparative perspective.* New York: Elsevier. pp. 255 - 280

Goffman, E. 1959. *The presentation of self in everyday life.* Garden City, N.Y: Doubleday Press

Grasmuck, S and Espinal, R. 2000. Market success or female autonomy? Income, ideology, and empowerment among microentrepreneurs in the Dominican Republic. *Gender and Society.* 14 (2): 231 - 255

Guzman, F. 2008. *Common law marriage? DR1 Forums.* http://www.dr1.com/forums/legal/71876-common-law-marriage-legal-elements.html. 4/08/2008

hooks, B. 1992. *Black looks: Race and representation.* London: Turnaround

Human Rights Watch, 2004. *A Test of inequality: Discrimination against women living with HIV in the Dominican Republic.* http://www.hrw.org/en/node/12001/section/1. 1/5/09

Jimenez, D. and Santaolalla, A. 2008. *Dominican Republic-European community: Country strategy paper and national indicative programme for the period 2008-2013.* http://ec.europa.eu/development/icenter/repository/scanned_do_csp10_en.pdf

Jordan, M. 2009. Money sent home by Latin American expatriates to drop. *Wall Street Journal.* August 12th: A10

Kempadoo, K. 2004. *Sexing the Caribbean: Gender, race, and sexual labor.* New York: Routledge

Lingis, A. 2004 *Trust.* Minnesota: University of Minnesota Press

—. 2000. *Dangerous emotions.* Berkeley: University of California Press

Malik, B. 1989. Dominican Republic: The economy. R. A. Haggerty (ed). *Dominican Republic: A country study.* Washington: Federal Research Division of the Library of Congress

Pellarano and Herrera, Attorneys at Law. 2005. Legal framework for foreign persons: Important aspects of Dominican family law. *Dominican Today.* http://www.dominicantoday.com/dr/business-guide/2005/8/6/3443/IMPORTANT-ASPECTS-OF-DOMINICAN-FAMILY-LAW

Roth, P. 2001. *The dying animal.* New York: Houghton Mifflin

Rich, A. 1986. *Blood, bread, and poetry: Selected prose 1979-1985.* New York: W. W. Norton

Ryan, C and Hall, C. M. 2001. *Sex tourism: Marginal people and liminalities.* New York: Routledge

Safa, H. 1995. T*he myth of the male breadwinner: Women and industrialization in the Caribbean.* Boulder: Westview Press

Shakespeare, W. 2001. King Henry VI, Part III. J. D. Cox and E.
    Rasmussen (eds). *Arden Shakespeare third series*. London: Thomson
    Learning
Sheller, M. 2003. *Consuming the Caribbean: From arawaks to zombies*.
    London: Routledge
Shildrick, M. 2002. *Embodying the monster: Encounters with the
    vulnerable self*. London: Sage
TW. 2002. Warning to common wife junkies. *DR1 forums*.
    http://dr1.com/forums/legal/16341-common-law-wife.html. 4/08/2008
World Travel & Tourism Council, 2010. *Travel & tourism economic
    impact: Dominican Republic*.
    http://www.wttc.org/bin/pdf/original_pdf_file/dominicanrepublic.pdf.
    4/5/10
Zelizer, V. 2005. *The purchase of intimacy*. Princeton: Princeton
    University Press
Zizek, S. 1994. How did Marx invent the symptom? S. Zizek (ed).
    Mapping ideology. London: Verso Press. pp. 296 – 331

CHAPTER FIVE

REGULATORY SPACE AND CHILD SEX TOURISM: THE CASE OF CANADA AND MEXICO

LINDA M. AMBROSIE

In 2002 three Canadian and nine American men on vacation in Acapulco were arrested for enticing young male street boys to their house. For several years over the winter months, these men had rented a house overlooking the bay where they held adolescent boys hostage while they took turns having sex with them and filming their activities. The pornographic material served not only to record their exploits but also to finance the trip through the sale of the images over the Internet. In 2007 in two separate incidents two Canadians were charged in Thailand. The Canadian, Christopher Paul Neil, now in prison in Thailand, was sentenced for sexually molesting at least three boys whereas a separate Canadian offender, Orville Mader, slipped across the border to Cambodia and flew back to Canada in order to be prosecuted under softer Canadian laws. Between 1993 and 2008 there were at least 156 Canadians charged overseas for offences relating to child sexual abuse and exploitation (Perrin, 2008), yet to date only one man has ever been successfully prosecuted in Canada under the Child Sex Tourism (CST) laws introduced in 1997.

An increase in the number of victims of trafficking suggests there are a growing number of tourists that engage in CST (ICE, 2008; UNHCR, 2008). It is estimated that in Mexico the number of children that are victims of prostitution, pornography and human trafficking increased from 16,000 to 20,000 between 2000 and 2008 (UNHCR, 2008). Most of the exploitation occurs in Mexican tourist resorts such as Cancun and Acapulco, and in border cities such as Tijuana (near San Diego) and Ciudad Juarez, near Tucson, Arizona (ICE, 2008; UNHCR, 2008). Among those who pay for sex with boys and girls are American, Canadian and European tourists (Mattar, 2007; UNHCR, 2008). Often they contact "sex tour operators" to assist their travel arrangements to American cities such

as Tucson, Arizona from where they are transported the 100 km to Ciudad
Juarez, Mexico to engage in sex with minors. In the past few years,
American Customs officers posing as sex tourism operators in Tucson
have arrested child sex tourists from Germany, France and Canada (ICE,
2007; 2008).

Although the actual numbers of children being commercially exploited
is disputed (Estes, 2001), UNICEF (2009) estimates that as many as 1.2
million children fall victims of trafficking, pornography and sex tourism
every year. Despite international efforts, there is no doubt that the practice
is on the rise as is its importance to some economies. A UN (International
Labour Office) report found that in countries such as Indonesia, Malaysia,
the Philippines and Thailand, the "sex sector" accounts for anywhere
between 2 to 14 percent of national income of which half is estimated to
come from child sex tourism (Song, 2003). Privilege and corruption, as
well as race and age, conspire to allow the often blatant commission of this
internationally denounced crime which remains nearly impossible to
prosecute despite the unanimity as to the necessity of enforcement.

CST is largely a phenomenon of poverty in the underdeveloped and
developing nations (hereinafter Less Developed Countries or LDCs).
Although the number of tourists that travel internationally to engage in
sexual activity is less than the national incidence of child sexual abuse
(NCMEC, 2009), nonetheless all the member states of the United Nations,
with the sole exception of the USA, have unanimously ratified the 1990
UN Convention on the Rights of the Child (hereinafter UNCRC) in which
article 34 binds signatories to incorporate appropriate measures to protect
children from sexual exploitation. Additionally, the Optional Protocol to
the UNCRC (hereinafter the Protocol) with broader binding obligations
than those set out in the UNCRC was opened for ratification in 2000 and
by 2009 117 countries were signatories with 135 countries party to the
Protocol (Treaties, 2009). The importance of arresting the growing
incidence of CST was so paramount that the preamble to the Protocol
states that one of the motivating factors is concern "at the widespread and
continuing practice of sex tourism, to which children are especially
vulnerable, as it directly promotes the sale of children, child prostitution
and child pornography." In the eight page Protocol reference is made to
the commercial sexual exploitation of children no less than 12 times and
an entire article (Art. 10) is devoted specifically to the subject.

In addition to these important landmark conventions, there have been
many other voices denouncing the crime of child sex tourism including the
United Nations World Tourism Organisation (hereinafter UNWTO) whose
members have signed a statement calling for ethical behaviour in tourism,

and ECPAT's[1] efforts to have tourism companies such as airlines, hotels and tour operators sign a Code of Conduct. This chapter seeks to answer the question as to what has been the real effect at the international, bilateral and domestic levels of this concern. Have there been significant modifications to domestic legislation and a corresponding increase in investigations, prosecutions and convictions? In view of the widespread agreement as to the obvious violation of human rights what are the social and legal constructions of CST complicating the battle to thwart this growing side of the tourism industry? Using the analytical device of "regulatory space" the articulation of formal authority and discursive legitimacy is examined in order to determine who dictates the (im)mobilization of critical resources that have made any final act of enforcing CST laws a rarity.

Despite a plethora of conventions and domestic extraterritorial legislation, the record of prosecution of child sex tourists has been limited for three reasons. Firstly, is the increasing irrelevance of the nation-state in a globalizing world where enforcement depends on domestic efforts to prosecute trans-national crimes. Secondly, webs of NGOs such as ECPAT and UNICEF can highlight the issues but have no control over the resources to enforce. Finally, domestic legislation focuses on the offender alone with little regard to the chain of tourism-related activities promoting and facilitating access to children. New forms of technologies such as the Internet and better modes of travel are making the world a smaller place and shortening the chains between the offender and his victim. Without a serious attempt to address these key links, the overall impact of domestic legislation will be minimal and these children will remain in bondage.

One of the misconceptions this chapter hopes to dispel is the assumption that wealthy developed nations, in particular Canada, are proactive in preventing and prosecuting the crime of CST. Despite a growing recognition of online and real-time sexual predators in Canada resources are minimal to combat this trans-national crime and resources are deployed almost exclusively to prosecute online predators of Canadian minors. Mexico is also the focus of this chapter as it ranks in the top ten tourist destinations worldwide based on international tourist arrivals. Canadians comprise 5-10% of those arrivals (UNWTO, 2008).

---

[1] ECPAT stands for 'End Child Prostitution in Asian Tourism', later broadened to 'End Child Prostitution, Child Pornography and Trafficking in Children for Sexual Purposes'. ECPAT originated in Thailand and now has representatives around the world. The organization works closely with UNICEF, the UNWTO and theCode.org.

What is Regulatory Space?

More than simply regulation, regulatory space is the institutional arrangement that arises from relations of power which determines what constitutes public and private domains (Hancher & Moran, 1989). This distinction is important because only that which is considered to be in the public domain, and therefore in the public interest, will be regulated by formal authority. Regulatory space is comprised of the subjects to be regulated, the issues to be regulated and the sanctions imposed for deviance from the norms established. The subjects to be regulated are a nation's citizens comprised of men, and less equally women and children. The issues regulated are a set of activities which are formulated as problems (problematised) based on the ideological constructions by dominant stakeholders who are able to dictate, or strongly influence, what needs to be regulated when, where and how. In other words, these influential members determine the limits of the public and therefore what is harmful to society. They determine what is visible and therefore regulated and enforced. They also have the power to deflect or even silence opinions and perspectives surrounding contested issues. It is the range of issues in a community that defines the boundaries of a particular regulatory space and therefore struggles are inevitable.

> ...occupants [of a particular regulatory space] are involved in an often ferocious struggle for advantage. Any investigation of the concept involves examining the outcomes of competitive struggles, the resources used in those struggles, and the distribution of those resources between the different involved institutions. In other words, the play of power is at the centre of this process (Hancher & Moran, 1989: 288)

Enforcement of formal regulation highlights ruptures in and the limits of a particular regulatory space. To enforce requires a definition of what is "public" and what issues in that public space are regulatable. Furthermore, costs and benefits of the mobilization of limited resources are calculated. The resources, both material and social, which are apportioned to the problematisation and subsequent resolution of any particular issue(s) is the outcome of a decision by those stakeholders capable of imposing their priorities on that issue.

One domain of power is sex. It is impossible to address the acts of sex and the discourse of sexuality without reference to power which Foucault (1990: 92) defines as the "multiplicity of force relations immanent in the sphere in which they operate and which constitute their own organization." Foucault studied the history of the discourse of sexuality through the analysis of the intersection of discursive production, power and dissemination of knowledge which he terms "knowledge production." More important than the simple proliferation of the discourses of sex was "the multiplication of discourses concerning sex in the field of exercise of power itself: an institutional incitement to speak about, and to do so more and more; a determination on the part of the agencies of power to hear it spoken about, and to cause *it* to speak through explicit articulation and endlessly accumulated detail" (Foucault, 1990: 18). The institutional incitement to speak about sex is a negotiation between the private sphere and public interest to determine which acts are considered "harmful to society as a whole and prohibited by statute, and prosecuted and punished by government;" the general definition of criminal law (Duhaime, 2009). Despite the plethora of international and national legislation, it is the resources that are deployed for enforcement that render visible the "force relations" of power. These power struggles are visible at the juncture of the technologies that facilitate CST and the juridico-institutional crystallization and law formulation with its exclusive focus on the offender.

The domain of tourism

Rather than being an unwitting player in CST, the tourism industry has turned a blind eye to its role in facilitating the crime. The explosion of beach destinations in emerging economies and the increase in low-fare airlines to and hotel chains at these beach destinations has increased opportunities for access to children. Emerging economies such as Mexico and Costa Rica have preferred to ignore this growing crime for fear of sullying a pristine destination image and as such have been slow to introduce appropriate legislation (Andrews, 2004). Airline and other tourism companies have been slow to adopt the Code of Conduct[2] which requires signatories to establish an ethical policy regarding CST, train their personnel regarding that policy and to provide information to travellers (personal communication with ECPAT). Equally, few hotels have taken an active role in training their employees, especially bell boys, regarding this illegal activity. Occasional and opportunist tourists that failed to pre-emptively investigate prior to arrival are often informed by hotel bellboys and taxi drivers of the names and locations of local bars and brothels.

---

[2] The Code of Conduct for the Protection of Children from Sexual Exploitation in Travel and Tourism is an industry driven responsible tourism initiative in collaboration with ECPAT International, funded by UNICEF and supported by the UNWTO.

Last but not least is the facilitation provided by the Internet and tourism operators. Until one decade ago, the vast majority of travel planning and reservations were done with the assistance of a physical travel agency; the Internet is changing that landscape. Online travel services are one of the most successful and fastest-growing sectors of e-commerce. InterActiveCorp (IAC), the owner of expedia.com and hotels.com, alone sold US $10 billion-worth of travel in 2005 (Economist, 2004). Although the new technology and the leisure industry have not created the child sex tourist, in a globalizing world they contribute to a low-risk, low-cost environment in which child sex tourists can be cheaply and easily gratified.

Sex tourism

A functional definition of prostitution is "a business transaction understood as such by the parties involved and in the nature of a short term contract in which one or more people pay an agreed price to one or more other people for helping them attain sexual gratification by various methods" (Perkins & Bennett, 1985: 4). This definition suggests a consensual act understood as such for gain.

Sex tourists are defined as "persons who travels from their homes, usually across international borders, with the intent of engaging in sexual activities with others, including children" (Estes, 2001: 8). The UNWTO (1995) defines "sex tourism" as "trips organized from within the tourism sector, or from outside this sector but using its structures and networks, with the primary purpose of effecting a commercial sexual relationship by the tourist with residents at the destination." Although this definition does not distinguish between a child and an adult it is found under the sub-heading of "child protection."

Consensual sex is defined as "making the object of pleasure into a subject who has control over her/his pleasures" (Foucault, 1986: 225). In the absence of consent, or the denial to an individual the possibility to consent, under international law there is the presumption of negligence and harm. Unlike the situation of adult prostitutes, the act with minors does not need to involve means of coercion, deception, or any form of illicit influence in order to meet the conditions of criminality for CST. As to what age constitutes a child, the statutes of the UNCRC stipulates that "every human being below the age of 18 years unless, under the law applicable to the child, majority is attained earlier" (UNCRC, 1990, Art. 1). In short, international accords presume coercion and harm as children cannot consent to having sex.

Although CST is associated with paedophilia, it is far more pervasive. A child sex tourist falls into one of three categories: paedophiles, "preferentials" and "situationals" (opportunistic) (Estes, 2001). A paedophile is defined as an adult with sexual desires and arousal fantasies that often culminate in sexual acts with pre-pubescent children of the same or opposite sex. Preferentials are those sex offenders who travel abroad with the primary intent of having sex with a child. Situationals are those who abuse children out of convenience. The people who commit these crimes, predominantly men, come from all walks of life from plumbers to an Australian ambassador; are of all ages from early 20s to grandfathers in their late 60s; and many are married with their own children and grandchildren (ECPAT, 1999). It is estimated that 25% of all sex tourists are Americans and this proportion increases to 80% in Costa Rica (Song, 2003). In short, the problem of CST is broader than the psychopathy of paedophilia.

Rather than a static, recent phenomenon as some social scientists imply (e.g., Kempadoo & Ghuma, 1999), sex tourism has long historical roots. Prostitution in Asia and elsewhere has gone through four major stages: indigenous prostitution, economic colonialism, militarism (prostitutes who served the Asian and American soldiers during WWII and the Vietnam War) to now institutionalized sex tourism for foreign exchange earnings (Hall, 1992). Prior to 1920 Japan sent prostitutes (bonded women) to its ports to service merchants and sailors. When Japan legislated against the practice in the 1920 Overseas Prostitution Prohibition Order and then in 1958 criminalized prostitution in Japan, the Japanese mafia moved their operations overseas to the major Asian cities. With the Vietnam War and the American military, Phuket was the object of a specific agreement between the Thai government and the US military for the R&R of American soldiers. Popular sex tour destinations, such as Angeles City and Olongapo in the Philippines, were once the sites of large U.S. military installations. U.S.-based sex tour operators, in their advertising, frequently mention their sexual exploits in the service (IHRLI, 2003).

The number of sex tour travel agents and sex tour websites that exist worldwide is not known. In 1999 there were over twenty-six businesses in the United States that offered and arranged sex tours. Small-scale travel operators, very often one-man operations, arrange sex travels and indicate resorts where prostitution is available. They arrange for a 24 hour companion or book with hotels known to tolerate or actively promote prostitution. Customers can choose child escorts from catalogue pictures (Steinman, 2002). The broader tourist industry provides the vehicle for movements of sex tourists. Arrangements of the vast majority of sex tourists are organised by reputable travel agents and package tour operators, and all are transported by unsuspecting airlines.

Although the travel industry in general could deny its conscious participation, it is the travel industry, and legitimate tour operators in particular, that perpetuate the colonial core-periphery imagery of unchanged, sensual destinations where submissive peoples are there to do First World bidding, and where exploration and exploitation are unhindered by morality and legality. Destination marketing and the justification used by child sex exploiters correlate. In a recent study of 115 tourism brochures, three clusters of destination types were identified: historical (unchanged), luxuriant (unrestrained) and exploratory (uncivilized). The "unrestrained" destinations "are places where nature is pristine and never harsh, where the people are friendly and never unwilling to cater to every tourist need, and where the resorts offer amenities to satisfy every sensual desire, whether active or passive" (Echtner & Prasad, 2003: 672).

The justification of child sex tourists echoes much of the tourism marketing discourse: open cultures where sex is natural from a young age, offering financial benefits to destitute children, and the denial that their behaviour is immoral due to a racist ideology that the culture is different. Andrews (2004) gives examples of a sex tourist visiting the Dominican Republic who remarked; "Sex is the natural thing ...By the time a girl is 10 years old, she's had more experience than ...an American or an Irish woman won't ever have that much experience in her whole life...Girls learn it's the way to keep a man happy... it's natural to them." A Canadian expatriate living in Costa Rica described the country as "an open, natural culture. Girls are so willing and open, they want to please. They're sexual from the age of six" (Andrews, 2004: 423). In addition to sexual experience, children are perceived to be free from disease.

> In many countries a premium is placed on purchasing sex with virgins, who are prized not only for their youth, but also for their purity and expected lack of sexually transmitted diseases. This expectation of purity is often mistakenly extended to all children. Some abusers prize the innocence of children while others correlate youth with beauty or attractiveness. (Andrews, 2004: 422)

In view of the international condemnation (ex. ECPAT, UNCRC, UNWTO) and the negative destination image, more and more Asian countries are enforcing laws criminalizing CST. Due to this "push-down" in Asia, child sex tourists are now "popping-up" in Latin America where laws are still lax and enforcement non-existent (Steinman, 2002). The

Internet allows sex offenders, both paedophiles and preferentials, to engage in "jurisdictional shopping" to find the regions with the most lax laws (Teichmann, 2004). As such, Latin American humanitarian organizations are receiving more reports and one sex tourism newsletter, "Asia Files" once focused on providing information to sex tourists concerning travels and exploits in Asia, has expanded its coverage to include Latin America (Steinman, 2002).

Just like sex tourism, CST is not a recent phenomenon. As long as there has been human trafficking the practice has existed. However, as technological advances in communications accelerate and expand, CST accelerates and expands. Inexpensive long-haul flights preceded by Internet travel arrangements and information exchange enable a broader range of consumers to travel to all corners of the globe in search of sex with minors.

The Legal Construction

As mentioned above regulatory space is the institutional arrangement that arises from mentalities and relations of power which result in the successive web of organizations (private, public and professional) that offer a space for the regulation of a field (Foucault, 1991). This space is the outcome of continuous negotiation between social actors as to social meanings to delimit the public from the private, determine inclusion and exclusion and thus define compliance and deviance. This analytic device addresses the question of which actors (interest groups, states, communities or individuals) have the power to constitute and/or modify the space and determine the issues to be addressed or ignored.

Regulatory space, once established, is not static. The space is continuously reorganized through power relations. The outcome of these historical struggles can be "observed" through an analysis of formal authority, critical resources and discursive legitimacy (Hardy & Phillips, 1998). Formal authority is the recognized, legitimatized right to make a decision and impose legislation. Such authority can reside in domestic governments or in trans-national decision-makers such as an international consensus of lawmakers that arrive at agreements through the UN. Formal authority permits the control of critical or scarce resources such as expertise, money, equipment, or information. Finally, in the field of legal construction is discursive legitimacy which are actors or organizations such as UNICEF and ECPAT that are understood to be speaking on behalf of the voiceless, and whose interests are considered to be above the self-serving interests of private corporations or governments. As these groups rely on formal authorities for the apportionment and deployment of the resources, they are at an obvious power disadvantage. Despite a disadvantage, these NGOs play an important role in influencing the apportionment and mobilization of critical resources (Hardy & Phillips, 1998)

In short, the analysis of formal authority, resource control, and discursive legitimacy helps to explicate the observable acts of enforcement, a key element of legal construction. These acts provide clues to inter-organizational cooperation and conflict within a contested terrain such as enforcement of CST.

Formal Authority

In the Leviathan (1999: xiii), Thomas Hobbes wrote that in the *state of nature* (meaning life without a strong central authority) the lives of men [sic] are "solitary, poor, nasty, brutish and short." Based on this assumption Hobbes advanced social contract theory wherein there is a need for sovereign will to which all members of a society are bound in order to avoid conflict and war. In short, in return for protection from strife citizens within the bounds of a defined territory surrender some rights and freedoms to the institutions with authority over that territory. This seminal notion introduced almost half a millennium ago has led to jealously guarded bounded geographic space within which regulation is most often constructed and deployed (Scott & Stephan, 2006)

Regulation of "protection" is best exemplified by the construction and deployment of the criminal justice system within each nation-state. In general, before a criminal prosecution may proceed most states require that they have both jurisdiction over the offence (prescriptive jurisdiction) and jurisdiction over the person (enforcement jurisdiction). These two types of jurisdiction are founded primarily on the principle of territory and the principle of nationality. Briefly, the principle of territory refers to crimes committed within the territory of the state. Jurisdiction over the offence refers to a person of any nationality who commits a crime within a territory whether or not that person is still within the country. For example, although the person is no longer in Canadian territory, Canadian courts can enter a judgment against a person found guilty of such conduct and sentence him in absentia if s/he has left the country. In this situation even though the courts may have jurisdiction over the offence, they may not have jurisdiction over the person if the person is of another nationality. Continuing with our example above, a Canadian may commit the crime of CST in Mexico and return to Canada. Under these circumstances, although

"Canadian courts would then have jurisdiction *in personam* over him, it does not follow that under international law Canada has the right to prosecute such a person under a Canadian statute when the unlawful acts were committed entirely abroad" (Kindred & Saunders, 2006: 549).

To solve the dilemma of prescriptive and enforcement jurisdiction between countries, there are two orders of trans-national crimes: trans-national crimes of domestic concern and trans-national crimes of international concern. Trans-national crimes of domestic concern are those crimes occurring in more than one country and are considered "common" crimes such as prostitution and rape. The treatment of these crimes can be through domestic legislation or extraterritorial legislation wherein a bilateral treaty specifies the crimes covered and the persons prosecutable. However the form of jurisdiction (domestic or extraterritorial) is a state prerogative (Kindred & Saunders, 2006). On the other hand, trans-national crimes of international concern, which include international drug trafficking and terrorism, is not a prerogative. These crimes require the domestic implementation of international treaties binding the state to either prosecute or extradite the perpetrator to a territory where s/he will be prosecuted. In other words, the offender should not escape prosecution because the state is obliged to criminalize a certain kind of behaviour (Kindred & Saunders, 2006).

Although rape and prostitution are categorized as trans-national crimes of domestic concern, the Protocol elevated CST to the level of trans-national crime of international concern requiring of any nation that ratified the agreement the domestic prosecution or extradition of the child sex tourist. Canada is among 44 countries with extraterritorial legislation that allows for the prosecution of its own citizens for sexual crimes committed in other jurisdictions. Like all countries, Canadian authorities cannot conduct investigations of suspected child sex abuse perpetrated by Canadians in another jurisdiction. The foreign government must provide Canada with enough evidence to support charges. But unlike pro-active countries such as Australia and the US, Canadian officials often do not ask for any evidence from other jurisdictions and Canadian prosecutors are failing to lay charges against suspects (Perrin, 2008).

In an increasingly globalised world, the jealously guarded "sovereign nation-state" can be pernicious rather than protective. In the case of Canada, despite the existence of formal authority through government agencies, international agreements and domestic legislation, resources are not being deployed to investigate cases and enforce existing legislation. As Perrin (2008: 2) writes "Canada's extraterritorial child sex tourism provisions are amongst the most under-enforced of the entire [Canadian] *Criminal Code*."

Deployment of Resources

Enforcement includes the detection of what has been deemed a crime, the collection of evidence, the successful prosecution based on effective legislation and investigation, sentencing befitting the crime and then the criminal actually fulfilling the sentence (Tonry, 2001). Successful enforcement involves numerous actors and actions to bring just one criminal to justice. There is significant opportunity for enforcement to fail at any one of the numerous steps. From a short list of cases (and failures) involving Canadian authorities alone come the following:

- Detection: it took Interpol in Paris four years using new technology to unswirl Canadian Christopher Neil's face in over 200 pornographic photos and then track Neil down (Interpol, 2008). Another 2008 case of child-sex tourism involves a Quebec aid worker and another man who face multiple charges involving the sexual abuse of children in a Haitian orphanage between December 2006 and March of 2007. The case of Rochefort, 59, and Huard, 64, came to light only after the Haitian government contacted the United Nations which informed the RCMP (White, 2008).

- *Divergent Legal Interpretations:* a Canadian working in South Korea was investigated for numerous accounts of his activities and presented to a Canadian prosecutor for prosecution under Canadian sex-tourism laws that allow citizens to be tried in Canada for crimes committed abroad. The Canadian prosecutor chose not to prosecute claiming that the Canadian was not a tourist but an expatriate working in South Korea. Yet the Canadian Christopher Neil, an English teacher, was arrested and prosecuted in Thailand. And while Neil was in custody in Thailand awaiting sentencing, Neil's acquaintance, another Canadian English teacher, evaded police and returned to Canada. Orville Mader is currently under investigation and faces possible prosecution under Canadian sex-tourism laws (Theodore, 2009).

- *Ineffective legislation:* In February 1998, Yves Banville who travelled for months in Africa collecting hundreds of child pornography photos, and according to his own diaries, seized by the police, had sexually abused children as young as eight, was arrested at Vancouver airport. He received a minimal three hundred dollar fine and eighteen months probation for possession of child pornography. Although aware of the legislation on sex tourism, the police were unsure on how to proceed (Prober, 1999; Pynn, 1998). Since 1997, the Criminal Code in Canada was extended extraterritorially to include crimes against children. However, before a Canadian could be prosecuted for an extraterritorial child pornography or child sexual abuse offence, a letter of request was required from the country where the crimes were committed and the approval of the Attorney-General of the home province of the accused acquired (Hecht, 1997). This condition was finally repealed in 2002 but the constitutionality of the legislation itself is now being challenged by Kenneth Robert Klassen, an international art dealer who is married with three children. He was arrested in 2007 and charged with 35 sex tourism counts involving six underage girls in Colombia, eight in Cambodia and three in the Philippines (Hall, 2007; White, 2008).

- *Sentencing:* Bakker, the first and only Canadian to be prosecuted under Canada's revised CST laws was sentenced to ten years for sexually abusing at least seven children in Cambodia and Vietnam ranging in ages from 7 to 12, and brutally beating three sex workers in Vancouver. His sentence was reduced to six years for declaring his guilt and for time served of which he had only served 18 months at the time of sentencing in 2005 (Regina v. Don Michel Bakker, 2005).

Last, but not least, must be added the possibility of corruption of representatives of formal authority. In the state of Quintana Roo, Mexico the first person ever to be charged under the recent CST laws was a Canadian in 2007. Although the new law did not allow for bail when accused of such crimes, the Ontarian was released in less than two months allegedly due to errors in evidentiary collection by the local police (Noticaribe, 2007a; Noticaribe, 2007b).

The low priority in Canada to monitor and prosecute Canadian child sex tourists is evidenced by the few resources apportioned to the issue. Canada has only one very small group of federal officers involved in the Integrated Child Exploitation Unit (ICE) responsible for tracking sexual predators (Sher, 2007). Despite being overwhelmed by domestic cases requiring investigation of child exploitation, the staff is too small (only three) and resources too few to respond to anything except the most urgent and blatant (Sher, 2007). Although this unit works in coordination with the National Child Exploitation Coordination Centre in Ottawa, the latter's mission is limited to online exploitation only. The Toronto Police also has a Child Exploitation Section (CES) comprised of three teams of officers (Sher, 2007). However, their focus is on child victims of on-line sexual abuse. According to Sher (2007) Canada spends more money investigating stolen cars and credit cards which are already insured than on investigations of sexual predators.

In contrast, Operation Predator, part of Immigration and Customs Enforcement (ICE), harnesses important resources in the USA. There are also ICE agents stationed internationally in some US embassies (ICE, 2008). To date the US has arrested more than 65 and successfully prosecuted more than 45 American child sex tourists. Australia has also taken seriously investigating and prosecuting its child sex tourists and has successfully prosecuted 28 cases. Australia also stations an officer at its embassy in Thailand to assist in training local forensic specialists to gather evidence against Australian sex tourists. The UK has also sent teams of experts to train the police in Cambodia to collect evidence as well as train social workers to assist the abused but to date has only prosecuted 6 child sex tourists in the UK (Beddoe, 2008).

In short, historical conditions of the emergence of formal authority explicates the criminal justice system within each nation-state including differences in sentencing (Tonry, 2001). These mentalities combine with control over resources to determine how resources are deployed. However, an important factor in explicating modifications of mentalities and resource deployments is that of discursive legitimacy.

Discursive Legitimacy

Discursive legitimacy is the legitimacy accorded to those organizations considered to be above the self-serving interests of private corporations or governments. For example, following the introduction of the UN Convention of the Rights of the Child, ECPAT International and other NGOs pressed for a Protocol with broader binding obligations. In response to its international obligations as signatory to UN agreements (UNCRC and the Protocol) Canada adopted Bill C-27 in 1996 which modified Sec. 7 of the Criminal Code making CST a trans-national crime. However, Sec. 7(4)2 required that an official department of the country where the crime is committed request that the Canadian authorities investigate. Only after ECPAT Canada tirelessly lobbied the government was sec 7(4)2 repealed thereby removing an insurmountable obstacle to the prosecution of Canadian child sex tourists.

Canada's poor record of successful prosecutions is partially explained by discursive legitimacy. Whereas Canada has two loosely formed NGOs overseeing issues of age of consent, child exploitation, Internet child pornography and CST, Mexico has several well-coordinated organizations including ECPAT Mexico with a full-time staff member in Mexico City and volunteer representatives in Cancun. These offices receive financial and other support from such UN organizations as UNICEF, UNIFEM and the ILO. These organizations coordinate with certain government offices of the *Sistema Nacional para el Desarrollo Integral de la Familia* (DIF – National System of Integrated Family Development). To help refine legislation, the sociologist-criminologist Erick Gomez-Tagle from the *Instituto Nacional de Ciencias Penales* (INACIPE) works with federal legislators to change federal CST laws. Based on federal legislation Gomez-Tagle then works with each state to ensure harmonization of legislation between all states as well as with the federal code.3.

The web of NGOs such as ECPAT and INACIPE ensures the visibility of CST issues through information fed to the media as well as the lobbying of legislators. NGOs and individuals are working tirelessly to introduce CST legislation into the respective complex criminal codes of each of Mexico's 31 states and one federal district. These legislative changes including the difficult task of elevating CST to the level of a federal crime, are the result of numerous studies and intense lobbying efforts of ECPAT Mexico, UNICEF, ILO and researchers such as Erick Gomez Tagle and Elena Azaola (Azaola, 2003; Gomez-Tagle, 2006).

Internationally, TheCode.org in partnership with ECPAT, UNWTO and UNICEF is now in 32 countries and has 600 signatories to The Code of Conduct; most importantly private firms in the tourism industry. The goal of this NGO, active mostly in Europe, is to promote ethical behaviour through self-regulation of international tourism companies. In recognition of the industry as facilitators of CST and in lieu of formal authority to introduce command law, NGOs are promoting self-regulation of airlines, hotels and tour operators (see www.thecode.org).

In an increasingly globalised world where national governments become rule-takers of international conventions as opposed to rule-makers, as national governments concern themselves less and less with

---

[3] Unlike Canada and the US where CST falls under a federal criminal code, in Mexico each state legislates its own criminal code. With the exception of organized crime, the competent authority for the vast majority of criminal activity is the state police and courts. In addition to 32 state criminal codes, Mexico's police forces are organized by specialization as well as territory: municipal police for general municipal security; transit police for municipal traffic accidents and violations; federal transit police for federal (non-municipal) traffic security; state public ministry for criminal violations such as theft and rape committed within a state; and the federal police for federal crimes such as organized crime. Although this allows for specialization, it has the disadvantage of gaps and overlaps between agencies especially when the crimes are committed between states or between nations, as is the case of CST.

providing moral leadership but simply punctually manage assets, supra-national organizations such as ECPAT and other NGOs play an important role, "one where NGOs with direct citizen input are the emerging check and balance, adding value to the existing checks and balances of national and international courts, UN institutions and national legislatures" (Braithwaite & Drahos, 2000: 7).

Conclusion

It is well-known that the supply nations (often referred to as "hosts") for CST are underdeveloped or developing countries and that the tourist-generating countries are mainly the industrialized nations. High unemployment, poor access to affordable health services and the lack of social welfare programs marginalizes sectors of the population in underdeveloped countries forcing parents to make terrible choices: parents acting as an intermediary in the exploitation of their own child or the outright sale of their child to an intermediary. There is also the phenomenon of the runaway or "throwaway" children engaging in "survival sex" (Estes, 2001: 8). By whatever means these children find themselves on the street, wealthy tourists mainly from industrialized countries are attracted to these exotic destinations filled with people portrayed by the tourism industry as both passively and eagerly awaiting to fulfil their every desire. Easy access to these "bargain" child "commodities" combined with relative impunity of both the offender and the tourism industry, is transforming CST into a lucrative business.

Regulatory space is the outcome of a continuous process of negotiation of social meanings between social actors to define the boundary between compliance and deviance. Regulatory space in general and what constitutes harm to another individual in particular, is more often than not negotiated by and for adult males. Thus, the conduct considered harmful to society as a whole and prohibited by statute, and prosecuted and punished by government, the general definition of criminal law, is determined by constant struggle to define the limits of acceptable/unacceptable and in the case of sex tourism, when is a person's access to others' sexuality considered harmful and non-consensual. This access is determined by the "age of consent."

Unlike traditional feminist analysis that focuses on subordination, it is also revealing to view advocacy from the perspective of claiming and defending national and international regulatory space. The use of the analytic tool in the analysis of CST helps to direct our attention to issues surrounding the production of international conventions and national legislation as well as the seriousness of national and international efforts to enforce compliance of conceptually shared social meanings and crystallized in agreements that unanimously denounce female slavery and child exploitation. By exploring the boundaries of regulatory space (public, regulatable and enforceable) of the overlapping domains of tourism and child exploitation in the legal and leisure settings of Canada and Mexico, this chapter illustrates the increasingly important role in a globalizing world of those actors with discursive legitimacy such as ECPAT and the UN to influence the mobilization of critical resources held by nation-states in order to make final act of enforcement of CST less of a rarity.

Areas of future research could be the application of this framework to other contexts such as Australians visiting Thailand. Unlike Canada, Australia is very active in legislating and enforcing bans on tourists who travel for the purposes of engaging in child exploitation (ECPAT, 1999; Perrin, 2008). It is possible that differing concepts of regulatory space lead to greater engagement of resources. An examination of these two developed countries with similar histories and legal systems comparing and contrasting formal authority, deployment of resources and discursive legitimacy could serve to highlight differing conceptions of regulatory space which may explain differing levels of engagement.

References

Andrews, S. K. 2004. US domestic prosecution of the American international sex tourist: Efforts to protect children from sexual exploitation. *Journal of Criminal Law & Criminology*. 94 (2): 415 - 445

Azaola, E. 2003. La explotación sexual comercial de niños en México. E. Azaola & R. J. Estes (eds). *La infancia como mercancía sexual: México, Canadá, Estados Unidos*. Mexico, DF: Siglo XXI. pp. 140 - 155

Beddoe, C. 2008. Return to sender: British child sex offenders abroad - why more must be done. *ECPAT UK Annual Report*.
www.ecpat.org.uk

Braithwaite, J., and Drahos, P. 2000. *Global business regulation*. Cambridge: University of Cambridge Press

Duhaime, L. 2009. *Legal dictionary*.
http://duhaime.org/LegalDictionary/c/criminallaw.aspx. 1/12/09

Echtner, C. M. and Prasad, P. 2003. The context of third world tourism marketing, *Annals of Tourism Research*. 30 (3): 660 - 682

ECPAT. 1999. Extraterritorial legislation as a tool to combat sexual
    exploitation of children: A study of 15 cases. Amsterdam: ECPAT,
    Europe Law Enforcement Group
Economist. 2004. A perfect market. *The Economist.* 371 (8375): 3 - 5
Estes, R. J. 2001. *The sexual exploitation of children: A working guide to
    the empirical literature.*
    http://www.sp2.upenn.edu/~restes/CSEC_Files/CSEC_Bib_August_20
    01.pdf. 1/9/08
Foucault, M. 1991. Governmentality. G. Burchell, C. Gordon and P.
    Miller (eds). *The Foucault effect: Studies in governmentality.* Chicago,
    IL: University of Chicago Press. pp. 87 - 104
—. 1990. *The history of sexuality: Vol 1: An introduction.* New York:
    Random House
—. 1986. *The history of sexuality: Vol 2: The use of pleasure.* New York:
    Random House
Gomez-Tagle, E. 2006. Trata de personas y explotacion sexual: la agenda
    legislativa pendiente. *IterCriminis: Revista de Ciencias Penales.*
    Instituto Nacional de Ciencias Penales
Hall, M. C. 1992. Sex tourism in South-east Asia. D. Harrison (ed).
    Tourism & the less developed countries. London: Belhaven Press. pp.
    65 - 74
Hall, N. 2007. Art dealer accused of sex-tourism crimes gets bail on
    condition he post a $50,000 surety. *The Vancouver Sun.* March 30.
    p. B3. Retrieved from Canadian Newsstand Core. (Document
    ID: 1247795741)
Hancher, L., and Moran, M. 1989. Organizing regulatory space. L.
    Hancher and M. Moran (eds). *Capitalism, culture, and economic
    regulation.* Oxford: Clarendon Press
Hardy, C., and Phillips, N. 1998. Strategies of engagement: Lessons from
    the critical examination of collaboration and conflict in an
    interorganizational domain. *Organization Science.* 9 (2): 217 - 230
Hecht E. 1997. Canada's Bill C-27, how does it compare to extraterritorial
    legislation in other countries? *Human Rights Tribune.* 4 (1): 10ff
Hobbes, T. 1999. *Leviathan, or the matter, forme and power of a common-
    wealth, ecclesiasticall and civill.* Hamilton, Ontario: McMaster
    University
ICE. 2008. *U. S. immigration and customs enforcement, office of
    investigations.* http://www.ice.gov. 1/11/09
—. 2007. *U. S. immigration and customs enforcement, office of
    investigations.* http://www.ice.gov/pi/news/factsheets/sextourists.htm.
    1/9/07

IHRLI. 2003. *Demand dynamics: The forces of demand in global sex trafficking (conference report).* International Human Rights Law Institute, DePaul University College of Law. http://www.law.depaul.edu/institutes_centers/ihrli/publications/index.a sp#trafficking. 1/11/06

Interpol. 2008. Thai court jails pedophile arrested after INTERPOL global appeal. *Interpol.* http://www.interpol.int/public/thb/vico/default.asp. 1/2/10

Kempadoo, K., and Ghuma, R. 1999. For the children: Trends in international policies and law on sex tourism. K. Kempadoo (ed). *Sun, sex and gold: Tourism and sex work in the Caribbean.* Lanham: Rowman & Littlefield. pp. 291 - 308

Kindred, H. M. and Saunders, P. M. 2006. *International law: Chiefly as interpreted and applied in Canada.* Toronto: WordsWorth Communication

Mattar, M. 2007. *International child sex tourism: Scope of the problem and comparative case studies.* Baltimore: John Hopkins University, Paul H. Nitze School of Advanced International Studies. http://www.kmk-studio.com/JHU/JHU_Report.pdf. 1/12/09

NCMEC. 2009. *National center for missing and exploited children.* http://www.missingkids.com. 1/11/09

Noticaribe. 2007a. Formal prisión a canadiense por abuso de menor. *Noticaribe.* http://www.noticaribe.com.mx/chetumal/2007/04/formal_prision_a_ca nadiense_por_abuso_de_menor.html. 1/12/09

—. 2007b. Apelarán libertad a canadiense pedófilo. *Noticaribe.* http://www.noticaribe.com.mx/chetumal/2007/07/apelaran_libertad_a_ canadiense_pedofilo.html. 1/12/09

Perkins, R., and Bennett, G. 1985. *Being a prostitute.* Sydney: Allen & Unwin

Perrin, B. 2008. *Discussion paper: Sexual exploitation of children & adolescents (Canada).* Washington DC: Canada-US Consultation in Preparation for the World Congress III Against Sexual Exploitation of Children and Adolescents.

Prober, R. 1999. Children: Canada's child sex laws. *Human Rights Tribune* 3 (6). http://www.hri.ca/tribune.aspx. 1/10/06

Pynn, L. 1998. Child-porn importer fined $300: The man apprehended at Vancouver International Airport had a diary in which he alleged he had sex with girls as young as eight, raising questions about a law banning travellers from child sex. *Vancouver Sun.*

Regina v. Don Michel Bakker. 2005. BCPC 289, [2005] B.C.W.L.D. 5097, [2005] B.C.W.L.D. 5098, [2005] B.C.L.W.D. 5093, [2005] B.C.L.W.D. 5099; Decision June 2, 2005; referenced in 2005 CarswellBC 1758

Scott, R. E. and Stephan, P. B. 2006. *The limits of Leviathan: Contract theory and the enforcement of international law.* New York: Cambridge University Press

Sher, J. 2007. *One child at a time: The global fight to rescue children from online predators.* Toronto: Random House Canada

Steinman, K. J. 2002. Sex tourism and the child: Latin America's and the United States failure to prosecute sex tourists, *Hastings Women's Law Journal.* 13 (1): 53 - 76

Song, S. 2003. Children as tourist attractions, *Youth Advocate Program International Resource Paper*
http://www.yapi.org/rpchildsextourism.pdf. 1/11/09

Teichmann T. 2004. The market for criminal justice: Federalism, crime control, and jurisdictional competition. *Michigan Law Review.* 103: 1831

Theodore, T. 2009. B.C. court grants Mader bail *The Globe and Mail.* http://www.theglobeandmail.com/news/national/article796120.ece. 25/10/09

Tonry, M. H. 2001. Punishment policies and patterns in Western countries. M. H. Tonry (ed). *Sentencing and sanctions in Western countries.* Cary, NC, USA: Oxford University Press. pp. 3 - 28

Treaties. 2009. *United Nations treaty collection.*
http://treaties.un.org/Pages/ViewDetails.aspx?src=TREATY&mtdsg_no=IV-11-c&chapter=4&lang=en. 1/12/09

UNCRC. 1990. The United Nations convention on the rights of the child. *http://www.unhchr.ch/html/menu3/b/k2crc.htm*: Office of the High Commissioner for Human Rights. 1/11/06

UNHCR. 2008. *Trafficking in persons report 2008 - Mexico.* United States Department of State.
http://www.unhcr.org/refworld/docid/484f9a2cc.html. 1/11/09

UNICEF. 2009. *Child protection from violence, exploitation and abuse - Child trafficking.*
http://www.unicef.org/protection/index_exploitation.html. 1/11/09

UNWTO. 2008. *Tourism market trends, 2007 Edition - Americas.* Madrid: World Tourism Organization

UNWTO. 1995. World Tourism Organisation statement on the prevention of organized sex tourism. *Resolution A/RES/338 (XI)*

http://www.world-tourism.org/protect_children/statements/wto_a.htm.
    1/4/07
White, M. 2008. Canadian aid worker guilty of assaulting Haitian boys.
    Ottawa Citizen.
    http://www2.canada.com/ottawacitizen/news/story.html?id=ba814e0a-
    8f11-408d-b5c0-1b6af28ed000. 17/11/08

PART II:

SEXUAL BEHAVIOUR AND DESIRES IN THE LEISURE AND THE TOURISM EXPERIENCE

CHAPTER SIX

CASUAL SEX AND THE BACKPACKING EXPERIENCE: THE CASE OF ISRAELI WOMEN

LIZA BERDYCHEVSKY, YANIV PORIA AND NATAN URIELY

Introduction

Tourism is considered to provide individuals with opportunities and legitimacy to engage in sexual behaviours differing from those practiced within the constructs of the routine of everyday life (Bauer & McKercher, 2003; Ford & Eiser, 1995). This concept is the premise of both the "sex tourism" literature focusing on commercial sex between tourists and locals (Hall, 1992; Truong, 1990) and the few existing studies about sexual activity among tourists. The latter issue, termed "sex in tourism" (Bauer & McKercher, 2003; Oppermann, 1999), is this chapter's main focus. Specifically, the study presented here examines the role of non-commercial sexual behaviour in the backpacking experience among Jewish Israeli women.

Numerous studies suggest that backpacking is a distinctive type of tourist experience characterized by its adventurous nature (e.g., Cohen 1972; Lepp & Gibson 2003). Thus, the main question of the research on which this chapter is based is whether the backpacking experience is associated with particular sexual behaviours complying with its image as adventure tourism. Furthermore, the study investigates the place of sex in the backpacking experience and the attributes of the backpacking tourist experience related to women's sexual behaviour. The interviews, which were undertaken with 14 heterosexual Israeli women who engaged in backpacking, aim to provide additional insights to both the liminal nature of tourism in general, and the adventurous image of backpacking, in particular.

Sex and Tourism

Existing literature suggests that an individual's sexual behaviour changes during tourist activity. For instance, Ford and Eiser (1995: 323) explored the relationship between sexual activity and what the authors described as "situational disinhibition" – the feeling of being a different person on holiday. This feeling is attributed to the ability to perceive oneself as free and not responsible for one's actions. Likewise, Wickens (1997: 151) referred to women tourists that exhibited sexual permissiveness on holiday as "licensed to thrill" due to tourism's unique social environment. Clift and Forrest (1999) claim that the tourist experience reduces inhibitions and provides increased opportunities for sex, offering a liminal environment, not burdened by everyday constraints. According to Ford and Eiser (1996), liminality is a sense or space where social rights and obligations are temporarily suspended. Selänniemi (2003) suggests that the liminality effect encourages tourists to partake in sexual behaviour different from those practiced in everyday life and can be understood as a transition in terms of space, time, mind and senses. Finally, Poria (2006) argues that the anonymity, provided by the tourist environment, offers the gay and lesbian populations relief from everyday social pressures, a hiatus from sexuality concealment efforts and an opportunity to experience homosexual sex. However, most studies available in the literature are theoretical in nature and do not specifically address people's sexual behaviour during the backpacking experience.

Backpacking and Adventure Seeking

Historically, the study of backpacking began when Cohen (1972) differentiated between institutionalized tourists and their non-institutionalized counterparts. Tourists who comply with the latter roles are often addressed in the literature as backpackers (e.g., Loker-Murphy 1995; Pearce 1996) and are characterized by novelty seeking. The two categories were further classified by Cohen (1972) into organized-group and individual mass tourists within institutionalized tourism, and into explorers and drifters within non-institutionalized tourism. The terms "explorers" and "drifters" refer to spontaneous and unconstrained kinds of travellers who tend to shun regular tourist routes and use a minimum of tourism facilities during their predominantly unplanned travel. By applying Cohen's typology of tourist roles in terms of quest for familiarity/novelty, Lepp and Gibson (2003) concluded that potential sources of concern for conventional mass tourists may serve as sources of excitement for explorers and drifters (i.e., backpackers). This perspective is congruent with early conceptualizations of non-institutionalized tourists as adventure seekers (Cohen 1972). In line with this theory, Elsrud (2001) determined that risk and adventure are central to the construction of backpacker's identity. Specifically, her study indicates that backpackers' narratives tend to include accounts of their supposedly adventurous experiences as part of their attempt to distinguish themselves from conventional mass tourists.

The notion of backpacking as an adventurous form of tourism should be further examined with respect to various practices and attitudes associated with contemporary backpacking. In this context, it is worth mentioning that there has been a dearth of studies of the issue of sexual behaviour within the backpacking context, although it may be essential to the understanding of the backpacking experience as a social phenomenon.

Sex as a motive for tourist activity and the attributes of the tourist environment

Identification of the significance of sex as a motive for backpacking tourist activity and/or its links to the satisfaction with such activity has, to the best of our knowledge, received no specific research attention in the context of "sex in tourism." Nevertheless, sex presents an agreed upon motivator for tourism, when commercial "sex tourism" is discussed (Bauer & McKercher, 2003; Oppermann, 1999). Sex is also clearly a motivator for other forms of tourist activity. For example, a study of American students on spring break found that the opportunity for casual sex was among the most significant vacation motives (Sönmez et. al., 2006). Additionally, Sönmez et. al's study revealed that the destination choice was based on the potential for sexual opportunities. Similarly, young tourists travelling to Greece reported that sexual opportunity was a common motive in tourist destination choice (Wickens & Sönmez, 2007). Nevertheless, the abovementioned studies delineate sex as one of a diverse set of motivators for tourism activity instead of investigating it in-depth. In addition, the few attempts made to understand the attributes of the tourist experience as facilitators and/or inhibitors of sexual behaviour have not succeeded in painting a holistic picture (Opperman, 1999; Thomas, 2000). Moreover, almost none of the studies reported here considered the possibility that certain attributes of the tourist experience might inhibit

sexual behaviour, an issue deserving research attention. One exception is
Thomas' (2000) research that confronts this issue, suggesting a framework
of facilitating and/or inhibiting factors of casual sex in tourism.
Specifically, Thomas (2000) focuses on five facilitators and/or inhibitors
of women's sexual behaviour in the tourism context: relationships
(previous or existing), alcohol, space and privacy, anonymity, emotions of
fear and vulnerability. These factors do not have one unified meaning, nor
do they necessarily lead to one predictable outcome. However, Thomas'
study, which only concerns women, ignores the role of sex as a motivating
force for their involvement in tourist activity and the importance of casual
sex for the satisfaction derived from the tourism experience.

In line with the above, the study on which this chapter is based had
four main objectives: (1) clarifying the importance of sex as a motivating
force for involvement in backpacking activity; (2) investigating the
contribution of casual sex to women's satisfaction with backpacking
experiences; (3) describing changes in women's sexual behaviours during
the backpacking experience; and (4) exploring the attributes of the
backpacking experience that may facilitate and/or inhibit women's sexual
behaviour. These objectives have potential to illuminate the backpacking
experience as a social phenomenon by comparing women's sexual
behaviours at home and abroad, as well as by clarifying its role in
women's everyday life.

Research process

The complex and multi-dimensional nature of the studied phenomenon
requires a qualitative phenomenological paradigm, characterized by a
holistic vision. The findings reported here are based on in-depth interviews
with fourteen heterosexual Israeli women. The decision to focus on
women derives from the oppressive norms towards women's sexual
behaviour in Western society (Pines, 1998), suggesting that investigating
women's experiences in anonymous tourist environments might be a
source of richer findings in terms of transgression of boundaries as
compared to heterosexual men. Also, this choice aimed to minimize the
social bias between female interviewer and interviewees. The in-depth
interview was chosen as a research tool because of its flexibility and the
sensitivity of the explored topic. Also, the in-depth interview enables
personal interaction and assists in establishing relationships between
interviewer and interviewee, based on trust and confidence which are
essential for research on sensitive topics, just as this one, in order to
achieve trustability (Gubrium & Holstein, 2002) or trustworthiness

(Decrop, 2004); two measures of quality in qualitative research (Decrop, 2004). In addition, the effectiveness of interpersonal dynamics in face-to-face interview has a potential to reduce the problematic effect of the interviewees' social desirability response bias, denial of unpleasant memories and faulty estimation; especially with respect to such a sensitive topic as sexual behaviour.

Furthermore, the women who agreed to be interviewed on such an intimate topic may not be representative of the general population. With the aim of achieving diversity among the sampled population two tactics were implemented: (1) the snow-ball sampling was initiated from several different opening points (i.e., 4 women with different socio-demographic characteristics) and (2) the purposeful sample technique was implemented to identify interviewees possessing potential to illuminate the studied phenomenon. Data analysis was conducted simultaneously with data collection. The chosen strategy for data analysis was grounded theory (Strauss & Corbin, 1990), based on the combination of thematic analysis (Shkedi, 2003) and categorization (Arksey & Knight, 1999).

In general, the interviewees described the backpacking experience as a once in a lifetime experience—a "mind cleaning" subsequent to army service (military service is obligatory for both Jewish Israeli men and women), before entering the circle of post-secondary education and/or work. Nonetheless, four interviewees stated that they backpacked twice, of which three travelled to new destinations and one returned to their initial destination. The most frequently reported backpacking destinations were Thailand and South America; two participants' interviews centre on their backpacking experience in India and Australia. The length of the backpacking experiences ranged from one month to one year.

Data Analysis

The findings are presented with respect to three main themes which emerged from the data analysis: (1) women's anticipation for sex and sex's affects on the tourist experience; (2) alterations in sexual behaviours while backpacking; and (3) the features of backpacking that either facilitate or inhibit sexual behaviour.

Anticipation of sex and its effects on the backpacking experience

Data analysis reveals that sexual activity plays an important role in woman's backpacking tourist experience. The interviewees stated that the opportunities for sexual adventures offered by the backpacking experience served as a motivation for engagement in this specific kind of tourist experience, as exemplified in the citation from an interview with a 26 years old unmarried woman employed in the field of organizational consulting:

> Gila - (pseudonyms are used): "When I flew alone to South America, of course the opportunity for sex was one of the explicit motivations for this trip."

In some cases, the informants stated they had heard from friends about sexual opportunities at specific tourist destinations and were curious to experience such opportunities themselves. For instance, a 25 year old woman, employed at a telephone customer service company, stated:

> Anat: "After the army I needed some fresh air and I wanted to travel. I chose Thailand and I was quite prepared for what was waiting for me there and I was quite curious to try it. My friends have cued me in about all the sexual opportunities there and my best friend even gave me a pack of condoms and said: 'I want to see it empty when you come back'."

However, some interviewees mentioned that casual sex was not a motive for undertaking a backpacking experience, as might be inferred from the quotation of 29 year old unmarried human resources manager:

> Tal: "I can't say that sex was my motive for a trip or for choosing Thailand. I've have heard that it is a destination for sex, but I thought that is about prostitution and is mostly for men. But when I arrived there I realized that it is a place for fun, parties, alcohol and casual sex for everybody. So many temptations, you just can't resist!"

Furthermore, some respondents even stated their unwillingness to enter any kind of ongoing relationship while backpacking, as a commitment might damage the diversity of the opportunities for sexual adventures and even the backpacking experience itself, as inferred from the interview with a 27 year old woman employed in the hotel industry:

> Reut: "Ongoing relationship in backpacking? No way! It spoils the trip. Why would I do that? It's casual sex, or nothing. There are so many fish in the sea! It's forbidden to stop with one man! You have to keep on trying, the more the better!"

The importance of sex as a motivator for the backpacking experience is exemplified in its role during the planning process. The interviewees stated they designed their backpacking experience in a way that facilitated casual sex. For instance, most respondents designed a travel route providing opportunities to meet potential casual sex partners. Also, the interviewees reported that plans for intended casual sex defined the room type booked at the lodging venue (without, or at least with a few, room partners) in order to achieve some privacy. Respondents even stated that the chosen backpacking partners were selected according to participants intentions of being involved in sexual activity (participant were interested to travel with partners who were *"open minded"* and *"encouraging"* vs. *"conservative"* and *"oppressing"*).

Sexual behaviour when backpacking

Most of the respondents stated that casual sex is an integral part of their backpacking experience, describing casual sex for the purpose of physical satisfaction, feelings of adventure, curiosity and for accumulating sexual experiences. As a 27 years old student stated:

> Shira: *"I perceive sex differently when backpacking. It's sex for the sake of sex and I don't expect any continuity. I'll go home and he will too, thus there are no obligations and no expectations. I just want to enjoy and have fun."*

The interviewees also depicted a change in the quantity of casual sex while backpacking in comparison to their home experiences. Some even claimed that they would not agree to partake in casual sex in the home environment, but they perceived it as an integral part of the backpacking experience. A 27 year old sports instructor (Sigal) and a 27 years old woman employed in the field of marketing (Rona) exemplify the point:

> Sigal: *"You'll never catch me engaging in casual sex in Israel! Why would I do that? It's my reputation and I don't need a sexual disease! But in South America it was different. You can't stay without sex for a year! And you don't have to worry about your reputation. You just want to have fun, so you can find yourself four times a week with different sexual partners."*

> Rona: *"I had three casual affairs during two months of backpacking in Australia; while at home I can handle being without sex for two months without any problem."*

While the quantity of sexual partners increases while backpacking, the interviewees claimed that sexual quality decreases because of the lack of acquaintance, with gratification stemming from the excitement and variety of sexual partners and not from the sexual act itself. The findings also indicate significant diversity of sex experiences during backpacking. Specifically, women reported that they could adopt sexually permissive behaviours and practice a "different" type of sex, such as casual sex, frequent change of sexual partners, lesbian sex, orgies, and sex in public places; such behaviours may be looked down upon at home. The following citations of a 27 year old sports instructor (interview 3) and a 30 year old investment advisor (interview 26) exemplify the point:

> Sigal: "While backpacking in South America my friend and I were dragged into orgy. The next day, we didn't believe that we actually did this! But it was fun! Anyway, I would never do it here [in Israel]."

> Nona: "I'm not attracted to women, but during backpacking you collect memories and I've decided to try [lesbian sex]. It was fine but it's not me, and I didn't take it personal. It was just a nice episode."

Sexual behaviour and the features of backpacking

The interviewees described the backpacking environment as saturated with factors facilitating sexual behaviour. One dominant factor facilitating women's sexual behaviour during their holiday experience is the nature of the social atmosphere in the tourism environment. The interviewees claimed that the backpacking experience creates a unique social atmosphere and state of mind empowering women to feel free and become involved in sexual adventures different from everyday life, such as casual sex. The atmosphere was described by the means of *"parties and hormones"* (Sigal - 27 year old sport instructor), *"liberation from routine limitations"* (Shira - 27 year old student), *"dizziness and craziness"* (Sasha - 30 year old high-tech employee). However, the most common factor participants related to was perceived anonymity. The informants stated that a backpacking trip is the most typical tourist frame for casual sex, as this tourism experience usually occurs without a regular sexual partner (contributing to the extent of the anonymity in the tourism environment) and is long and geographically remote enough to foster feelings of detachment from routine everyday life. The respondents highlighted that the perception of the tourism environment as anonymous encouraged them to experience sexual behaviours that might have damaged their reputations in their home environments. The following citation of a 27 year old unmarried sport instructor exemplifies the idea:

> *Sigal: "Anonymity is extremely important to me! I'll never have casual sex at home, no way! It will damage my reputation and it's just not me! But in South America, of course I did it. Who cares? Nobody knows me. I don't have to explain anything!"*

The interviewees also referred to the comfortable physical conditions (e.g., room and privacy) as contributing to their decision to become involved in sexual activity. For instance, a room without roommates and possessing the requisite hygiene conditions were depicted as facilitators of sexual activity. The respondents also stated that alcohol and drug consumption while backpacking is significantly higher in comparison to everyday life. The interviewees reported that alcohol and drugs provided them with legitimization to feel less responsible for their actions and/or to perceive themselves as a different person, free to participate in sexual adventures. Quotes from a 36 year old marketing worker (Shula) and a 26 year old organizational consultant (Gila) exemplify these points:

> *Shula: "Vacation [backpacking] and alcohol are synonyms and alcohol stimulates senses and desire. If I don't drink too much, I will go far beyond the boundaries and I don't have to feel responsible for what I do because I'm drunk. I have an excuse; it's not me it's the alcohol."*

> *Gila: "I've tried MDMA [methylenedioxymethamphetamine/Ecstasy—a mood and mind altering amphetamine derivative] in Thailand and the sex was awesome! You wouldn't believe what this drug does! You love everybody! After this drug I could even kiss a girl, I've seen a [straight] man kissing a man and a man who was embracing a bench."*

Another facilitating factor is the supporting and/or encouraging attitudes of trip partners regarding sexual permissiveness and creative sexual behaviours. The citation from a 27 year old sports instructor exemplifies the point:

> *Sigal: "While backpacking in South America with my friends [girls] we had kind of a 'battle slogan': 'Use him and loose him!' In this way, we encouraged each other not to give up the opportunities, in order not to regret afterwards. It also helped me to overcome the hesitations and to feel in charge of the situation."*

The respondents referred not only to the trip partners' supportive feedback regarding permissive sexual behaviour as a facilitating factor, but also to the confidence that the trip partners would not reveal their sexual behaviour back at home.

However, further findings refute the thought that the tourism environment is characterized exclusively by facilitating factors and suggests several factors inhibiting women's sexual behaviour. Interestingly, most of the inhibiting factors are identical to the facilitating factors, but the context is different. The interviewees described poor physical conditions as a factor inhibiting sexual activity and they described the following elements as crucial: cleanliness, sense of privacy (although, the interviewees also stated that sometimes they did have sex in a room with roommates) and an accessible condom. Additionally, excessive alcohol consumption and several types of drugs were delineated as inhibiting factors, as can be inferred from the citations of a 29 year old student working as an administrative clerk at a hospital (Dana) and a 26 years old woman employed in the field of organizational consulting (Gila):

> Dana: "If I drink too much, I throw up and it surely oppresses the desire for sex. In alcohol there is a stage between an excellent feeling and then at some point it's too late, you are like a dead wood!"

> Gila: "Some drugs are uppers and encourage sex and others are downers and suppress it. Grass and hashish are downers, as they make you feel exhausted, you don't want to move. I've heard that ecstasy encourages, but when I tried it, it was awful. It was the only evening [in Thailand] when I didn't want to have sex."

In addition, the interviewees stated that conservative trip partners and uncooperative behaviours (i.e., suggesting such trip partners will inform others back home of one's involvement in casual sex, or will cause a sense of guilt) suppresses their involvement in casual sex. Feelings of vulnerability in foreign and unfamiliar environments were also described as inhibiting sexual behaviour. The respondents explained that possible sources of perceived vulnerability include: the fear of not being able to understand and/or foresee whether the situation becomes threatening due to cultural differences; perceived sexual permissiveness of tourists and/or locals (caused by fear of harassment and the feeling of disgust from the environment that is perceived as dirty); and the fear of sexually transmitted diseases. The following citations regarding Thailand from interviews with two backpackers aged 36 (Shula - marketing worker) and 30 (Nona - investment advisor) demonstrate this concept:

Shula: "There is some scary effect, because you are in an unfamiliar country, you don't trust men and you are actually helpless. These men are strangers with a different mentality and you have no idea what they have on their minds."

Nona: "In Thailand you have plenty of opportunities for casual sex, but I was deterred by this permissiveness. I was afraid of diseases and felt disgusted from people."

Conclusion

The findings reveal several important issues that have not gained previous research attention. First, the findings delineate significant changes in women's sexual behaviours during the backpacking experience. Furthermore, most interviewees cite sex as constituting a considerable motive for involvement in backpacking tourist activity. In addition, the study emphasizes the role of casual sex as a crucial factor to women's satisfaction with the backpacking experience. Casual sex and other sexual behaviours that participants perceive as extraordinary are considered as integral parts of the backpacking adventure. Moreover, participants stated that the tourist experience is designed in a manner that facilitates casual sex. Namely, the destination, trip partners and recreational and lodging places are often chosen in accordance with their appropriateness for casual sex.

The study suggests insights to the dual effect (facilitating and/or inhibiting) of the attributes of backpacking experience on women's sexual behaviour. First, the liminal social atmosphere in the backpacking tourism environment is attributed as a facilitating factor, providing an anonymous, temporarily constrained, socially tolerated period of wish fulfilment; a form of fantasy enactment that is normally denied to people, as suggested earlier by Ryan and Kinder (1996). Simultaneously, in line with Thomas (2000), the backpacking environment might yield feelings of vulnerability and helplessness in an unfamiliar environment Second, the influence of physical conditions is rather expectable and depends on the perceived quality of those conditions. Third, the influence of alcohol on sexual behaviour depends on the quantity consumed. However, several participants explained that the alcohol affect during the backpacking experience is mostly psychological, rather than physiological. Fourth, with respect to drugs, while researchers usually refer to their effect as facilitating sexual behaviour (e.g., Bellis, et al, 2004), the present study indicates that certain types of drugs have inhibiting effects on sexual behaviour. Finally, the fifth factor refers to the potential influence of trip partners, which varies according to their specific character and personality traits. Partners may either be supportive and encouraging or conservative and inhibiting.

With respect to the particular nature of backpacking, the data analysis demonstrates that Cohen's (1972) non-institutionalized tourists' quest for novelty is expressed in women's unconstrained sexual behaviour during their backpacking experiences. The findings suggest that the liminal nature of the backpacking tourist experience offers women opportunities to fulfil aspects of sexual life they perceive as reputation damaging in their everyday reality. Namely, the respondents perceived their sexual behaviour while backpacking (with regard to choice of partners or the nature of sexual activity) as inappropriate, radical and sometimes even deviant for everyday life as well as for other types of tourism experiences. Sexual adventures that might be a source of social discomfort and concern for a woman under other circumstances, transform into a source of excitement, self-investigation and, in certain cases, even fulfilment, when a woman adopts the backpacking role. It seems that backpacking stimulates women's curiosity and encourages them to satisfy their sexual desires. Casual sex was described as an integral part of the backpacking experience; an additional adventure in an adventurous liminal tourist experience. In line with Elsrud (2001) who claims that adventure is central to the construction of backpacking identity, the findings reveal that sexual adventures might play an important role in the construction of the backpacking experience and identity. While this observation does not refute recent studies that point to the "massification" of backpacking, it clearly stresses the notion of backpacking as a distinctive tourism category characterized by a promise of adventure and a liminal timeframe during which people have the opportunity to take "time out" from daily life norms (e.g., Cohen, 1972; Elsrud, 2001; Lepp & Gibson 2003).

Although this study did not aim to reveal managerial recommendations, the findings may contribute to establishing intervention programs against sexually transmitted diseases, as they address the significance of sexual behaviour in tourism and identify the attributes of the tourist experience that facilitate and/or inhibit it. However, the findings derived from Jewish Israeli women might not be relevant to women in other environments. Thus, future studies should be conducted with women from other countries and cultures. In addition, many issues remain to be investigated about the link between sex and tourism. For instance, applying similar research to other types of tourism experiences, such as rest and relaxation vacations, business and sightseeing trips, might be insightful. In addition, further research could focus on the most prevalent form of sexual activity within tourism; namely, sexual behaviour among couples who are involved in long-term relationships. Such a study would contribute important insights about the mainstream.

References

Arksey, H. and Knight, P. 1999. *Interviewing for social scientists*. London: Sage Publication

Bauer, T. G. and McKercher, B. 2003. Conceptual framework of the nexus between tourism, romance, and sex. T. G. Bauer and B. McKercher (eds). *Sex and tourism: Journeys of romance, love, and lust*. New York: Haworth Hospitality Press. pp. 3 - 17

Bellis, M. A., Hughes, K., Thomson, R. and Bennett, A. 2004. Sexual behaviour of young people in international tourist resorts. *Sexually Transmitted Infections*. 80: 43 - 47

Clift, S. and Forrest, S. 1999. Gay men and tourism: Destinations and holiday motivations. *Tourism Management*. 20: 615 - 625

Cohen, E. 1972. Toward a sociology of international tourism. *Social Research*. 39 (1): 164 - 189

Decrop, A. 2004. Trustworthiness in qualitative tourism research. J. Phillimore and L. Goodson (eds). *Qualitative research in tourism: Ontologies, epistemologies and methodologies*. London: Routledge. pp 156 - 169

Elsrud, T. 2001. Risk creation in traveling: Backpacker adventure narration. Annals *of Tourism Research* 28 (3): 597 – 617

Ford, N. and Eiser, J. R. 1996. Risk and liminality: The HIV-related socio-sexual interaction of young tourists. S. Clift and S. Page (eds). *Health and the international tourist*. London: Routledge. pp. 152 - 178

Ford, N. and Eiser, R. 1995. Sexual relationships on holiday: A case of situational disinhibition? *Journal of Social and Personal Relationships*. 12 (3): 323 - 339

Gubrium, N. J. and Holstein, J. A. 2002. *Handbook of interview research: Context and method*. Thousand Oaks: Sage Publications

Hall, C. M., 1992. Sex tourism in Southeast Asia. D. Harrison (ed). *Tourism and the less developed countries*. London: Belhaven Press. pp. 65 - 74

Lepp, A. and Gibson, H. 2003. Tourist roles, perceived risk and international tourism. *Annals of Tourism Research*. 30 (3): 606 - 624

Loker-Murphy, L. and Pearce, P. 1995. Young budget travelers: Backpackers in Australia. *Annals of Tourism Research*. 22 (4): 819 - 843

Oppermann, M. 1999. Sex tourism. *Annals of Tourism Research.* 26 (2): 251 - 266

Pearce, P. 1996. Recent research in tourist behaviour. *Asia-Pacific Journal of Tourism Research.* 1: 7 - 17

Pines. A. M. 1998. *Psychology of gender.* (Hebrew) Tel-Aviv: Open University Press

Poria, Y. 2006. Assessing gay men and lesbian women's hotel experiences: An exploratory study of sexual orientation in the travel industry. *Journal of Travel Research.* 44 (3): 327 - 334

Ryan, C. and Kinder, R. 1996. Sex, tourism and sex tourism: Fulfilling similar needs? *Tourism Management* 17 (7): 507-518

Selänniemi,, T. 2003. On holiday in the liminoid playground: place, time, and self in tourism. In T. G. Bauer and B. McKercher (eds). *Sex and tourism: Journeys of romance, love, and lust.* New York: Haworth Hospitality Press. pp. 19 - 31

Shkedi, A. 2003. *Qualitative research – Theory and practice: Words trying to touch.* (Hebrew) Ramot: The University of Tel-Aviv

Sönmez, S., Apostolopoulos, Y., Yu, C. H., Yang, S. Y., Mattila, A. and Yu, L. C. 2006. Binge drinking and casual sex on spring break. *Annals of Tourism Research.* 33 (4): 895 - 917

Strauss, A. and Corbin, J. 1990. *Basics of qualitative research: Grounded theory procedures and techniques.* Newbury Park, California: Sage Publications

Thomas, M. 2000. Exploring the contexts and meanings of women's experiences of sexual intercourse on holiday. S. Clift and S. Carter (eds). *Tourism and sex: Culture, commerce and coercion.* London: Pinter. pp. 200 - 220

Truong, T. 1990. *Sex, money and morality: Prostitution and tourism in Southeast Asia.* London: Zed Books

Wickens, E. 1997. Licensed for thrills: Risk-taking tourism. S. Clift and P. Grabowski (eds). *Tourism and health; Risks, research and responses.* London: Pinter. pp. 151 - 164

Wickens, E. and Sönmez, S. 2007. Casual sex in the sun makes the holiday: Young tourists' perspectives. Y. Apostolopoulos and S. Sönmez (eds). *Population mobility and infectious disease.* US: Springer. pp. 199 - 214

CHAPTER SEVEN

SEXUAL ENCOUNTERS BETWEEN MEN IN A TOURIST ENVIRONMENT: A COMPARATIVE STUDY IN SEVEN MEXICAN LOCALITIES

ÁLVARO LÓPEZ LÓPEZ AND ANNE MARIE VAN BROECK

Introduction

This chapter presents partial results of a project, entitled "The Territorial Dimension of Male-sex Tourism in Mexico," which started in 2006 at the Instituto de Geografía of the Universidad Nacional Autónoma de México (UNAM), and which by 2008 had brought together more than fourteen specialists and thirteen students from the fields of geography, anthropology, psychology and tourism studies. The authors of the chapter are the project coordinators, and the data they discuss here come from the findings of seven place-specific research studies, carried out by different research teams. The research addresses the territorial dimensions and the dynamics of commercial sexual encounters between street male sex workers and male tourists, from the perspective of the sex worker.

Prostitution in Mexico has not been sufficiently studied, and though male-to-male prostitution has received some attention by writers on sexual diversity, the practices of adult male prostitutes in tourist contexts remain virtually unexplored. Aside from the work of Cantú (2002), the few existing texts on the subject are very recent and emanate from the abovementioned project (List & Teutle, 2008; López & Carmona, 2008; Monterrubio, 2008; Vargas & Alcalá 2008).

As for the sexual identities of men who engage in homo-erotic practices, the works of Carrier (1985; 1995; 2003) and Lumsden (1991) on bisexuality and homosexuality in Western and Central Mexico, threw some light on the subject, even though they came up with rather essentialist discourses which the works of Núñez (1994; 2005; 2007), Hernández (2001; 2004; 2005) and Vendrell (2001) later helped overcome. These latter studies focused on the cultural construction of sexual identities in the context of homo-erotic practices, and their specific and particular denominations in the geographical spaces where they take place—Central and Northern Mexico in this case.

Among the existing studies on adult male-to-male prostitution, the ethnographic work of Liguori and Aggleton (1999) analyzes the practices of *masajistas* (masseurs) at the saunas of Mexico City who, among other services, offer sex to their clients. Lara (2005) studies the night clubs visited by military men stationed in the capital, and the different activities—including male prostitution—that take place there. In Western Mexico, the sexual life and identity of men who practise sex with other men—some of them prostitutes—is explored by the wide ethnographic study conducted by Carrillo (2002) in Guadalajara. Finally, male-to-male prostitution in the city of Xalapa (Eastern Mexico) and the sexual identities that arise are explored by Córdova (2003; 2005).

The studies of De Ocampo and Van Broeck on the island of Cozumel (De Ocampo, 2003; Van Broeck & De Ocampo, 2003; Van Broeck & De Ocampo, 2010) explore the lives of local beach boys who "hang around" with tourists. Carried out from the perspective of "sharks," as these young men call themselves, this research contrasts sharply with other studies about "springbreakers" in which prejudice and sensationalist perceptions stand in the way of objective knowledge about sex and tourism (*Cf.* Palma, 2007).

The literature hitherto referred to provides basic elements to build a theoretical framework for the interpretation of the relations between sex and tourism in homo-erotic contexts. Though hardly visible at all in geographical space, the presence of male-to-male prostitution in tourist contexts in Mexico is a fact that deserves attention. The relevance of this chapter, the authors believe, stems from its wide territorial scope, encompassing seven major towns—from the northern borderlands to the coasts through the interior—with an important tourist component in their economies. The text delves into the visions of sex workers who, despite their differences in origins, motivations and identities, share common territorial behaviour patterns in the practice of their trade.

Theoretical aspects of tourism, sexuality and homo-eroticism

For decades, mass tourism has been related to the famous three S's of sun, sea and sand. To these, a fourth S was added to account for sex (Crick, 2001). It is understandable that, as a basic human activity, sex be considered a part of holiday-making. However, as some studies demonstrate (Carter & Clift, 2000; Hughes, 2006; Ryan & Hall, 2001), tourists, during their holidays, tend to be even more prone to engage in sexual activity. Being away from home and far from their habitual restrictions, many of them feel encouraged to lift certain inhibitions, which results in an increase in the frequency of sexual practices, not only among those travelling together (existing partners), but also among tourists who meet at their destination point, or between tourists and local people. Norms about having sex with unknown people are more relaxed while on a holiday, since holidaying is considered as a "liminal" phase (Ryan & Hall, 2001).

> The customary courting relationships were abandoned during the holiday period and individuals were more apt to engage in sexual relationships with strangers (Hall, 2001: 101).

> ...holidays are opportunities for relaxing behavioural norms and [...] tourists do make new sexual contacts and may take greater risks in those contacts. Holidaymakers have reduced perceptions of the consequences of sexual activity and some—especially heterosexually-oriented holiday companies—encourage sexual activity. Most papers [in Clift and Page, 1996] agreed that casual sexual encounters appear to be part of the desired holiday experience (Hughes, 2006: 62).

Furthermore, some tourists even travel "with the primary purpose of having sexual encounters while away, and this usually on a commercial basis" (Hughes, 2002: 65). Travel with the specific purpose of engaging in commercial sexual relationships has generally been called "sex tourism." According to Oppermann (1999), the sex tourist is generally seen as a person who "purposely takes a holiday to have sex, stays away from home at least 24 hours, meets the sex provider for the first time, has sexual intercourse as a result of direct monetary exchange, and obtains sexual gratification in encounters which last a relatively short time" (Oppermann, 1999: 261). According to this view, sex tourism is a form of prostitution, and some authors (such as Sanchez Taylor, 2001) have indeed used the term "prostitution tourism."

Oppermann (1999) criticizes this narrow view and demonstrates that sex tourism may take multiple forms, depending on the stand of the tourist on the following six considerations: 1) having sexual relationships is either his/her main motivation to travel, not the main motivation, or not at all a motivation; 2) sexual encounters happen either with a direct monetary exchange, without any form of recompense, or with only an indirect one, 3) the sexual encounter is either a short one or a long one, and happens either just once or takes place on several occasions; 4) the sexual encounter takes place in the context of either a short-lived relationship, or a long-term one—leading even to marriage, 5) sexual activity is not confined to intercourse and includes, for instance, voyeurism; 6) both tourist and sex worker may either be travellers—the latter being at the tourist destination either looking for clients or on holidays—or none of them travels, like in "virtual" sex encounters.

Other authors have likewise brought the complexity of sex tourism to the fore. Ryan and Hall (2001) describe the sex-tourism relationship according to three similar parameters: First, the sexual practice may be anywhere between completely commercial and completely non-commercial; next, the engagement in the sexual encounter can be either with mutual consent or, at the other end, completely involuntary; finally, the third parameter refers to the level of personal integrity. McKercher and Bauer (2003), for their part, have looked at the degree of "romance" that may be present in the relationship, as well as the positive—i.e., beneficial—versus the negative—exploitative—character of the sex experience. They also consider the degree in which the infrastructure and organization of tourism influences the relationship under scrutiny.

Oppermann's (1999) analysis evidenced that not all sexual relations between tourists and local individuals could be considered as prostitution (as had hitherto been implicit in the usage of "sex tourism"), and that the term should therefore be expanded to account for the diversity and complexity of these relations. Understood in this way, "sex tourism" could then be used to describe virtually any occurrence of sex in tourism, which consequently lead some authors to avoid the term altogether and talk instead of "sex-and-tourism" (Clift & Carter, 2000; Bauer & McKercher, 2003).

Most of the aforementioned studies on sex tourism, and on the relations between sex and tourism, have centred their analysis on heterosexual sexuality—particularly male tourists and female sex labourers. However, in more recent research and literature—especially that which encompasses all aspects of sex-and-tourism, or sex *within* tourism—a strong homosexual theme has started to emerge, and there is also an increasing interest in female tourists in search of sex and romance. This chapter—and the research on which it is based—scrutinises the sexual interactions that happen between males. As writers on queer theory have rightly warned (Butler, 1993; Jagose, 1996; Núñez, 1994), it is important, when dealing with this subject matter, to differentiate between practices and identities. It would be utterly incorrect to consider that all male tourists and male locals implicated in the phenomenon of sex-and-tourism are either "homosexual" or "gay," both terms coined and widely used in the West, but not necessarily elsewhere. Sexual practice is understood here as nothing else but the exercise of sex, and therefore we refer to the sexual interaction between two males as "homo-erotic practices," or "homo-eroticism." Identity, on the other hand, relates to the feeling of belonging to a certain social group; in this case, a group defined by the sexual practices of its members, with its specific cultural constructions.

Throughout the West, from the second half of the nineteenth century up until the 1980s, the most widespread sexual identity among men who engaged in homo-erotic practices was the "homosexual" identity. However, as early as the 1960s another identity—namely "gay"—started to gather more legitimacy. This identity presupposes not only the proud assumption of the homo-erotic condition—to "come out of the closet"—and the adoption of a specific iconography (e.g., the rainbow flag, the pink triangle) but, more importantly, the conformity to a way of life associated to a conspicuous consumption behaviour that has given way to the "pink economy," in which tourist consumption occupies a relevant position (Herdt, 1992; Hernández, 2004; 2005; Jagose, 1996).

The growing diffusion in Mexico of a "global" gay identity through the expansion of globalised phenomena—such as tourism—has not yet eliminated traditional homo-erotic identities. In the towns selected for the research conducted for this report, many of the sex workers interviewed—hailing from both urban and rural contexts—use other categories to refer to those involved in sexual interaction between males, such as "*chacales*," "*mayates*," "*chichifos*," "*machos*" and "*hombres*" (Cantú, 2002; Carrillo, 2002; Córdova, 2003). These are identities that seldom relate to the idea of openly expressing sexual desire for other males—as happens with gay identity—but rather the opposite. Diverse though they may be in their meaning and associated behaviour, these regional identities share one thing in common: the males who assume them are convinced that as long as they play the role of the "*activo*" (i.e., "top") their masculinity—their "manhood"—remains intact and therefore they will not lose their privileged, "superior" position. This means that they will have assigned uses and prohibitions to three specific areas of their bodies: A) the penis is available to other men for oral and anal sex; B) the anus—and, consequently, the buttocks—can never be touched by another man—or woman, for that matter—and C) the mouth is not available to other men for kissing. At the other end of the logical spectrum, "*pasivos*" (i.e., 'bottom') occupy a "feminine" and therefore "weak" position, in clear disadvantage to the socially-tolerated—and even acclaimed—behaviour of the "*activo*" in certain sectors.

One cannot ignore the multiple sexual identities that, in the context of tourism (and sex), exist side by side with the cultural particularities of both tourists and local dwellers. Therefore, when Puar (2002: 2) talks about "the growth and expansion of gay and lesbian tourism and other emerging forms of queer travel" she acknowledges the existence of other sexual identities apart from the most recognized ones, and uses "queer travel" as a more inclusive term. Likewise, the term "tourism of homo-erotic practices" used by the authors of this chapter is an inclusive term that encompasses all forms of tourism by men who engage in sex with other men, regardless of their sexual identities. Although not the only one, the dominating identity related to "tourism of homo-erotic practices" is usually the gay identity. This is because gays in general—especially in the West—enjoy a high purchasing power and, for many of them, travel and tourism have become a way of joining the world of the cosmopolitan gay (Hughes, 1997; 2006).

In the literature to which we have had access, the answer to the question of whether "tourism and sex" is typical of, or strongly related to gay tourism—or, in broader terms, to tourism of homo-erotic practices— varies widely. As happens with heterosexual tourists, sexual activity is part of the daily life of men who engage in homo-erotic practices, and therefore not only present during holidays but, as might be expected, even augmented by it.

According to Ryan and Hall (2001: 103), "one of the great myths of gay lifestyles [is] that it is full of single gays and lesbians who are seeking casual sex." However, other authors, such as Clift and Forrest (1999b), illustrate that the gay men they interviewed had frequent new partners when not on holidays—which suggests that they might have even more during the holidays. In another study (Clift & Forrest, 2000), the same researchers added that half of their informants agreed that there were more opportunities for sex on holidays, and that nearly forty percent of them were more active on holidays than at home. Not surprisingly, men holidaying in gay destinations searched for and found more opportunities for sex with other males. For others, however, having sex during holidays was less important in planning a holiday than being able to socialize with other gay men in gay places; both opportunities often being unavailable at home (Clift & Forrest, 1999a). As with other tourists, some people with homo-erotic practices travel with the only and prime motive of having sexual encounters.

Generally speaking, the sexual behaviour of men who engage in homo-erotic practices, whether or not on holidays, has not been sufficiently researched. Comparative research with single non-gay men on this theme would be very interesting, although according to Clift and Forrest "Gay men are considerably more likely than heterosexuals to have sex with new partners on holiday" (Clift & Forrest 1999b: 290).

Finally, in this chapter—and the research on which it is based—the terms "sex service," "prostitution" and "sex work" are used indistinctively, as are their derivatives "*sexo-servidor*" (Spanish for a person offering sex services), "prostitute" and "sex worker." We have found equal arguments for and against the use of each one of these terms. For example, although "sex worker" might sound more politically correct, in the case of Mexico its use may give the reader the wrong impression that it has acquired a legal meaning. Also, by using this "clean" term, one obscures the causes that bring many of the sex workers to the practice (poverty, hunger and despair), as well as the effects of practising it (degradation, stigmatization, marginalization). For many of them, sex for money is the only feasible way of subsistence (Khan, 1999). On the other hand, the term "prostitution," notwithstanding its pejorative and incriminating connotation, is preferred by some authors for its re-signification as a tool for empowerment. Adult persons have the right to rent out their body as a *modus vivendi* (Altman, 2001: 100). For the purpose of this work, any of these terms will simply refer to the acts of selling and buying sexual services, with no political, moral or any other connotation whatsoever.

Methodology

The first step of the research on which this chapter is based was the selection of the Mexican towns. Those towns with a major influx of tourism that present specific sectors for homo-erotic recreation as well as male prostitution were favoured (Figure 7.1). Mexico City and Guadalajara were chosen from among the big metropolises; Acapulco, Puerto Vallarta, Veracruz and Cancun from among the coastal towns, and Tijuana from the border towns.

Figure 7. 1: Main tourist destinations in Mexico, 2005

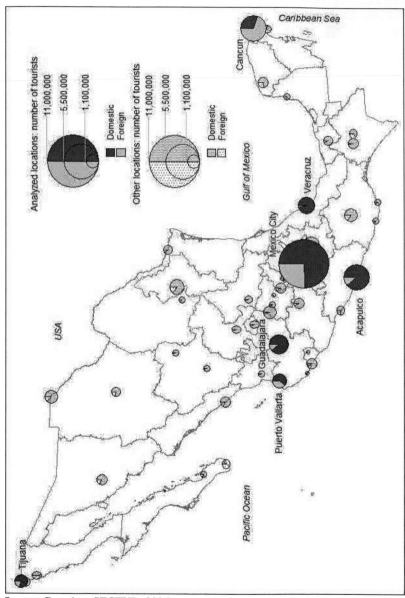

Source: Based on SECTUR, 2006.

In each of the localities under study, a team of researchers conducted the investigation, involving in total more than fourteen specialist and thirteen students from the fields of geography, anthropology, psychology and tourism studies. The fieldwork and the collection of data were carried out in several periods from late 2006 to early 2008, mostly during high tourist seasons. Although basically a general shared methodology was determined, the teams and researchers had certain autonomy and freedom to adapt it to the specific site characteristics.

Although the goal was at first to obtain information from both sex workers and tourists, the existing anthropological literature on sex tourism evidenced the difficulties in getting access to the latter, as tourists tend to deny their involvement in this kind of sexual practice, even though they engage in them (Aramberri, 2005). It was therefore decided to focus the research on prostitutes, and basically on those working fundamentally in open spaces. It should be pointed out that various sex workers covered both "open" and "closed" spaces to contact clients, meaning that they also made contacts, for instance in discotheques and bars, or by phone or the Internet, besides the open public spaces.

For each of the towns, the following three aspects were established and mapped: 1) The tourist areas (i.e., spaces with a high concentration of tourist infrastructure, such as hotels and restaurants); 2) The areas of homo-erotic socialization related to the tourist areas; 3) The areas where male-to-male prostitution takes place, particularly the "open spaces" (e.g., streets, beaches, main squares, shopping malls) in which, occasionally or permanently, men offer their sexual services to other men.

An exploratory investigation of the dynamics of the sexual encounter required a qualitative approach. Therefore, participant observation and an in-depth, semi-structured personal interview were chosen as the main research procedures, thereby allowing methodological triangulation. Participant observation took place at several moments in places where tourists would meet sex workers. No observation was carried out at the sites where the actual sexual act was consummated, or at the sex workers' place of residence. Following theoretical as well as judgemental criteria, the investigators sampled their subjects at the public and "open" spaces of the locality in question, and observed them. Attention was fixed not only on the persons sharing this space, but on their use of it and, in particular, the dynamics taking place in the context of sexual encounters.

Semi-structured interviews were conducted with sex workers. Inasmuch as their vision and experiences were considered important for the understanding of the phenomenon under study, an "emic" perspective was favoured (Harris, 2001; 1979). An interview protocol with possible research topics and some related questions was drawn up. Although basically all topics were to be covered, the different teams had a certain freedom of choice to explore them, or to study them more in depth, according to the location. The interview protocol allowed for more detailed probing in: 1) the socio-demographic characteristics of the prostitute, 2) his mobility, 3) his family and personal life, 4) his work as sex server, 5) his perspective on the organization of labour, 6) his perspective on clients, 7) the forms and places in which the sex worker contacts clients, 8) the supply and demand of sex services, 9) the places where the sex act is consummated, 10) the economic aspects of sex service, 11) the risks and power relations involved in the exercise of male prostitution, 12) health aspects, 13) sexual identity and self-esteem issues, 14) the sex worker's perception of his own marginality and exclusion, and 15) his own expectations and opinions.

For each town, between seven and fifteen interviews were carried out by the local team of researchers. In total, eighty four interviews were conducted. Many interviewees were found through snow-ball and judgmental sampling. The interviews took place either at the open spaces where the sex worker was met—bars, restaurants—or in hotel rooms or hotel lobbies—where researchers were staying. The interviews lasted on average from forty five to sixty minutes and were recorded. The sex workers received, according to the town, between 150 and 400 Mexican pesos. The interviews were transcribed, referring to the sex worker with a pseudonym.

The research data were complemented with information from web site analysis, informal conversations, and historical documents. Some investigating teams included other informants apart from the street sex worker, such as personnel from government or non-government institutions, and a few prostitutes who made their contact mainly in "closed" space, to contextualize the basic information.

Each research team analyzed their data, using content analysis, semiotic analysis or grounded theory analysis, trying to get below the surface of the communication, noticing trends and developing categories and themes inductively from the reading of the interviews. The analysis presented in this chapter is based on our interpretation of the information contained in the research reports from the different teams, which will be published as chapters in a forthcoming book (Lopez & Van Broeck, forthcoming).

Tourism of homo-erotic practices in Mexico

Throughout the present century and a significant portion of the 20th century, Mexico has occupied a privileged position in the world of tourism in terms of both number of visitors and the revenue derived from tourist activities (WTO, 2008). This performance is even more outstanding if one considers that tourism has represented almost ten percent of the country's GDP in the last decade and generated five percent of direct employment. The impact of tourism is felt as much in the economic as in the social and cultural spheres.

In 2005, Mexican hotels lodged about forty five million tourists (SECTUR, 2006).[1] The seven towns included in the study on which this chapter is based, accounted for fifty four percent of that total, as well as fifty two percent of domestic tourists, and sixty two percent of international tourists (Figure 7.1).

Tijuana, a northern border town, received in 2007 around 53.4 million visitors from the US who on average remained in town for six hours (Camarena, 2007). Though these visitors are not classified as "tourists" in official records (such as the World Tourism Organisation), they have similar consumption patterns and behaviour: they eat in restaurants, visit bars, lounges and casinos, they stay in "hourly hotels" (usually with no check-in process or registry) and buy sexual services (Bringas, 1991), which was a reason to include Tijuana in this research as another important Mexican tourist destination.

An indicator of the relevance of the tourism of homo-erotic practices in the economy of the selected towns is the concentration of gay businesses. The *Spartacus Guide* (Gmünder & Bedford, 2007), a leading international gay travel guidebook, showcases Mexico City, Puerto Vallarta, Guadalajara, Monterrey, Tijuana, Acapulco and Cancun as the Mexican towns with the widest array of places for gay tourists, such as restaurants, tour operators and entertainment (Figure 7.2). However, this guide caters mostly to tourists—domestic and international—belonging to the global "pink tourism" prototype (Hughes, 2006) and leaves out a large number of non-gay, homo-erotic socialization places that are frequented by national tourists and some international tourists. The "Clandestino" Internet guide (www.clandestino.com) offers information on the location and activities of "clandestine" places for homo-erotic encounters for these tourists.

---

[1] Data refers to the fifty-five tourist destinations in the country that keep tourist registries (SECTUR, 2006).

The port of Veracruz, known nationally for its tolerance of prostitution and homo-erotic practices, in the *Spartacus Guide* is featured as having remarkably few "gay" places. This town also offers the special, "temporary" open spaces of mass festivities such as the Carnival, where national and some international male tourists seek sexual encounters with other males. The Veracruz Carnival enjoys a relatively established tolerance for sexual interaction. While the popular night party dominates the scene, many non-gay places, such as streets, public plazas, beer parlours, traditional bars, etc., are the stage in which flirting takes place between male tourists and local males willing to interact sexually in exchange for gifts or money.

Coastal tourist destinations—Acapulco and Cancun, but especially Puerto Vallarta—have, in absolute as well as relative terms (i.e., as per total number of visitors as well as total local population) a great number of gay places. Acapulco, one of Mexico's oldest resort cities, was promoted throughout the world as a first class-tourist destination whose profile included male sex tourism and gay tourism (Vargas & Alcalá, 2008). However, in the last two decades, having passed the consolidation and stagnation phases of Butler's life cycle of tourist area evolution (Butler, 1980), Acapulco has been receiving more national tourists than international tourists. Cancun and Puerto Vallarta, on the other hand, have from their relatively recent inception as tourist destinations been directed to the foreign tourist market and continue to be so. This has significantly influenced the emergence of gay places in those towns. The *Spartacus Guide* list of such places in Puerto Vallarta rivals that of Mexico City, even though the latter has, by far, a much larger population and number of visitors.

Mexico City, Guadalajara and Monterrey, the three largest urban agglomerations in Mexico—all with an inland location—have a large number of gay places (in Figure 7.2 Monterrey, a town not included in this study, has the largest circle in grey). However, when compared to smaller towns, these metropolises show a lower degree of relative concentration of such places. Finally, a border town like Tijuana shows a larger proportion of gay places per inhabitant than the large metropolises on account of the many short-term international visitors it registers.

Figure 7.2: Gay places in Mexican towns, as per an international tourism gay guide

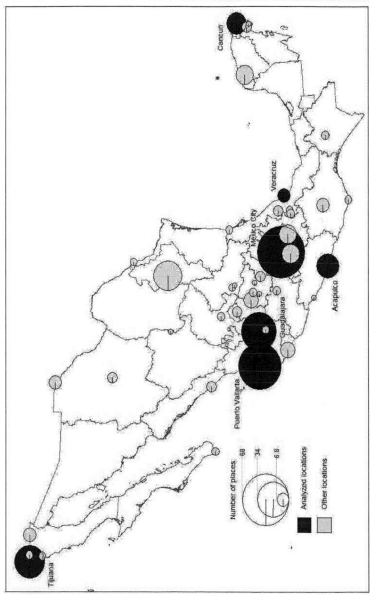

Source: Based on Gmünder & Bedford, 2007.

Space, tourism and sex: the case of Mexican sex workers

The information obtained from the eighty four interviews mentioned above, as well as the researchers' ethnographic observations in the selected towns, allow us to identify two different "types" of space—which by no means are disconnected— where male sexual commerce in tourist contexts takes place; namely, "traditional" and "gay" spaces. The differences between these two types of space relate to factors such as the sex workers' socio-economic level and degree of social segregation, the sexual practices involved, the identity of the sex worker, his way of marketing sexual services, and his general health condition.

"Traditional" spaces are typically urban public spaces, such as parks and central squares—known in Mexico as "*zócalos*," the site of civil and religious buildings—and neighbouring streets, bars and *cantinas*, where homo-erotic socialization between people of middle and lower-middle class has been taking place. This confirmed the results of other studies (Córdova, 2003; 2005; Valenzuela, 2008; Sánchez & López, 1997; 2000; López & Sánchez, 2004), in which it was found that in various Mexican cities the main square (*zócalo*), as well as parks and other green areas become in the evening a meeting point for street youngsters, as well as for gays and men who are looking for someone of the same sex.

"Gay" spaces, on the other hand, are a more recent phenomenon, coinciding with the introduction in the 1980s of "gay" identity into the country (Sánchez & López, 1997; 2000). Gay identity and a proud and evident adherence to a sexual orientation have had important territorial repercussions. People of the upper classes, who used to socialize in private, unidentifiable spaces such as parties and gatherings, began to meet in these new places of gay socialization, in whose proximity (streets, plazas, parks, beaches) sex workers often circulate or stalk their clients. In this sense, the emergence of these private spaces has contributed to a greater occupation of public spaces by both prostitutes and wandering clients.

In almost all the selected towns, "gay" spaces are located either close to tourist areas or right inside them, where they benefit from the best transport, communications, hotel and entertainment infrastructure available. The emergence of these new places of gay socialization was almost simultaneous with the growth of mass tourism in these towns. However, it is impossible to determine whether the emergence of gay spaces came as a result of the activities of gay tourists in a given locality, or gay tourism was attracted to pre-existing gay spaces in the tourist areas.

In the "traditional" spaces, sex services are offered in the open by means of a more-or-less concealed set of codified gestures. The sex server will typically stand in one place waiting for a client, or walk around or towards a nearby bar to facilitate the encounter. While suggestively staring at a potential client, he will express his disposition to have sex by placing his hand on his crotch. When the time comes to discuss with his client his willingness to exchange sex for money or other favours (e.g., drinks, food, entrance fees to places of entertainment) he must make sure that his "manhood" is not in any way diminished, even though he may openly agree to sexual practices regarded as non-masculine (e.g., anal sex, oral sex, kissing).

> **Interviewee**: Some [sex workers, to catch clients] grab their crotch like that...or even stick their cock out...or they take off their T-shirts... I've never found it necessary... I am not as unattractive as to having to provoke them [the tourists] that way...
> (**Interviewee**: Eduardo, eighteen years old, Mexico City).

> **Interviewee**: There's lots of little tricks to attract the client's attention: how you stand, how you look at them... Some [sex workers] are rather boorish and they pull down their pants and show it all to the clients...
> (**Interviewee**: Ángel, twenty years old, Mexico City).

Interaction between tourists and prostitutes in the "gay" spaces (streets, beaches, as well as discos and bars) is more straightforward than it is in "traditional" spaces, since both the prostitute and the tourist involved recognise themselves and each other as "gay." The sexual services and terms of agreement (e.g., price, duration, meeting place and limits of sexual practices) are more openly and directly discussed. Though by no means considered set in stone, the commercial contract is acknowledged as such and the process is usually more expedite.

Even though some of them may accept the "gay" or "homosexual" labels, male prostitutes who offer their services in "traditional" spaces are usually men who see themselves as heterosexual or bisexual, more at ease with local descriptive terms such as *"activos," "chichifos," "mayates"* or *"chacales"* when talking about their identity.

> **Interviewee**: No, *they* do it [oral sex] to me; I am hundred percent *activo*; '*activo*' means manly! I don't like to suck dick, nor do I like to be fucked or anything, or to be penetrated. I like to penetrate and to have oral sex performed on me, and that's it.
> (**Interviewee**: David, nineteen years old, Mexico City).

Interviewee: God no! What 'you mean…?! No way! They've sometimes tried to touch my butt, but I tell them [the tourists] *nel*[2] you stick to this [my cock]! Because this is all I like, to be sucked, oh yes! I am hundred percent active. Not for nothing am I dark and black, of Latin race: hotter!
(**Interviewee**: Kalimán, twenty four years old, Veracruz).

The sex workers described themselves as "real men" and declared that, though their desire was focused on women, their virility was such that they were capable of having an erection when it came to having sex with another man. For many of the prostitutes, this performance of the "hyper-masculine" is very important. However, in the event that a tourist expresses his desire to go over the stated limits and asks the sex worker to adopt a "passive" role (that is, to perform oral sex on the client, or to be penetrated by him), some will be willing to comply in exchange for a significant amount of extra money. Charging more gives the sex worker the possibility to justify his engagement in "non-masculine" sexual activities and keep up appearances as a "real man." That is, even though he may act as "*pasivo*," a sex worker will never stop claiming that he is, in essence, an "*activo*."

Interviewers: How do you define yourself?
Interviewee: *Mayate*.
Interviewers: And if they were to offer you extra money to penetrate you or to have you perform oral sex on them, would you do it?
Interviewee: Well, it depends… But I would charge a lot.
Interviewers: To do what?
Interviewee: To be penetrated…but I don't like it; I would do it just for the money, because I need it.
(**Interviewee**: Fernando, twenty years old, Puerto Vallarta).

Differences aside, in both types of spaces the ideal of masculinity plays an important role in the assignment of monetary value to the sexual services by individuals who self-identify as "men." The relative conformity of the sex server to this ideal is negotiated and resolved between himself and his client—the tourist. For many of the workers interviewed—coming from widely diverse socio-cultural contexts—masculinity is among other things associated to the possession of a big and potent sex organ, as well as with having a muscular body and showing gestures, voice inflexions and language characteristic of the male prototype.

---

[2] Slang for 'no' throughout Mexico, chiefly amongst youngsters.

Interviewee: As far as they've told me, they [the tourists] like the way Mexicans do it [sex]... Yes because...um, they are well-endowed and because generally back there [the tourists' places of origin] people are not so hot...
(**Interviewee**: Jonathan, twenty seven years old, Acapulco).

Interviewers: But what do you think they find attractive in you?
Interviewee: The masculinity they see in me.
Interviewers: Because you're always, so to speak, the macho, aren't you?
Interviewee: 'So to speak' no! *I* am!
(**Interviewee**: Iván, twenty eight years old, Puerto Vallarta).

Interviewers: What do you think clients look for in you?
Interviewee: Well, you could say...masculinity, my body, my cock!
(**Interviewee**: Alberto, seventeen years old, Puerto Vallarta).

Age is another intervening aspect in the negotiation of sex services. Many sex workers thought that being over thirty five (or even thirty) years old made one less "competitive" in the sex market. Indeed, none of the prostitutes interviewed exceeded thirty three years of age, and the great majority of them were under twenty seven (Figure 7.3).

Interviewee: There's a mate [sex worker] who is over thirty five and even so he gets clients; I would feel ashamed to be a prostitute when I am over thirty... At that age it's time for you to ask for the [sex] services instead!
(**Interviewee**: Mike, seventeen years old, Cancún).

Those interviewed who belonged to the lower and lower-middle class sectors, often had given up their studies and found themselves lacking the necessary skills to opt for a paying job. Even if they could find one, the salary would not be sufficient to make a living. They regarded prostitution as practically the only solution at hand, sometimes combined with other informal activities.

Interviewee: Honestly, I do it out of need...to get an extra buck. If I get thousand pesos a week doing construction work, and if I have to spend fifteen hundred pesos a month on rent, it is but natural that I have to look for other ways of making money; 'cause stealing I would not do...
(**Interviewee**: Jorge, twenty two years old, Veracruz).

Figure 7.3: Age of the interviewed sex workers

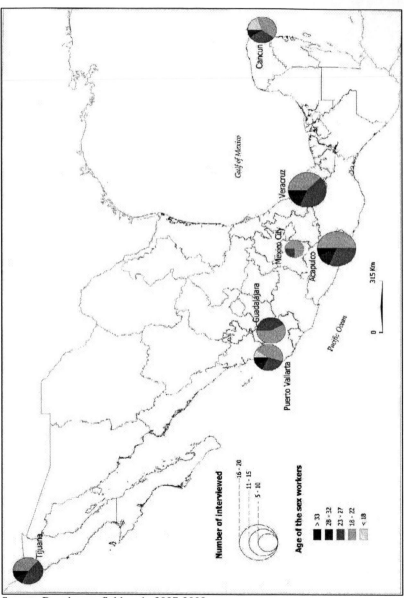

Source: Based upon fieldwork, 2007-2008.

However, some of the interviewed—especially those who see themselves as gay, often with a higher educational level—did admit to have the possibility of finding a well-paid job, but they preferred and enjoyed offering their sex services, which affords them sexual gratification while allowing them to make "a lot of money" in little time.

> **Interviewee**: I practise prostitution for various reasons: it's fun, it's pleasant and it is a paid-for pastime... Need is not so much a reason... But of course a little money is always welcome..!
> (**Interviewee**: Eduardo, eighteen years old, Mexico City).

Though not as important as masculinity and age, ethnic appearance was also detected as an intervening factor in the negotiation of sex services with tourists. Many of those interviewed revealed that "white" foreign tourists predominantly seek a "dark-skinned" prototype of sex worker, especially when they visit coastal areas, while national tourists seem to prefer those with a "lighter" skin.

> **Interviewee**: Since most people in the US are really blond, Americans find brown-skinned people very attractive...they love them! They [white tourists] are tired of blond people and come here to find brown people. I...used to say oh, why wasn't I white..! But now I say thank goodness!
> (**Interviewee**: Carlos, twenty four years old, Puerto Vallarta).

Conclusions

In Mexico, commercial homo-erotic sex in the context of tourism had not hitherto been directly addressed. The research results presented in this chapter not only throw light on the subject, but offer an understanding of the territorial dimensions and dynamics of these practices from the perspective of the sex workers. The findings derive from cross-examination of the seven towns under study.

Notwithstanding their historical, cultural, socio-demographic and other differences, these towns share in common the presence of two different "types" of spaces where commercial homo-erotic sex is offered to tourists: the "traditional" spaces of the old central areas, and the "gay" spaces of the modern areas, located mostly within or nearby the spaces of tourist activity. These two spatially-differentiated areas of commercial homo-erotic sexual activity are differentiated also in terms of the different sexual identities of the sex workers who operate in them, and the ways in which they relate to their clients. In the traditional spaces, prostitutes tend to assume a regional or local identity and therefore they do not necessarily see or define themselves as "gay"—but rather as "*chacales*," "*mayates*," "*chichifos*," "*machos*," "*hombres*" or "*activos*"—whereas those working in gay spaces do adopt more readily the more "international" gay identity.

It is significant that a considerable part of the interviewed sex workers are immersed in structurally marginal socio-economic conditions. Their access to a formal job with sufficient pay to satisfy their needs and those of their dependants is at best limited, and this is usually one of the reasons why they turn to this money-making activity. Nevertheless, a few of those who operate in the gay areas consider this a rather enjoyable occupation affording them some extra cash.

In the "traditional" spaces, sex services are offered in a rather concealed way, by means of a codified set of gestures, while in the "gay" spaces the interaction between tourists and prostitutes is more straightforward, since both parties recognize themselves and each other as "gay."

Further research on these two kinds of spaces—either in the same towns or other towns—will allow for a better understanding of how they are shaped, the public that frequents them, and the dynamics of the relations that take place in them. It would also be interesting to expand the research so as to include the tourists' viewpoint. From the interviews, we could detect that customers in the traditional zones are more frequently local or regional visitors who often conceal their homo-erotic practices and to whom the sex workers often refer as "*tapados*" (that is, "closeted"), while international tourists, often more at ease with their being "gay," are more frequently found in the areas dominated by "gay culture."

A relationship between the presence of gay travellers and gay spaces or sectors could easily be established. As gay travellers look for or include themselves in the already-constituted spaces of gay socialization—or in those under formation by the local territorial dynamics—their presence and specific demands will undoubtedly have an impact on the emergence, consolidation and expansion of gay areas. We can expect that this increase in gay spaces will also have an impact on the local dynamics and on the multiple identities that are currently under negotiation.

Acknowledgments

Interviews to sex workers referred to in this chapter were conducted by Alfonso Jiménez, Álvaro López, Anne Marie Van Broeck, Brenda Alcalá, Cristóbal Mendoza, Karina Amador, Lucinda Arroyo, Napoleón Glockner, Orlando Merino, Patricia Medina, Rosío Córdova.

References

Altman, D. 2001. *Global sex*. Chicago: The University of Chicago Press

Aramberri, J. 2005. Nuevas andanzas de rostro pálido. Dimensiones del turismo sexual. *Política y Sociedad*. 42 (1): 101 - 116

Bauer, T. and McKercher, B. (Eds.) 2003. *Sex and tourism: Journeys of romance, love and lust*. New York: The Haworth Hospitality Press

Bringas, N. 1991. Diagnóstico del sector turístico en Tijuana. N. Bringas, N. and J. Carrillo (eds). *Grupos devisitantes y actividades turísticas en Tijuana*, Mexico: El Colegio de la Frontera Norte. pp. 17 - 46

Butler, J. 1993. *Bodies that matter*. New York: Routledge

Butler, R. 1980. The concept of a tourist area cycle of evolution: Implications for management of resources. *Canadian Geographer*. 24 (1): 5 - 12

Camarena, G. 2007. Realidades del turismo fronterizo, *Primera Sesión Plenaria de Ciudades Fronterizas del Norte de México*, Tijuana. http://www.tijuana.gob.mx/dependencias/sedeti/SDE/Turismo.pdf. 1/7/08

Cantú, L. 2002. De ambiente: Queer tourism and the shifting boundaries of Mexican male sexualities. *GLQ: A journal of Lesbian and Gay Studies*. 8 (1/2): 139 - 166

Carrier, J. 1985. Mexican male bisexuality. *Journal of Homosexuality*. 11 (1/2): 75 - 86

—. 1995. *De los otros: Intimacy and homosexuality among Mexican men*. New York: Columbia University

—. 2003. *De los otros. Intimidad y homosexualidad entre los hombres del occidente y el noroeste de México* (Updated version). Mexico: Pandora

Carrillo, H. 2002. *The night is young: Sexuality in Mexico in the time of AIDS*. Chicago: University of Chicago Press

Carter, S. and Clift, S. 2000. Tourism, international travel and sex: Themes and research. S. Clift and S. Carter (ed). *Tourism and sex: Culture, commerce and coercion*. London: Pinter. pp. 1 - 19

Clift, S. and Carter, S. (Ed.), 2000. *Tourism and sex: Culture, commerce and coercion*. London: Pinter

Clift, S. and Forrest, S. 1999a. Gay men and tourism: Destinations and holiday motivations. *Tourism Management*. 20 (5): 615 - 625

Clift, S. and Forrest, S. 1999b. Factors associated with gay men's sexual behaviours and risk on holiday. *AIDS Care*. 11 (3): 281 - 295

Clift, S. and Forrest, S. 2000. Tourism and the sexual ecology of gay men, S. Clift and S. Carter (eds). *Tourism and sex: Culture, commerce and coercion*. London: Pinter. pp. 179 - 199

Córdova, R. 2003. Mayates, chichifos y chacales: Trabajo sexual masculino en la ciudad de Xalapa, Veracruz, M. Miano (ed). *Caminos inciertos de las masculinidades.* Mexico: INAH/CONACULTA. pp. 141 - 160
—. 2005. Vida en los márgenes: La experiencia corporal como anclaje identitario entre sexoservidores de la ciudad de Xalapa, Veracruz. *Cuicuilco.* 12 (34): 217 - 238
Crick, M. 2001. Representations of international tourism in the social sciences: Sun, sex, sights, savings and servility. Y. Apostolopoulos, S. Leivadi and A. Yiannakis (eds). *The sociology of tourism: Theoretical and empirical investigations.* London: Routledge. pp. 15 - 50
De Ocampo, I. 2003. *El paquete shark: Turismo de sexo y romance en Cozumel.* Undergraduate dissertation, Cozumel, Mexico, Universidad de Quintana Roo
Gmünder, B. and Bedford, B. 2007. *Spartacus international gay guide 2007.* Berlin: Bruno Gmünder Verlag GmbH
Hall, C. M. 2001. Gender and economic interests in tourism prostitution: The nature, development and implications of sex tourism in South-East Asia, Y. Apostolopoulos, S. Leivadi and A. Yiannakis (eds). *The sociology of tourism: Theoretical and empirical investigations.* London: Routledge. pp. 265 - 280
Harris, M. 2001. 1979. *Cultural materialism.* Walnut Creek: Alta Mira Press
Herdt, G. 1992. 'Coming out' as a rite of passage: A Chicago study. G. Herdt. (ed). *Gay culture in America: Essays from the field.* Boston: Beacon Press. pp. 29 - 67
Hernández, P. 2005. El movimiento lésbico, gay, bisexual y transgenérico y la construcción social de la identidad gay en la Ciudad de México. *Memorias de la II Semana Cultural de la Diversidad Sexual.* Mexico: Instituto Nacional de Antropología e Historial. pp. 287 - 304
—. 2004. Los estudios sobre diversidad sexual en el PUEG. G. Careaga and S. Cruz (eds). *Sexualidades diversas: Aproximaciones para su análisis,* Mexico: Programa Universitario de Estudios de Género (Universidad Nacional Autónoma de México) and Miguel Ángel Porrúa. pp. 21 - 33
—. 2001. La construcción de la identidad gay en un grupo gay de jóvenes de la Ciudad de Mexico: Algunos ejes de análisis para el estudio etnográfico. *Desacatos. Revista de antropología social.* 6: 63 - 96
Hughes, H. 1997. Holidays and homosexual identity. *Tourism management.* 18 (1): 3 - 7
—. 2002. Gay man's holiday destination choice: A case of risk and avoidance. *International Journal of Tourism Research.* 4 (4): 299 - 312

—. 2006. *Pink tourism: Holidays of gay men and lesbians*. Wallingford: CABI

Jagose, A. 1996. *Queer theory. An introduction*. New York: New York University Press

Khan, S. 1999. Through a window darkly? Men who sell sex to men in India and Bangladesh. P. Aggleton (ed). *Men who sell sex: International perspectives on male prostitution and HIV/AIDS*. Philadelphia: Temple University Press. pp. 195 - 212

Lara, M. 2005. Placeres marciales. *Proceso*. 1499: 36 - 40

Liguori, A. and Aggleton, P. 1999. Aspects of male sex work in Mexico City. P. Aggleton (ed). *Men who sell sex: International perspectives on male prostitution and HIV/AIDS*. Philadelphia: Temple University Press. pp. 103 - 126

List, M. and Teutle, A. 2008. Turismo sexual: Saunas para varones en la ciudad de Puebla. *Teoría y Praxis*. 5: 113-122

López, A. and Carmona, R. 2008. Turismo sexual masculino-masculino en la Ciudad de México. *Teoría y Praxis*. 5: 99 - 112

López, A. and Sánchez, A. 2004. Dinámica territorial del deseo *queer* en Monterrey, Nuevo León. *Ciudades*. 62: 25 - 33

López, A. and Van Broeck, A. (eds). Forthcoming. *Turismo sexual en México. Hombres que se vinculan con hombres. Una perspectiva multidisciplinaria*. Mexico: Instituto de Geografía (Universidad Nacional Autónoma de México)

Lumsden, I. 1991. *Homosexuality, society and the state in Mexico*. Toronto: Canadian Gay Archives

McKercher, B. and Bauer, T. 2003. Conceptual framework of the nexus between tourism, romance and sex. Bauer, T. and McKercher, B. (eds). *Sex and tourism: Journeys of romance, love and lust*. New York: Haworth Hospitality Press. pp. 3 - 17

Monterrubio, J. 2008. Comunidades receptoras y percepciones: un estudio sobre turismo y sexualidad. *Teoría y Praxis*. 5: 145 - 160

Núñez, G. 2007. *Masculinidad e intimidad: Identidad, sexualidad y sida*. Mexico: Miguel Ángel Porrúa, Programa Universitario de Estudios de Género (Universidad Nacional Autónoma de México) and El Colegio de Sonora

—. 2005. Significados y políticas de la 'diversidad sexual': sanización de la otredad o reivindicaciones de lo polimorfo? Reflexiones teóricas para el activismo. *Memorias de la II semana de la diversidad sexual*. Mexico: Instituto Nacional de Antropología e Historia. pp. 225 - 239

—. 1994. *Sexo entre varones. Poder y resistencia en el campo sexual*. Mexico: El Colegio de Sonora and Programa Universitario de Estudios de Género (Universidad Nacional Autónoma de México)

Oppermann, M. 1999. Sex tourism. *Annals of Tourism Research*. 26 (2): 251 - 266

Palma, G. 2007. *Springbreakers. Turismo salvaje en playas mexicanas*. Mexico: Grijalvo

Puar J. 2002. Introduction. *GLQ: A Journal of Lesbian and Gay Studies*. 8 (1/2): 1 - 6

Ryan, C. and Hall, C. 2001. *Sex tourism: Marginal people and liminalities*. London: Routledge

Sánchez, A. and López, A. 2000. Visión geográfica de los lugares gays de la Ciudad de México. *Cuicuilco*. 7 (18): 271 - 286

—. 1997. Gay male places of Mexico City, G. B. Ingram, A. M. Bouthillette and Y. Retter (eds). *Queers in space: Communities, public places, sites of resistance*. Washington: Bay Press. pp. 197 - 212

SECTUR. 2006. *Compendio estadístico de turismo en México, 2006*. Mexico: Secretaría de Turismo

Taylor, J. S. 2001. Dollars are a girl's best friend: Female tourists' sexual behaviour in the Caribbean. *Sociology*. 34 (3): 749 – 964

Valenzuela, E. 2008. *Construcción, evolución y organización del espacio turístico de Acapulco, Guerrero*, doctoral dissertation, Mexico: Facultad de Filosofía y Letras (Universidad Nacional Autónoma de México)

Van Broeck, A. and De Ocampo, I. 2003. Sun, sea, sand and sharks. *American Anthropological Association, 102nd Annual Meeting*. Chicago, USA

—. 2010. Turismo, romance y sexo: relaciones temporales entre hombres jóvenes (sharks) y mujeres turistas en la isla de Cozumel. *Teoría y Praxis*. 7

Vargas, S. and Alcalá, B. 2008. Espacios homoeróticos y turismo sexual en Acapulco. *Esencia y espacio*. 26: 26 - 34

Vendrell, J. 2001. La homosexualidad no evoluciona, se construye: Para una crítica antropológica del esencialismo (homo)sexual. *Cuiculco*. 8 (23): 31 - 50

WTO. 2008. *Yearbook of tourism Statistics. Data 2002-2006*. Madrid: World Tourism Organization

CHAPTER EIGHT

WHITE GAY WOMEN'S LEISURE SPACES IN BLOEMFONTEIN, SOUTH AFRICA

GUSTAV VISSER

Introducing gay women, leisure and space

Space has emerged as a difficult, uneasy concept which, as Shurmer-Smith and Hannam (1994: 13) suggest, does not exist other than in a cultural sense. According to them, spaces appear and disappear and change size, character and meaning according to the manner in which people construct them. Place, like space, is an intersubjective reality in what have been referred to as "emotional geographies" (Shields, 1991: 6). As a consequence, spaces are seen as negotiated socio-cultural constructions (Aitchison & Reeves, 1998: 51). However, some groups are more powerful than others in the negotiation of space and place, and appear to claim and dominate both physical and social space (Bell & Valentine, 1995). This has been particularly strongly demonstrated in a range of investigations (Bell & Binnie, 2000; Valentine, 1993) that show how space is racialized, gendered and heterosexualized.

The importance of gender as a shaper of leisure experiences has been the subject of considerable research interest (Bell, et al., 1994; Valentine, 1993). In much of this work it has been established that gender shapes leisure experiences, but also space and place. In addition, this body of research has explored how human status characteristics such as class, race and ethnicity, sexuality and disability have combined to create points of empowerment or oppression, particularly in women's leisure worlds (Pritchard, et al., 2002: 106). The general contention in both past and present research is that gay women have been marginalized in physical and symbolic realms; among them leisure space (Bell, et al: 1994). This does not always appear to be the case, as many investigations suggest that the homosexual community is becoming more integrated with other groups in what used to be exclusively heterosexual leisure space (Aitkenhead, 1997; Kirkey & Forsyth, 2001; Visser, 2008a). However, this ignores the fact that the so-called "homosexual community" is a heterogeneous, culturally diverse group of men and women who, despite sharing same common bonds, have diverse identities and use diverse spatial realms to explore these bonds (Greene, 1997: vi).

Gay identities are gendered and reflect the significant power differentials between gay men and women, while also linking to various forms of gender performativity. Most current work suggests that a homogeneous "gay community" and "gay space" potentially obscures gay men's oppression of gay women while reinforcing a tendency of patriarchal society by which male experience subsumes female experience and becomes regarded as some gender-neutral "norm" (Pritchard, et al., 2002: 106). Considerable work (for a review see Bell & Binnie, 2000) has been undertaken to expand on the contention that the traditional conceptualization of leisure processes and spaces is both heterosexist and androcentric. The ways in which gay male presence, power and control dominates gay space and threatens gay women's space have been remarked on (Bell, et al., 1994). There has also been limited investigation into the impact of gender on gay women's use of public, particularly gay, leisure space, in their relationships and negotiations with gay men and in their encounters with heterosexuals of both genders (Browne, et al., 2006). It has been suggested that apartheid heteropatriarchy complicated formal research into homosexual identities generally, and gay leisure space in particular (Visser, 2003a). Early exceptions to the lack of research on homosexual identities were sociological investigations (cf. Muntingh, 1967; Schurink, 1979) on "femme lesbians" included, for example, in an edited collection ominously entitled *Social Problems in South Africa* (Lotter, 1979). There were further early studies focused on gay men and women's "illegal, abnormal traits," typically conducted in psychology or psychiatry departments. Not surprisingly, a focus on issues such as gay leisure or tourism did not feature in this discourse at all.

However, during the 1990s the paucity of research into homosexuality in South Africa began to be addressed. Gevisser and Cameron's (1993) edited collection, *Defiant Desire: Gay and Lesbian Lives in South Africa*, along with a number of papers, begun to address themes of sexuality in South Africa. Notable research includes Achmat's (1993) analysis of the emergence of homosexual practices in male prisons, Dirsuweit's (1999) in-depth analysis of sexuality in female prisons, and Moodie's (1993) study of migrancy and male homosexuality the context of South African mines. The most recent and arguably most sophisticated research into homosexuality is found in Van Zyl and Steyn's (2005) collection, *Performing Queer: Shaping Sexualities 1994–2004*. To date, this anthology certainly represents the most comprehensive investigations into queer sexuality and identity in South Africa. Although there are repeated references to leisure throughout the text, gay leisure per se is not really a central theme of these investigations.

Nevertheless, the contribution by Leap (2005) to Van Zyl and Steyn's (2005) collection does address queer life in a spatial context. It examines the intersection of same-sex sexualities and geography in metropolitan Cape Town, focusing specifically on depictions of space and spatial practices during the 1990s. The multiple spaces and places that contribute to the formation, development and reconfiguration of homosexual identities are insightfully revealed. The imprint of racial, economic, social and political histories on the meaning of various spaces informs the use of urban space. Perhaps most importantly, the different geographies (including leisure geographies) of homosexual persons are separated according to race, class and gender. Of note to this investigation is the retention of the city centre as the space for mainly middle-class white, gay men, and the exclusion of most other homosexual groups from this space.

Subsequent research by Oswin (2005) and Rink (2007), though focusing on gay internationalization and localized responses to it, has found a similar hegemony in which particular groups of gay men dominate gay women in "gay space" and the generation of such leisure spaces. As will be seen later, the process of gay leisure space development in the Bloemfontein context is fundamentally different to that described in this research. It is the aim of this investigation to call for a more nuanced interpretation of gay women's relationship to homosexual, mainly gay male-dominated leisure spaces. Indeed, it is suggested that in some contexts gay female appropriation of gay leisure space is possible, although the creation of these spaces is ultimately underpinned by a more general heteropatriarchy. Drawing on the historical and current status of gay women's leisure spaces in the secondary city of Bloemfontein in South Africa, it is argued that some of the debates referred to above, which emanate from the developed North, are perhaps not always universally applicable. These debates should be more specific about the contexts in which claims are made about gay women's space development.

This contention is developed through four sections of discussion and analysis. First, a brief overview of the methodology employed in this investigation is set out. The second section provides a historical sketch of how Bloemfontein's gay leisure spaces have developed over the past two decades or so. The third section provides an analysis of the dynamics of contemporary gay women's leisure spaces in Bloemfontein, whilst the final section provides some concluding comments.

Methodology

The primary sources of data for the investigation on which this chapter is based are in-depth, semi-structured interviews with 54 white gay women, 30 of which were undertaken in 2006 and a further 24 in 2008. This augments 40 interviews of gay men undertaken in 2006. In all cases a snowball technique was employed to identify and interview survey participants. Survey participants completed a short structured questionnaire covering biographic information, as well as geo-referenced matrices which aimed at describing a typical week's activities, including the participants' leisure behaviour. Life-histories were then constructed from the semi-structured interviews and these life-histories were subsequently analysed.[1] Table 8.1 provides an outline of the biographical data collected, and Appendix 1 gives a list of the interviewees cited in this chapter.

It is important to note that the gay women interviewed are mainly well-educated, white, broadly-speaking middle-class individuals, aged between 20 and 40. The participants self-identify in the main as "gay women" and not "lesbian," a term which most of them find offensive. In addition, participants describe themselves as different types of gay women, including "butch," "femme," "lipstick lesbian," and "diesel dyke."[2] Thus a broad range of ways of sexual expression and gender performativity are included in the investigation. In addition, the participants are not overly socially-oriented, in the sense that most of them "go out" between once and three times during an average week, owing to a range of demands on their time. In contrast to many similar studies (Aitchison & Reeves, 1998), these participants represent an "out" group, the vast majority of who have revealed their sexual identities to family, friends and co-workers. In the literature (cf. Bell & Binnie, 2000), it is suggested that "out" gay women are more likely to be active in formal gay leisure development than those

---

[1] The views of some of the leisure venues mentioned were obtained. The quality and value of the responses were, however, not deemed sufficient to include in this investigation.

[2] Lipstick lesbian describes lesbian and bisexual women who exhibit feminine gender attributes, such as wearing make-up, wearing dresses or skirts and perhaps having other characteristics associated with feminine women. Diesel dyke is generally seen as derogatory slang for lesbians whose gender performativity is particularly male like, although in the broader literature the term is being appropriated regardless of individual gender expression.

who are still "in the closet," although "out" gay women are less likely to be active in formal gay leisure development than their male counterparts.

Table 8.1: Biographical details of participants				
Age	20–29 years 50%	30–39 years 30%	40+ years 20%		
Education level	High School certificate 70%	Bachelors degree / National diploma 22%	Postgraduate qualification 8%		
Occupation	Professions 33%	Services 22%	Administration 41%	Business ownership 4%	
Relationship status	In a relationship 70%	Not in a relationship 30%			
Private vehicle ownership	Yes 89%	No 11%			
Neighbourhood of residence	Middle– low income 22%	Middle income 70%	Middle–high income 8%	High income 0%	
Income per month	<R5000 30%	R5001– R10000 41%	R10001– R15000 15%	R15001– R20000 4%	>R20 000 10%
Leisure budget per month	<R500 15%	R500– R999 7%	R1000–R1499 19%	R1500– R2000 59%	
Frequency of "going out"	1/week 22%	2/week 41%	3/week 22%	4/week 11%	>4/week 4%

Historical notes on white gay men's and women's leisure spaces in Bloemfontein

The brief historical review of white gay men's and women's leisure spaces in South Africa contrasts sharply with a key claim made in this chapter: that gay leisure spaces in Bloemfontein, unlike in Cape Town and Johannesburg, for example, have always had a gay female, as opposed to male, character. However, issues of class, race, and gender which have been shown to be key variables in explaining gay leisure space development in the broader literature (Bell & Binnie, 2000) are nevertheless also shown to be important in the Bloemfontein context.

It is reported that at least since the 1960s there have been a number of leisure spaces which have provided some figurative and literal space for local gay men in South Africa (Visser, 2006; 2008a). In Bloemfontein, gay men and women mainly met one another through personal contacts, or chance encounters in different types of public (heterosexual) leisure spaces, as is typical of conservative small towns and cities elsewhere. Towards the late 1980s, during a time in which anti-homosexual legislation was seldom applied, according to Du Pisani (2001: 170), formal gay venues started to develop as spaces of defiance against the hegemonic white heteropatriarchal society of Bloemfontein, and South Africa more generally.

In contrast to the situation in the large metropolitan cities of Cape Town and Johannesburg (cf. Visser, 2003a; 2003b; 2008a; 2008b), there were no gay venues in Bloemfontein until recently. However, one venue outside of the city boundary started to cater for queer leisure needs in 1989: Orange Grove (later renamed Buzerant), located some 10km from the CBD (Central Business District). It is described as a very poor venue by those interviewees old enough to have participated in the gay leisure scene at the time of its opening. It was principally a farm barn that was converted to accommodate a dance floor, and the venue had no liquor licence. Importantly, this leisure space was in part initiated and supported by a national non-governmental organization, the Gay Association of South Africa (GASA), which recognized that there were no dedicated gay venues in Bloemfontein, unlike other cities in South Africa. In this sense they aimed to assist in the development of an inclusive queer leisure space.

Gay men and gay women have very different recollections of the early years of Buzerant. Two men interviewed, Adam and Dizzy, say it was a space they preferred to avoid, mainly owing to the disproportionate number of gay women there. The woman interviewees, however, hold fond memories. Fiona was quite nostalgic about those times. She recalled that it was mostly females who attended the parties at Buzerant, bringing cooler bags with drinks, snacks and meat. She said that when one arrived, it was customary to go around and greet each woman individually with a kiss. She noted that Buzerant was not as cliquey as she experiences it to be now. It was a welcoming space away from men generally, and heterosexual men in particular. Echoing the sentiments of Rush in 1950s America (Bullough, 2002) she is of the opinion that "the traditional butch and femme roles were much stronger [than they are now] and if you wanted to dance with someone you had to ask the butch's permission first."

South Africa does not have a history of pronounced gay activism, relative to 1950s America where an increasingly strong and defiant culture resulted as a response to heterosexual hegemony (Rothenberg, 1995). Nor is there evidence to support Rothenberg's (1995) suggestion that specifically gay female entertainment spaces were unlikely to establish themselves unless there was already a protective gay male population in the area.[3] This contention is particularly inaccurate in the Bloemfontein context. Indeed, queer leisure space developed in an isolated venue located far from heterosexual leisure spaces and was appropriated by gay women from the outset. By contrast, gay men supported heterosexual leisure venues in the CBD (Central Business District), and for them some leisure spaces were to an extent accepting of their presence. At the time (late 1980s and early 1990s) there was one nightclub in the city centre, Reds, that developed a reputation for being gay-friendly, according to Peter, a male interviewee. Another interviewee, Phoenix, says that Reds evolved as an alternative leisure space for gay men, while the gay women remained in the formal gay space of Buzerant.

While Buzerant developed as a gay women's leisure venue, it was not a commercial venture. After all, it was in part a project of GASA, a non-profit organization. Towards the mid-1990s a husband-and-wife team made a bid to redevelop Buzerant as a formal, commercial leisure venue, fulfilling the appropriate planning and licensing requirements, according to Mariaan. Fiona said that this resulted in changes in music styles (with rave music being introduced) and interior design. Subsequently, she noted, "a lot more men attended." A darkroom[4] was also added, which really put off gay woman patrons, according to Janine. Indeed, as a result of their protestations the darkroom was subsequently closed. The commercialization drive introduced to Buzerant the trappings of gay male clubs seen

---

[3] It must be noted that the history of gay men and gay women suggests that gay women were in the fact, the first to fight for their rights.

[4] A darkroom is a darkened room, sometimes located in a nightclub, gay bathhouse or sex club, where sexual activity can take place.

elsewhere, and a more overt sexualisation of this leisure space. At the time, however, there was still no dedicated gay leisure venue in the city centre or any of the decentralized business and entertainment nodes. Sporadic attempts were made to establish gay men's nightclubs and/or bars in the CBD, although none of these ventures ever lasted. They were neither particularly attractive leisure spaces, nor was the gay male market large enough to support such venues. Meanwhile, the gay women did not want to socialize in close proximity to heterosexuals, particularly straight men. Buzerant, which only operated during the weekends, held well-publicized and keenly anticipated "theme evenings," drawing crowds away from gay bars and nightclubs in the CBD. This added to their lack of financial viability.

However, this period (early 1990s) also saw changes in the local club scene. The implosion of the apartheid regime during the late 1980s opened up opportunities to satisfy the long-denied demand of a far broader range of people for "all things international," including previously banned items ranging from clothing and club venues to literature, movies, music, and even drugs. The style of music was starting to change and rave music appeared on the local club scene. Along with rave clubs and trance music came new drugs that were marketed as complementing this new clubbing experience. In addition, alternative sexualities suddenly seemed to be regarded as just another part of a broader transition to an as-yet undefined "new" South African dispensation (Visser, 2003a; 2003b; 2008a). This claim must, however, be qualified, in the sense that "homosexuality" was primarily understood as "gay male." In this context of political and social flux, gay men in particular felt less fearful of heterosexual patriarchy as expressed in formal leisure spaces. Moreover, a range of anti-gay legal measures were not being enforced to any great extent by the authorities, who had different priorities, given the instability in township areas. The interview material confirms that this experience of greater freedom was not shared by the woman interviewees, who mostly indicated that they only really started to feel less marginalized far more recently. In some ways this might explain the subsequent development of a new gay space in Bloemfontein.

An action bar, Roxy's, was established in 1993 as the first gay venue *in* the city that was open six days a week. Roxy's was located adjacent to the CBD in a high-density residential neighbourhood. What is particularly striking is that from the outset it was also predominantly a gay women's space. Again, this challenges Rothenberg's (1995) contention that women are unlikely to develop a gay female leisure space without the protection of gay men. None of the survey participants are absolutely clear on why

Roxy's became a gay women's space. Three interlinked explanations are made nevertheless. Firstly, Buzerant is not conveniently located, although its distance from heterosexual leisure venues presents patrons with the perceived advantage of safety and less contact with heterosexual men. Secondly, the fact that the women interviewees felt uncomfortable in a variety of heterosexual leisure environments meant that the possibility of a queer space more conveniently located and open during the week was extremely attractive. Thirdly, the main shareholder in Roxy's was a gay woman. Subsequently, the bar drew a large crowd of both gay men and women, but the women were always in the majority. Weekday evenings could be spent at Roxy's while on the weekend's people could "warm up" at Roxy's and then proceed to Buzerant.

Before long, the changing racial, social and investment geographies of Bloemfontein started to impact on Roxy's. Increased societal acceptance of gay men as opposed to gay women, along with greater gay male mobility in the local leisure scene (cf. Visser, 2008a), started to undermine the financial viability of Roxy's. Greater financial pressures lead to underinvestment in the bar's facilities, the neighbourhood started to desegregate racially, leading to white capital flight, and crime in the area increased noticeably. The first patrons to leave were the gay men, and thereafter the wealthier gay women. In the end Roxy's closed (2007). Janine remembered it as a hideous, common place, dirty, with bathrooms which never had lockable doors or toilet paper, and in a low-class neighbourhood (see also Visser, 2006; 2008a). While most interviewees highlight that they became fearful of the neighbourhood in which Roxy's was located (in the main because it had racially desegregated significantly), and certainly took issue with the physical condition of the venue, most of the woman participants have some nostalgic soft spot for it. For many this was the first place they visited when they "came out," where they met their first girlfriends and experienced their first sexual encounters, and became socialized into a broader community of gay women. Gay men did not have similar fond memories of Roxy's. Indeed, they mainly remember it as being aggressively a gay women's space, in which their presence was at best tolerated.

Bloemfontein and contemporary gay women's leisure spaces

Figure 8.1: Gay women's leisure spaces of support and avoidance (2006)

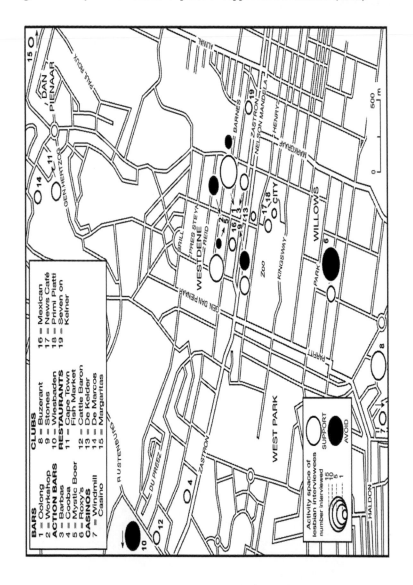

Figure 8.2: Gay women's leisure spaces of support and avoidance (2008)

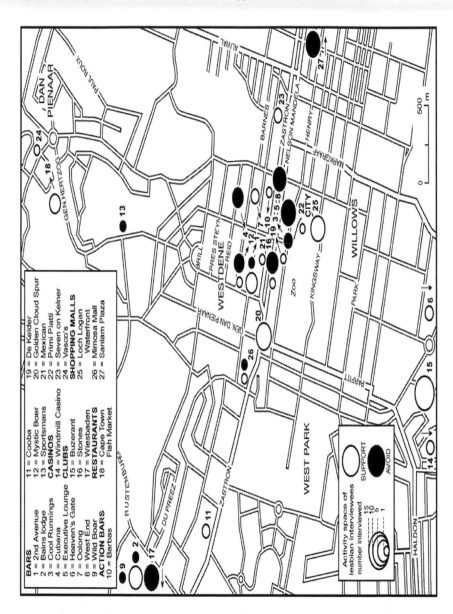

Drawing on the interview material, Figures 8.1 and 8.2 reveal the main leisure venues that members of the survey group of gay women frequented on a regular basis in 2006 and 2008 respectively. These two maps are not directly comparable, since the 2008 map is based on interviews with a different group of participants to those interviewed in 2006. In these maps, reference is made to leisure time spent "going out," mainly in the evenings when participants seek like-minded company and often not-so-clearly-stated possibilities of sexual adventure. In these figures, no mention is made of any regular daytime recreational activities such as organized sport, gym visits and so on, in which the interviewees might participate and which, at least in some cases, might provide opportunities for meeting potential sexual partners. Recreational activities that do not occur on a regular basis, such as going to the cinema or theatre and spectating at sports events, are also excluded. It is clear from the maps that white gay women's leisure time is concentrated mainly in three specific venues, all located in the historically (and still) mainly white leisure environment of Bloemfontein. Unlike gay men (see Figure 8.3), the woman participants do not support a wide range of different leisure venues. It has been shown elsewhere (Visser, 2006; 2008a) that gay men have been quite successful in sharing a range of predominantly heterosexual leisure spaces. Indeed, the argument has been made that many gay men actively avoid queer-coded spaces, and have found homo-normalized spaces in which sexual orientation is not a salient consideration in deciding who is or is not socially accepted (Rushbrook, 2002). Thus for these gay men, sexual orientation appears less important than other factors in their choices of where to seek leisure (see Visser, 2008a; 2008b).

Figures 8.1 and 8.2 also reveal those spaces that the survey group specifically avoided in 2006 and 2008. Counter-intuitively, one of the spaces that was avoided was a new queer venue, Executive Lounge (number 5. in Figure 8.2), which closed after only three months in operation. It was clear that issues of class played a critical role in its collapse. It was widely reported among the survey participants that the class position of the average patrons was problematic to them. It is clear that spaces to avoid are dispersed over the study area. The women participants, like the men, consistently describe Wiesbaden, located 10km to the west of the CBD, as homophobic. One survey participant, Candice, described it as being filled with "tappet" (stupid and unsophisticated), sweaty, Castle Lager-drinking, rugby-watching *boere* (farmers), that "perv over" (look lustfully at) her. Another participant, Olivia, remarked that she avoids the place because she "does not want to get hit over the head, or looked at funny." Woman participants,

Figure 8.3: Gay men's leisure spaces of support and avoidance (2006)

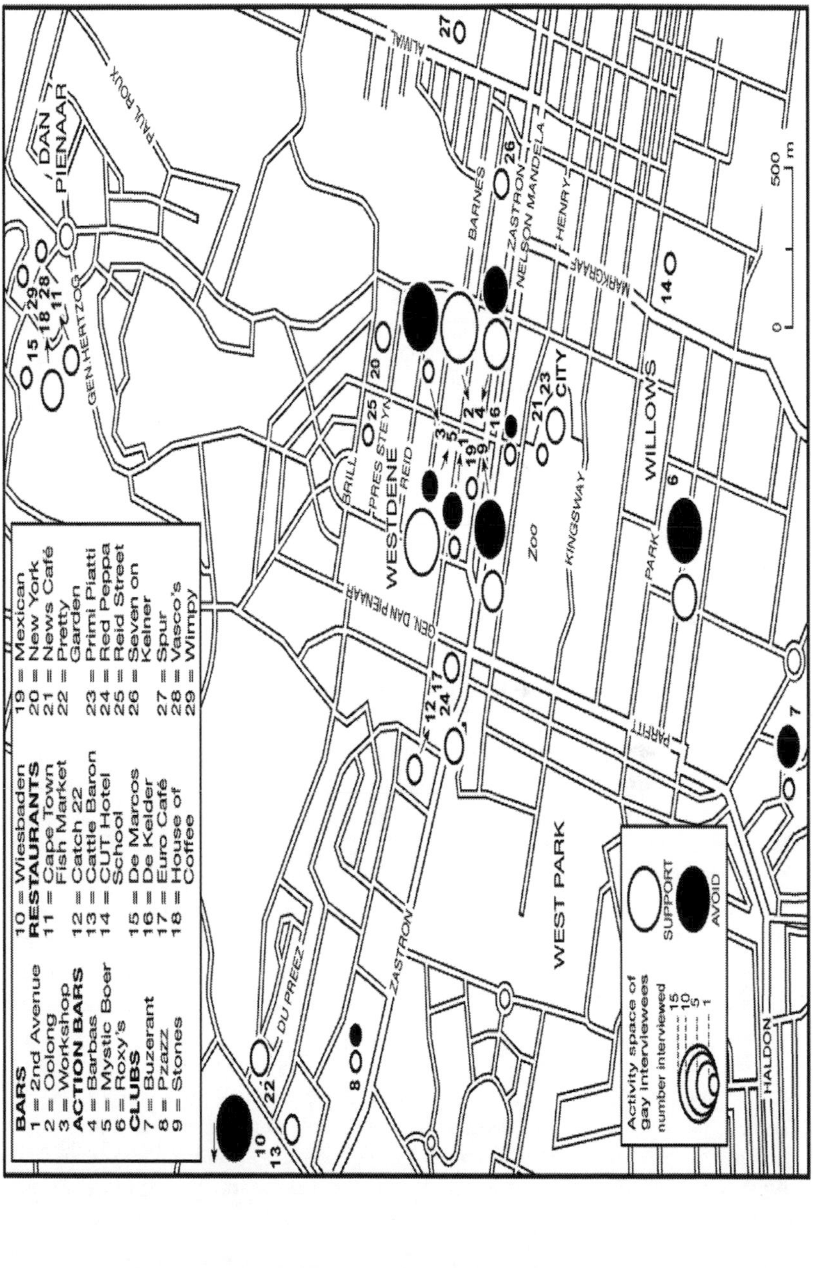

unlike their male counterparts, show very strong support for a single dedicated gay leisure space—Buzerant, located outside of Bloemfontein's main white leisure area in Westdene. In the next section of this chapter, an attempt will be made to explain this particular leisure geography. Attention is placed on why certain leisure spaces are supported and others avoided. In the main a highly complex leisure geography will be revealed.

Spaces of desire

It has been suggested that the lack of a permanent, regular, defined and recognized gay women's space in many settlements has meant that gay women have tended to organize leisure among friends and acquaintances, in their domestic home environments (Skeggs, 1999). The survey group often mentioned using their own and friends' homes as leisure spaces, especially as places where introductions with potential sexual partners could occur. However, they are not confined to domestic environments—after all, Buzerant is gay female-coded.

Buzerant remains after nearly two decades the undisputed leisure space of choice for gay women. In total contrast to gay male views, these women shower Buzerant with positive superlatives. They describe this space as one in which gay women can be themselves, enjoy good music, meet new people and be safe from heterosexual men. Generally, the literature is relatively quiet surrounding how desirable leisure spaces might translate into sexual activity. In this respect, the woman interviewees mentioned Buzerant as a place where the general style of music is more appropriate to close dancing, including ballads and the very popular *langarm* music (mainstream and "golden oldie" songs that can be danced as a two-set or quick-step). This presents the opportunity for "controlled" intimacy which can be further explored off the dance floor. In fact, the style of music could be seen as being a potential mediator with other sexual desires. Consequently, Buzerant, certainly creates opportunities to meet potential sexual partners. Indeed, for some it was not only a place to meet potential sexual partners but also a place of sexual encounter and engagement. Yet, as indicated in the included maps spaces of desire are not confined to overtly "gay space."

In contrast, and this is something of an anomaly in the geography of gay female leisure seeking, there is significant support through frequent visits for two overtly heterosexual leisure venues: a national family restaurant franchise—Spur—located in Westdene, an area many participants reported to avoid; and Bains' Lodge in the far westerly neighbourhood of

Langenhoven Park. Langenhoven Park, as well as the Spur, is unmistakably a space of heterosexual middle-class social, cultural and economic reproduction. In some ways it is supremely ironic that gay women should choose to frequent these venues. Despite this large-scale support, survey participants noted that when they met at these venues in any great numbers, "looks" were exchanged among other patrons. This was often acknowledged to be the result of someone in the group dropping her "guard" in terms of appropriate gender performativity relative to the expectations of the majority of heterosexual patrons. However, it was generally felt that there was some form of "safety in numbers" which did not deter the participants from enjoying these venues and returning to them. In addition, as was the case with gay men at other Bloemfontein venues in the 1990s, the owners of these establishments appear to be very welcoming of their gay female patrons, in part because at least some of the waiter and management staff are gay men and women, which provides some form of "protection."

Contradictory spaces of fear and loathing

In the view of the survey participants, one of the reasons behind what they describe at times as their aggressive defence of gay (female) spaces such as Buzerant relates directly to the sense of discrimination / oppression they experience in the heterosexual leisure environment. As seen in the following section, a range of narratives have been produced in which a number of white leisure spaces are described as undesirable. Here exclusion or forms of discrimination have links to both gender and gender performativity, relative to the predominant heterosexual crowd. Thus, the presence of straight men and women plays a role in the woman participants' avoidance of the main leisure space offerings of the city. For white gay women in Bloemfontein there are several spaces that are experienced as overtly forbidding. Westdene is the key "white" entertainment node of the city and is supported by the vast majority of students from the two local universities, as well as young working adults. Yet, most woman participants feel uncomfortable and even fearful of the area. This is linked a range of issues. First, participants held very particular views of sexuality and their own gender performativity, race and class positions. Linda and Belinda, for example, argued that 90% of the time they socialized with other gay women because for Belinda, "straight people are just weird," whilst for Linda heterosexual men are always trying to "chat one up ... and all the questions make her feel uncomfortable." Jay observed that straight men "want to change your sexuality as gay women [by having sex with one], or they want a threesome with you and your girlfriend." Gerda said "I hate it when straight people (not only men) look at me" whilst Ilse went so far as to say "I don't fear men, I hate them!" She also raised the issue of how the participants felt while around straight women in particular venues (see Pritchard, et al., 2002 for a related debate). There was a feeling that straight women looked down on them for not being "normal women" and were in some ways aggressive. Reference was made, for example, to feelings of discrimination when meeting straight women in the bathroom. Feelings of discrimination were also reported when participants encountered straight women on the dance floors and in bars. Ilse said that straight women in these encounters appeared to be fearful of gay women "as if we are going to seduce them at any moment." This in turn made the woman participants feel unwelcome, uncomfortable and undesirable in the mainstream white leisure venues.

But these feelings of fear and loathing are not unique to "straight" leisure spaces. For example, it is important to note that loathing (rather than fear) extends to gay men who are seen as "irritating moffies" (gay men) or "aggressive muscle Mary's." This is the case in both gay leisure spaces and heterosexual leisure spaces where gay men congregate (see Visser, 2008a). However, although one interviewee, Linda, preferred social interaction nearly exclusively with gay women, she did add that in those few venues (heterosexual, homo-normalized, or gay) where she socialized, she was "also careful of the 'dykes' because they generally argue *'Moer my of ek moer jou.'* (Hit me or I will hit you.)." Elmarie also expresses caution, stating that she was careful of "butch Tempe Tigers (gay women from the local military base)." In fact, butch gender perfomativity by gay women themselves was highlighted by some as a reason why they would support ostensibly heterosexual leisure venues. Carien remarked that "The female gay youth are just getting more and more butch, although there are still a handful of femmes too."

Thus, there is a feeling that some participants feel more comfortable among other gay women who practised certain types of gender performativity, than among others. Whilst Buzerant is undoubtedly the preferred venue of gay women, it is for some a space they, nevertheless, want to avoid and loathe. It would seem that intergenerational conflict is partly responsible for this situation. For example, Heidi, in her 40s, felt that whilst it is good to have a dedicated gay venue such as Buzerant, "it's just a load of kids that fuck around, which is problematic at times."

Discrimination and exclusionary behaviour is certainly not reserved for heterosexuals, for some survey participants themselves exhibited considerable discriminatory opinions. For example, some certainly disliked seeing non-white gay men and women at Buzerant, and a similar dislike was in large part a contributing reason behind the closure of Roxy's. In addition, class position, or perception thereof, certainly plays a role in participants' decisions on which places to support. This factor first undermined the viability of Roxy's and then directly led to the closure of the short-lived Executive Lounge.

Second, the gay woman participants on the whole have little desire to spend time, or share space, with gay men. Some found the "shared" aspect of Buzerant problematic. Fay, for example, bemoaned the fact that it was not exclusively a gay women's venue and did not appreciate the presence of gay men there. Indeed, for some participants, the fact that there is no dedicated gay women's leisure space equates to the notion that there are no gay leisure spaces in Bloemfontein at all. This observation cuts in different directions. Fiona pointed out that Buzerant is now supported by far more (gay) men than in the early years, something which she and apparently her friends and acquaintances, do not enjoy. Some gay women disapprove of seeing "straight-acting" gay men there because they feel they could support any leisure space. On the other hand, some "queens," or overtly effeminate gay men, were experienced as particularly irritating.

Conclusions

Since space is an uneasy concept, the idea of gay women's leisure space is equally, if not more, difficult to describe and understand. Indeed, it is intersubjective and leads to the generation of a range of emotional geographies of desire, fear and loathing which are often contradictory in terms of their status as systems of spaces or places of desire. The key contention of this investigation is that seemingly unlike their counterparts in places such as Manchester or Newcastle in the United Kingdom, lesbian women in Bloemfontein do create leisure spaces of their own, and are not dependent upon gay men to first "open up" homosexual leisure spaces for them. Indeed, perhaps the most important conclusion one can draw from the interview data is that gay women have taken both figurative and literal ownership of a particular leisure space, Buzerant, and would like the exclusion of gay men, and heterosexual men and women, from that space. In fact, they appear to be maintaining the key homosexual leisure spaces of this city. This might be because in Bloemfontein, the gay-coded spaces have been from the outset gay women's spaces, and still carry that general meaning. This calls for far more empirical work that seeks out places in

which gay women are in complex ways able to create, develop and
maintain homosexual leisure spaces.

While this might appear to suggest some sort of collective power that
challenges heteropatriarchy, it is in fact the result of the fact that gay
women bear the brunt of heteropatriarchy more intensely than many gay
men, and subsequently have worked hard to "defend" their spaces of
desire. The extremely restricted range of gay women's leisure geographies
in Bloemfontein, particularly in comparison to those of gay men, suggests
that gay women feel significant oppression in this urban area. Such a claim,
however, implies a future research agenda, of which the following is only
suggestive.

Firstly, the investigation on which this chapter is based was limited to
white gay women, to the exclusion of black gay women. Numerically, in
the case of Bloemfontein and South Africa generally, the largest number
of gay women's experiences have not been recorded in this investigation.
A key question would relate to the manner in which that cohort of gay
women supports the findings of this investigation. Secondly, this question
can be scaled both up and down the urban hierarchy, for one wonders in
what way the issues highlighted here apply to either larger or smaller
urban, and indeed, rural contexts. Thirdly, issues of class, although in the
South African context closely linked to race, need to be investigated in
greater detail. Could it be that gay women, like gay men, of a higher class
position, have different expectations, and also experiences, of spaces of
desire? Finally, this investigation looked at gay women in the South
African context, that whilst challenging, does not at all reflect the
repressive realities of most developing world countries. Indeed, spaces of
desire in the majority gay population of the world, whether women or men,
remains under-investigated and something of a mystery to the academic
gaze.

References

Achmat, Z. 1993. Apostles of civilized vice: Immoral practices and
    unnatural vice in South African prisons and compounds, 1890-1920.
    Social Dynamics. 19 (2): 92 – 110
Aitchison, C. and Reeves, C. 1998. Gendered (bed)spaces: The culture and
    commerce of women-only tourism. C. Aitchison and F. Jordan (eds).
    Gender, space and identity: leisure, culture and commerce. Eastbourne:
    Leisure Studies Association. pp. 47 – 68
Aitkenhead, D. 1997. The queen is dead. *The Modern Review*. November:
    23 – 26

Bell, D. and Binnie, J. 2000. *The sexual citizen: Queer politics and beyond.* London: Routledge

Bell, D., Binnie, J., Cream, J. and Valentine, G. 1994. All hyped up and no place to go. *Gender Pace and Culture: A Journal of Feminist Geography.* 1: 31 - 48

Bell, D. and G. Valentine, ed. 1995. *Mapping desire: Geographies of sexualities.* London: Routledge

Browne, K., G. Brown and Lim, J. (eds). 2006. *Sexy spaces.* London: Ashgate

Bullough, V. 2002. *Before Stonewall: Activists in lesbian and gay rights in historical context.* New York: Harrington Park Press

Dirsuweit, T. 1999. Carceral spaces in South Africa: A case study of institutional power, sexuality and transgression. *Geoforum.* 30: 71 – 83

Du Pisani, K. 2001. Puritanism-transformed Afrikaner masculinities in the apartheid and post-apartheid period. R. Morell (ed). *Changing men in southern Africa.* Pietermaritzburg: University of Natal Press. pp. 157 – 176

Gevisser, M. and Cameron, E. (eds). 1993. *Defiant desire: Gay and lesbian lives in South Africa.* Johannesburg: Raven

Greene, B. 1997. *Ethnic and cultural diversity among lesbians and gay men.* Thousand Oaks: Sage

Kirkey, K. and Forsyth A. 2001. Men in the valley: Gay male life on the suburban-rural fringe. *Journal of Rural Studies* .17 (4): 421 – 441

Leap, W. 2005. Finding the centre: Claiming gay space in Cape Town. M. Van Zyl and M. Steyn (eds). *Performing queer: Shaping sexualities 1994–2004.* Cape Town: Kwela. pp. 235 – 266

Lotter, J. M., ed. 1979. *Sosiale probleme in Suid-Afrika.* Pretoria: Raad vir Geestewetenskaplike Navorsing, Instituut vir Sosiologiese, Demografiese en Kriminologiese Navorsing

Moodie, T. D. 1993. Migrancy and male sexuality on the South African gold mines. *Journal of Southern African Studies.* 14 (2): 494 – 514

Muntingh, D. 1967. *Lesbinisme: 'n sosiologiese studie.* MA thesis, University of Pretoria

Oswin, N. 2005. Researching 'gay Cape Town', finding value-added queerness. *Social and Cultural Geography.* 6 (4): 567 – 586

Pritchard, A., N. Morgan. and Sedgley, D. 2002. In search of lesbian space? The experience of Manchester's gay village. *Leisure Studies.* 21 (2): 105 – 123

Rink, B. 2007. Community as utopia: Reflections on De Waterkant. *Urban Forum.* 19 (2): 205 – 220

Rothenberg, T. 1995. 'And she told two friends': Lesbians creating urban space. D. Bell and Valentine, G. (eds). *Mapping desire: Geographies of sexualities*. London: Routledge. pp. 165 – 181

Rushbrook, D. 2002. Cities, queer space, and the cosmopolitan tourist. GLQ*: A Journal of Lesbian and Gay Studies*. 8 (1/2): 183 – 206

Schurink, W. J. 1979. Gay-vroue: 'n sosiologiese verkenning van die leefwyse van 'n aantal lesbiers aan die hand van outobiografiese sketse. J. M. Lotter (ed). *Sosiale probleme in Suid-Afrika*. Pretoria: Raad vir Geesteswetenskaplike Navorsing, Instituut vir Sosiologiese, Demografiese en Kriminologiese Navorsing

Shields, R. 1991. *Places on the margin*. London: Routledge

Shurmer-Smith, P. and Hannam, K. 1994. *Worlds of desire, realms of power: A cultural geography*. London: Arnold

Skeggs, B. 1999. Matter out of place: Visibility and sexualities in leisure spaces. *Leisure Studies*. 18 (3): 213 – 232

Van Zyl, M and Steyn, M. eds. 2005. *Performing queer: Shaping sexualities 1994–2004*. Cape Town: Kwela

Valentine, G. 1993. (Hetero)sexing space: Lesbian perceptions and experiences of everyday spaces. *Environment and Planning D: Society and Space*. 11: 395 - 413

Visser, G. 2003a. Gay men, leisure space and South African cities: The case of Cape Town. *Geoforum*. 34 (1): 123 – 137

—. 2003b. Gay men, tourism and urban space: reflections on Africa's 'gay capital'. *Tourism Geographies*. 5 (2): 168 – 189

—. 2006. *Homonormalising heterosexual leisure spaces: The case of Bloemfontein*. Published report, University of the Free State

—. 2008a. The homonormalisation of white heterosexual leisure spaces in Bloemfontein, South Africa. *Geoforum*. 39 (3): 1347 – 1361.

—. 2008b. Exploratory notes on the geography of black gay leisure spaces in Bloemfontein, South Africa. *Urban Forum*. 19 (4): 413 – 423

Appendix 1: Interviewees cited in this paper

Interviewed in 2006

Men:
Adam, 28 years old, medical representative, in a relationship.
Dizzy, 36 years old, hair stylist, single.
Peter, 44 years old, teacher, in a relationship.
Phoenix, 25 years old, lecturer, single.

Interviewed in 2008

Women:
Belinda, 23 years old, sales coordinator, in a relationship.
Carien, 30 years old, sales representative, in a relationship.
Driekie, 28 years old, personal assistant, in a relationship.
Elmarie, 24 years old, receptionist, in a relationship.
Fay, 43 years old, training manager, in a relationship.
Heidi, 27 years old, lecturer, in a relationship.
Gerda, 26 years old, receptionist, single.
Ilse, 20 years old, administrative clerk, in a relationship.
Jay, 20 years old, shop assistant, in a relationship.
Karien, 27 years old, electrical retail, in a relationship.
Linda, 24 years old, article clerk, in a relationship.

CHAPTER NINE

QUEERING THE PITCH:
AN EXPLORATION OF GAY MEN'S
AMATEUR FOOTBALL IN THE UK

LOUISA JONES AND MAC MCCARTHY

Introduction

In the context of men's professional football (soccer), sexuality remains a difficult aspect of diversity for the game to embrace. To date, only one professional footballer, the late Justin Fashanu, has come out; a revelation largely resulting from pressures from various sources. Speculation of others remains rife and attracts much media interest. Against this backdrop, this chapter seeks to explore the recent growth and popularity of gay men's amateur football in the UK from a number of perspectives but most importantly from that of its players. Gay football clubs have provided for many men the opportunity to play football in a safe space; one without concern of being open about their sexuality regardless of whether they are "out" in other aspects of their lives. For many, it provides a sense of emancipation from closeted identities, negative experiences and homophobic incidents encountered often as far back as school days. Amateur gay football may be regarded as evidence of the increasing visibility of gay men in team sports and as such may be viewed as contesting heteronormativity and the prevailing masculine hegemony whilst also challenging views held by some in the gay community about football being a non-gay activity.

Gay Football Clubs in the UK

Currently, in 2010, there are 19 gay football clubs in the UK, the first being formed in 1991. Of this number, 6 have emerged within the last 2 years indicating not only a significant growth rate but also an increased visibility of gay men wishing to play football (albeit within a gay environment). Amongst the UK's gay football clubs, Leftfooters has arguably the most participative philosophy whilst others such as Village Manchester and Stonewall are highly competitive (to the extent both clubs field teams in mainstream Sunday Leagues). The rest, such as Yorkshire Terriers, Leicester Wildecats, Hot Scots, Mersey Marauders and Nottingham Ball Bois, find themselves on a continuum between these two extremes.

Linking teams together is the Gay Football Supporters' Network (GFSN). Established in 1989 as a membership based community for gay supporters of professional clubs to network, socialise and attend matches together, its emphasis has gradually shifted towards playing rather than supporting as evidenced by the emergence of gay clubs and later a specifically gay league. Most recently, the GFSN has adopted a profile-raising campaigning stance on key issues and has made links with The English Football Association (FA). Wellard (2002) points out that many gay sports organisations seek to legitimise themselves through association with similar authorities. The GFSN has appointed volunteer Liaison Officers from its membership to work with professional clubs in addressing issues of homophobia. This initiative has also begun to result in the formation of club specific gay supporters' clubs such as the Gay Villans, attached to and endorsed by Aston Villa FC, a well-known Premier League club.

Methodological Approach

Underpinning the research on which this chapter is based was the imperative of gaining an understanding as to why gay and bisexual men choose to join and play for specifically gay or gay-friendly teams, focusing on the motivations of the individuals, the team and the context of the wider gay community. Methods used included video diaries, participant observation, and pre-arranged semi-structured focus groups and were specifically chosen to enable the narrative to emerge such that the players' "thoughts and feelings [were] at the forefront of any discussion" (Harris, 2005: 185).

Phenomenology and interpretivism underpinned a largely heuristic approach (Walton, 2007). Robertson (2003: 707) suggests this enables "the exploration of lay narratives through recourse to existing social theory." In keeping with the views of other researchers such as Hammersley and Atkinson (1995) and Maykut and Morehouse (1994), we allowed elements of the research design to evolve over time, particularly with regard to the video diary interviews which were conducted at various tournaments over a three year period. Each time, a different set of questions was used in order to record a developmental narrative and as an attempt to chart the evolution of gay football itself.

Initial difficulties were encountered in establishing contact with players, possibly due to the sensitivity of the issues and uncertainties or reservations regarding the underlying motivations of both the study and the researchers who were, at that point, unknown in the world of gay football. An initial meeting in August 2005 with Steve Hess, the founder of the Mersey Marauders (himself a former Stonewall FC player) yielded a number of key contacts including Mikey Collins, the then player-manager of Leftfooters whom we met at The FA's Homophobia Summit in Coventry, November 2005. He subsequently introduced us to his club and, through the GFSN, other clubs, by what Ryan (1995) refers to as a process of "snow-balling." It became obvious early on that gaining the trust of teams was vital, primarily due to concerns about how thoughts and views might be portrayed. Participant observation took the form of supporting at matches and attending social events which earned us acceptance, such that our experience mirrored that of Barbara Cox who noted it enabled players to be "very open and honest with their thoughts, particularly on sensitive and personal issues" (Cox, 1998 cited in Cox & Thompson, 2000: 9).

Focus group content was analysed, a process which developed inductively from a series of emerging themes which, as Kitzinger (1995) suggests, helps to identify "sensitizing concepts." Many of these were subsequently further explored in the video diary interviews. Smith and Deemer (2002) note the difficulty in attempting to separate descriptive narratives from individuals' interpretations, supporting our own view regarding theory-free observation. Data gathered were considered separately by both researchers who identified and subsequently agreed emergent key themes. Interestingly, some degree of external affirmation came from a number of players themselves who expressed on-going interest in the research and commented on issues from their own focus group. Echoing Krane, et al's (2002: 32) experience, some players "thanked the investigator[s] for [their] interest in this often marginalised athletic population" noting the thought-provoking and sometimes therapeutic experience of the interviews.

The School Experience

School has played an important part in linking sport to healthy development in largely heterosexist terms. It was, and to an extent, still is seen as an arena in which character and moral values may be built (Kimmel, 1990). Given that a boy's prowess in competitive school sport provides a significant basis upon which he is judged (Messner, 1992), boys who do not possess such abilities or interests are branded "girls," "sissies," "poofters," "fags," "gays," and "queers" to describe them (Burgess, et al., 2003: 201).

Burgess, et al. (2003: 201) go on to suggest that peers will stigmatise non-participants, often with the tacit support of teachers thus "reinforcing notions of females and homosexuals as inferior to heterosexual men." Pronger (1999: 382) suggests that competitive sports encourage the desire to "take space away from others and jealously guard it for themselves." Thus competition becomes acquisitive; it is the desire to conquer and to be considered a victor over others, to achieve dominance which, he suggests is linked with the sexual imperative of the heterosexual male. This requires the male to take and to avoid, at all costs, being taken, something which is equated with homosexuality. Boys are thus subjected to an overwhelming pressure to conform to male stereotypes, to embrace heteronormativity and to accept, without question, society's view of what it means to be a proper boy. In so doing, they learn to reject and to pour scorn on alternatives. The players' recollections of their perceptions of school sport and football, especially, are important here:

"... a very straight masculine sport, with, you know, dads and sons and everyone at school pushing you to play and you weren't really good or accepted unless you were good at football."

"you're naturally judged at school by your ability at football and nothing else as a boy your status, who you are, is judged by how you play."

Thus, players who demonstrated competence in sport were aware that they had not appeared to be gay in any way, ensuring a more positive school experience than others: Craig recalled: "I was a rugby player and I've never felt intimidated by sport whatsoever—I never felt I ever had a problem with being gay, so it wasn't a big deal to me, but I don't think I acted particularly gay at school so people didn't think of me as gay. But then again I didn't have a boyfriend!"

Challenging Masculinities

Sport, in common with society in general, may be regarded as heteronormative, a view supported by Anderson (2002: 862) who claims that it is "a bastion of hegemonic masculinity, hetero-sexism and homophobia." Whitson (1990) regard team sports, in particular, as providing an environment in which masculinity is clearly defined around a set of norms, whilst Burgess, et al. (2003: 202) draw on Young, et al's (1994 cited in Burgess, et al., 2003) view that sport provides "a proving ground" for heteronormative masculinity, thus becoming a space where clear norms are established which then form the basis for "legitimate tests of manhood which have been the catalyst for idolisation." Mennesson and Clement (2003: 312) add to this by noting the frequent definition of sport in gender terms with an emphasis on "virile, heterosexual masculinity." In so doing, the legitimacy of gay men in sport is surely questioned. A recurring view held by players was expressed by Oli: "the whole football scene generally [is] very straight macho masculine" something which was felt to extend beyond the pitch too: "I think [gay players] feel alienated from, and not totally at home on the social side of a club, not feeling that they can be themselves so it's a bit of a relief to be themselves socially with the [gay] team." Significantly, most players identified the post-match showers to be possibly the most problematic aspect. The so-called "shower thing" was a widespread issue stemming from a concern that straight players would inaccurately perceive gay players' participation in football as having a sexual motive. Darren responded: "people think it's all about cock action definitely, that's what they associate it with … like it's some kind of a fetish, but it's not."

Straight teams were perceived by gay players to be more interested in winning than socialising and indeed many gay players also regarded this as highly important. Where opportunities arose for post-match socialising, gay players elected mostly to do so within their gay team. Damien observed "I don't socialise other than going for a quick drink after playing with my straight team, whereas in the last 6 months I've been a member of this [gay] team – I go out with them all the time." Ed's comments were typical:

> "It's nice to be able when you go out for a drink afterwards, to be yourself whereas I'm conscious all the time when I'm out with straight teams in the pub that I'm not being my true self. I'm, well I hope, I'm fairly straight acting anyway but I'm ultra conscious of it when I'm in a social environment with a predominately straight group of men."

This sense of needing to hide or adopt a different identity or set of behaviours was widely evident. The following comment by Andrew typified these views: "it would be nice if say on the social side in the pub after the match to be able to say "Oh yes, my boyfriend's doing such and such a thing…""

Robertson (2003: 708) suggests hegemonic masculinity becomes "the form by which other masculinities are measured and represented as subordinated to, or marginalized from, this hegemony," defining what it means to be a real boy or man, and how other forms of masculinity are seen in relation to this (Connell, 1995). Skelton (2000: 9) makes reference to the notion that football has been considered "in relation to further aspects of hegemonic masculinity: specifically, that it is constructed in relation to women and subordinated masculinities and is heterosexual." Arguably, the effect of this may be to exclude men who do not fit within defining norms; most notably those men who fall outside the gay stereotype. However this view was not shared by players interviewed: "we're just as masculine as [straight players] are." John from Village Manchester FC commented: "When we play a straight team, we've got a little bit more to prove, and we definitely up our game even more I think." Thus gay men would seem to be regarded as an implicit threat to the masculine norms enshrined football – one of the factors which may arguably be said to underpin the prevailing homophobia in the sport. Indeed, comments made in April 2008 by Luciano Moggi, former Managing Director of the Italian football club, Juventus, would seem to support this view:

> "A homosexual cannot do the job of a footballer. The football world is not designed for them, it's a special atmosphere, one in which you stand naked under the showers………. I never wanted to have a homosexual player and I still wouldn't sign one." (Anonymous. 2008)

Homophobia and the Gay Footballer

Associated with heteronormative views of masculinity has been an overwhelming degree of homophobia notably within team sports. Clarke (1998: 145) refers to the perception of gay men as "deviant and dangerous participants on the sporting turf" with Anderson (2002: 861) suggesting that gay men "defy culturally defined structures of hegemonic masculinity." Gay players thus challenge the orthodoxy and with it the notion of sport as the site upon which that particular masculinity has grown and developed. Sport, as an institution, is seen to "resist gay male participation through overt and covert homophobia" (Anderson 2005: 43). The space provided by sport thus withstands broader or alternative views of masculinity and offers an arena where there is certainty in and about the conventionality and rejection of other masculinities. This may be through aggressive behaviour or offensive humour. Chris, from Leftfooters, recounted a significant experience when he played in his works team:

"At first, I was only out to close friends at work. Gradually, they found out. I wrote a match report which I really camped up – and I'm not camp normally. It was a mistake if I wanted to continue to enjoy playing and being part of the team. They took me to a strip bar and set me up with a stripper. It was so embarrassing. They did it to make me feel small. They were laughing at me, I think. I was furious. The veteran on the team apologised – he said it was unacceptable. He said it's not what they're about. I never played for them again."

Skelton (2000) reviews the work of a number of authors who have identified football as a place where homophobic behaviours and attitudes are pervasive. Sexuality is a defining factor in establishing the sporting view of maleness, taking heterosexuality as given and thus treating any alternative as alien (Parker, 1996). Interviewees suggested that straight teams were committed to winning and consequently would use homophobic comments to deliberately undermine opponents. Gareth explained:

"I've played most of my life in straight teams, and if they want to win a game, they'll use whatever—people always mouth off in your ear just to wind you up, to put you off the game—that's part of it. If we're going to join a competitive league, then people have to be aware that they're going to say stuff like 'Oh you flouncing queen!' It's going to happen."

For some gay men, wanting to play sport and not wishing to be openly gay can be advantageous: "… sport becomes a safe space for those desiring to deeply conceal their same-sex desires" (Anderson, 2005: 43). Contact adverts in the gay press demonstrate the large numbers of gay men defining themselves as "straight acting," indicating a desire, it would seem, for their sexuality to go unnoticed. Aggressive team sports offer an arena for exemplifying straightness by association – how can he possibly be gay when he plays football? A minority of the players we interviewed were concerned that they should be perceived as "straight-acting" in their everyday lives and, therefore, considered it to be a natural response to play football in a straight team. Interestingly, though, all of those players had elected also to play in a space where homophobia was uncommon and, in their view, there was negligible adherence to hegemonic masculinity; they had chosen a more gay-friendly environment that was less intrinsically hostile (Hekma 1994; Pronger, 1990; Whitson, 1990;).

Anderson (2005: 14) cites Pronger's (1990) argument that competitive team sports provide a place to hide "as athletics are shrouded in a cloud of scripted heterosexuality." Anderson (2005: 37) further suggests that by accepting the prevailing hegemony gay players are "prevented from critically examining the effect sport has on society and on the stigmatizing of homosexuality." Thus, the very people who could challenge the orthodoxy and offer evidence for a different view of participation in sport that encompasses alternative masculinities have kept silent, and have, albeit inadvertently, helped to maintain the hegemony. Carl agreed: "the banter [in straight clubs] is frequently sexual – it's about picking up girls and mocking queers. Well, 'queer' is used to criticise anyone who hasn't played well or who doesn't quite fit the norm. You're not going to come out in an atmosphere like that, are you?"

Some players with experience of straight teams have consciously chosen, with the collusion of straight friends who knew of their sexuality, to maintain silence. Graham agreed: "Yes, I just don't think straight men react very well to the idea of playing in a football team with gay men…whereas my friends who knew I was gay before I joined the team don't have a problem with it obviously—but we just haven't told anyone else about it." Inevitably, numerous players interviewed felt a degree of anger and frustration at their frequent dismissal by many straight players as lacking competence. Pete's feelings were commonplace: "Eventually, it has to change … they've got to start somewhere and if we could get an acceptance that we could play football and we're not just a bunch of freaks then we would be getting somewhere."

An important challenge that gay men pose in football is the fact that they may prove to be proficient, contradicting the perceived stereotypes. Numerous players saw this as highly significant when they played against straight teams as Liam confirmed: "....that was their biggest problem— they're playing this bunch of poofs that they couldn't beat." Interestingly, some players who had previously played only straight football recalled their own misconceptions about playing with other gay men. Mark said:

"I was curious – I'd played in a straight team since I was about 16 or 17 – football mad. I was quite happy with that till I saw an advert for a gay team and then I was amazed to think that there were more people out there like me. My suspicions were that they'd be very camp, mincing queens, not really taking it seriously. I walked in and there were all these guys, and one person walked up to me and asked me if I was playing and showed me where to get changed and once I was there – I forgot about my worries really."

Surprisingly, some players saw homophobic comments from straight teams as simply part of the banter associated with the game, with the result that their own responses were a mix of humour, dismissiveness and counter-attack. Richie commented:

"It's not said because that person is actively thinking, 'that player is a homosexual and I don't like homosexuals.' He's thinking 'this term 'homosexual,' is kind of a weapon and I'm just going to say it, hoping it's going to put him off his game.' Now the fact that that guy thinks using 'homo' is a weapon, it doesn't really affect me, even though I know it's not right."

Steve recalled:

"One particular [straight] team were fighting hard against us and were getting beat, and one of them said to one of his team-mates, 'you want to watch that number nine, he's trying to get up your arse.' And our lad turned round and said to him, 'No, I'm not but I wouldn't mind getting up number three's arse!'"

Some players found this aspect satisfying. Mike said: "I used to say to my defender, 'grab him like that, back into him, alright sweetheart?' I find it hilarious, they're getting really offended by it, and I'm fucking laughing in their faces...."

Why Gay Football?

Clearly, there are gay men playing professional and amateur competitive team sports including football. As Anderson (2005) pointed out, gay boys and men do not necessarily avoid competitive team sports, despite the homophobia. Nor do the types and degrees of masculinity associated with sports uniformly deter them in seeking to participate (Pronger, 1999). Elling, et al. (2003: 443) suggest they play in what are perceived to be straight teams, often maintaining a "culture of silence" to avoid the consequences of coming out. Drawing support from Griffin (1998 cited in Elling, et al., 2003), Hekma (1994) and Pronger (1990), Elling, et al. (2003) further suggest that the closet remains a more comfortable place to be and represents more of a survival strategy than an individual choice. In so doing, currently in 2009 all professional football players (along with the vast majority of amateurs) remain tacit about their sexuality in the UK.

Siegal and Lowe (1995) refer to the creativity and adaptive strategies employed by gay men through their developmental years and in circumstances that have led them to choose to remain closeted; he believes that their journey to embracing a gay identity is thus difficult and painful suggesting its postponement leads to increased agony and insecurity. Confiding one's hidden identity runs the risk of homophobic reaction and it is not unreasonable to suggest, therefore, that doing so within the realms of football, in particular, is an especially fraught experience. Many players believed that saying "I am gay" can mean compartmentalising oneself. In terms of identity, this is a significant step, reaching the point where one's level of self-acceptance is such that the label itself is challenged. Thus some players believe gay teams present a challenge to misperceptions of gay men. Richard agreed: "I also like the idea that we're allowing straight people to see that we're just normal people as well and to try to break down some of the stereotypes that straight people have about gay men ....that we're all sort of flouncing about."

From a historical position of what Anderson (2002) describes as self-marginalisation where the tendency of gay men was to retreat from sport, it is evident that some gay men have started being open about their sexuality in this context by joining gay sports clubs. Deane-Young (1994: 11) reports the views of participants in the Gay Games, for example, who testify to "the joy of being *wholly* who they are and joining hands with a circle of comrades." Elling, et al. (2003) report one reason for this, also cited by lesbians, is not so much the fear of homophobia as the feeling of discomfort at being in an overtly heterosexual environment when in straight teams. Nathan noted that "it's a more relaxed atmosphere,... whether it's gay, gay friendly, you can just be yourself. You don't have to worry."

Research by Elling, et al. (2003) in the Netherlands proposes that society's gradually increasing acceptance of different sexualities may be one reason for the increased number of LGBT sports groups – a trend which has been noted in other countries too. However, Anderson (2005: 48) contradicts this view, suggesting that the challenge to hegemony "only takes place in the context of their [the LGBT sports groups'] sporting space and does not challenge the dominant structure of heterosexual sports because gay athletes are removed from it." Our findings indicate the phenomenon may well be part of a growing liberalisation rather than solely a challenge to the hegemony, as evidenced by a number of gay football teams' participation in Gay Pride marches across the UK.

Elling, et al. (2003: 444) note that "the low degree of acceptance of homosexuality among straight men is a [stronger] push factor for gay men," whilst acknowledging "the importance of the social factor of belonging to a gay club" as the basis upon which a stronger sense of belonging and community is being constructed. Comments such as Brian's were commonplace: "I guess it has to be because I felt more comfortable in the team – I can be me. I don't have to pretend or hide. Here my sexuality isn't an issue." Paul concurred: "It's not about being gay; it's about playing football. But playing with people who share a similar set of values."

A study by Elling and Janssens (2003) for the Mulier Sport Institute concluded that participation in gay sport was the result of both preference and pressure; that is, the desire to play with others who shared one's sexuality, coupled with the desire to avoid the discomfort of possible discrimination in presumed straight teams. A gay man whose identity remains hidden in an assumed straight team lacks what Crocker and Luhtanen (1990 cited in Krane, et al., 2002: 28) describe as "the feeling of self-worth derived from the collective aspects of the self, or group membership." Elling, et al. (2003) view integration within one's own group as a key feature of categorical clubs and importantly demonstrate that this was true regardless of sexuality. This was illustrated graphically in the case of a black player in one team. Ashley explained: "One lad was black as well [as gay] and he got quite a lot of abuse, physically and verbally from a black straight team. None of the rest of us [white gay] lads did – it was like it was the worst thing for the black guys, being black *and* gay." Our findings echo this view, suggesting affinity is of primary significance in players' choice of club.

An Alternative to the Scene?

Many gay men gravitate to the gay scene as part of their initial exploration of self and it remains their location of choice for developing a clearer gay identity. It also provides an escape from pressures that may be felt from family and friends. Sanderson (1999: 147) refers to "the creation of 'gay villages' in London and Manchester which seem to revolve mostly around hedonistic indulgence." However, as he points out, the gay scene is not only limiting in what it provides, it may well offer real risks in the form of recreational drugs and for many, be a source of growing dissatisfaction with its restricted forms of interacting. Gay football has, in numerous cases, been a conscious alternative choice offering a place for personal growth and development. Joe remarked "… the reason I actually joined the Blaze was to partly get away from the gay scene, because it's such a fickle place to be. To be honest, it's nice to go and do something completely, totally different, different sort of gay from what the scene expects from you." Stuart responded: "I take your point, you asked if it provided a space where you can be a gay but forget being gay, I don't think it's about forgetting being gay, it's about kind of a different type of gay." The reality seems to be that the scene remains a strong part of the culture, with players going to venues as a team, thus redefining the way in which the scene is perceived and used.

Whilst Elling and Janssens (2003) noted that the increased range of commercial sports facilities has attracted the gay community, this does not account for the growth of gay football. Our research suggests contributing factors may include the obvious popularity of football and its continued growth as an economic and social phenomenon over the last forty years combined with societal shifts which have meant gay men and women in public life have become increasingly more visible. Even so, socio-cultural shifts are complex. The UK government that legislated in support of gay people has also supported health promotion policies for men based around sport that emphasise maleness (Wilkins, 2001) and employed hegemonic images (Department of Health, 1998; Department for Culture, Media and Sport, 2001). In so doing, it has not addressed the physical and mental health benefits that might accrue to gay men. Conflict exists within the gay community with some resistance to their emergence into sports being encountered by players from other gay men. Chris explained:

> "I was in Cardiff handing out GFSN flyers and approached a group of lads and asked whether any of them were interested in football. The immediate response was 'We are in a gay club, does that not give you a clue?' Sums up the prevailing attitude nicely, but I think we might be beginning to change that!"

Whilst Deane-Young (1994) asserts that discrimination underlies the creation of gay teams and leagues, Krane, et al. (2002: 29) draw on work by Crocker and Major (1994) suggesting that "when stigmatized, individuals perceive discrimination as unjustified, they are likely to be motivated to engage in some form of social change activity." Within the perceived "safe space" of gay football, players identified the emergence of a new set of values not normally associated with competitive team sports, namely the rejection of aggressive behaviour and exclusion on the basis of proficiency or indeed (hetero)sexuality. Whilst many teams do play competitively, underpinning all teams appears to be a highly inclusive, supportive ethos, something which Pronger (1990: 383) terms as an element of "gay sensibility" brought to sport by gay people. Wellard (2002: 245) has identified the need for investigation into "new sporting practices which incorporate an inclusive, non-competitive framework," suggesting other forms of physical activity should be considered that eliminate the "risk of humiliation or shame." Mikey from Leftfooters explained:

"When we select the teams, we don't select on the basis of ability. We choose according to people wanting to play football. Everyone gets the chance to be chosen.....we weren't sure if we wanted to have a man of the match award because it's promoting ability on the pitch. Eventually, we supported the idea for people who had most improved or scored their first goal."

Anderson (2005: 161) found that "out" gay athletes were "just as eager to participate in this culture of hypermasculinity and competitiveness" whilst competing in the mainstream. However he notes that in self-segregated (gay) spaces, a greater focus on cooperation and reduced emphasis on competitiveness prevails. Anthony's comments provide some insight in to this:

"...in the changing rooms, no matter how the match has gone, we'll always be quite happy and chatty about everything. In straight teams, if you lose the match you have the manager shouting at you, and it's all pressure";

and

"... the relationship with the other teams also, there's a lot stronger bond than between straight teams. There's a lot more rivalry between straight teams."

Conclusion

The research identified a number of significant findings relating to the experiences of players in gay football teams, their reasons for joining and the perceived benefits of participating in gay team sports. It has been reported that, despite the barriers for gay men participating in sport, interest has grown significantly recently. The development of the GFSN and the burgeoning numbers of gay football teams in the UK are both testament to this. As gay men become more public, not only in their choices of careers and entertainment, but also in sport and recreational activities, they are challenging stereotypes, in both the straight and gay worlds. Sanderson (1999: 68) identifies that "a widespread desire for an alternative outlet to allow people expression of more than just their sexual urges" combined with an increased interest in health and fitness within the gay community has contributed to an increasingly pro-active interest in LGBT sports provision including the gay football phenomenon.

Personal growth, a sense of belonging, sharing one's interest in football with like minded people and finding a social life with other gay people away from the "scene" are benefits commonly cited by players in gay teams. A strong sense of community and for many, a feeling of affinity contributes to increased self-esteem and a notion of what Sanderson (1999: 66) refers to as "coming home." Thus there is a persuasive argument that gay football provides a unique opportunity for gay men not only to play a competitive team sport whilst challenging the traditional values underpinning the game – both implicitly or explicitly— but also to become whole. As Pronger (1990: 236) concludes "in gay sports, being gay is infused into an everyday activity rather than isolated as it is in gay politics, coming-out groups or other forms of gay activism."

References

Anderson, E 2005. *In the game: Gay athletes and the cult of masculinity.* Albany, New York: SUNY Press

—. 2002. Openly gay athletes: Contesting hegemonic masculinity in a homophobic environment. *Gender and Society.* 16: 860 - 877

Anonymous. 2008. 'A gay cannot do the job of a footballer,' says disgraced Italian football executive in bizarre TV rant. *Daily Mail.* http://www.dailymail.co.uk/news/article-1016353/A-gay-job-footballer-says-disgraced-Italian-football-executive-bizarre-TV-rant.html. 22/4/ 08

Burgess, I., Edwards, A. and Skinner J. 2003. Football culture in an Australian school setting: The construction of masculine identity. *Sport, Education and Society.* 8 (2): 199 - 212

Clarke, G. 1998. Queering the pitch and coming out to play: Lesbians and physical education in sport. *Sport, Education and Society.* 3 (2): 145 - 160

Connell, R. W. 1995. *Masculinities.* Berkeley: University of California Press

Cox, B. and Thompson, S. 2000. Multiple bodies: Sportswomen, soccer and sexuality. *International Review for the Sociology of Sport.* 35 (1): 5 - 20

Deane-Young, P. 1994. *Lesbians and gays in sports.* New York: Chelsea House Publications

Department for Culture, Media and Sport. 2001. *A sporting future for all.* London: HMSO

Department of Health. 1998. *Our healthier nation.* London: HMSO

Elling, A., De Knop, P. and Knoppers, A. 2003. Gay/lesbian sports clubs and events: Places of homo-social bonding and cultural resistance? *International Review for the Sociology of Sport.* 38: 441 - 456

Elling, A and Janssens, J. 2003. *"It's the Sport that counts"* – *Participation in sports by gays and lesbians*. Mulier Sport Institute commissioned by Initiated by the Dutch Ministry of Sport, Foundation of Homosport Nedeland and the Netherlands Cultural Sport Federation

Hammersley, M. and Atkinson, P. 1995. *Ethnography: Principles in practice* (2nd ed). London: Routledge

Harris, J. 2005. The image problem in women's football. *Journal of Sport & Social Issues*. 29 (2): 184 - 197

Hekma, G. 1994. *Als ze maar niet provoceren [As long as they don't provoke]*. Amsterdam: Het Spinhuis

Kimmel, M.S. 1990. Baseball and the reconstitution of American masculinity, 1880–1920. M.A. Messner and D.F. Sabo (eds). *Sport, men, and the gender order: Critical feminist perspectives*. Champaign, Human Kinetics. pp. 55 – 65

Kitzinger, J. 1995. Qualitative research: Introducing focus groups. *British Medical Journal*. 311: 299 - 302

Krane, V., Barber, H. and McClung, L. 2002. Social psychological benefits of Gay Games participation: A social identify theory explanation. *Journal of Applied Sport Psychology*. 14: 27 - 42

Maykut, P. and Morehouse, R. 1994. *Beginning qualitative research: A philosophical and practical guide*. London: Falmer

Mennesson, C. and Clement, J. 2003. Homosociability and homosexuality: The case of soccer played by women. *International Review for the Sociology of Sport*. 38: 311 - 330

Messner, M. A. 1992. Boyhood, organised sports, and the construction of masculinities, M. S. Kimmel and M. A. Messner. *Men's lives*. New York: Macmillan. pp. 161 – 176

Parker, A. 1996. Sporting masculinities: Gender and the body. M. Mac an Ghaill (ed). *Understanding masculinities: Social relations and cultural arenas*. Buckingham: Open University Press. pp. 126 - 138

Pronger, B. 1999. Outta my endzone: Sport and the territorial anus. *Journal of Sport and Social Issues*. 23: 373 - 389

—. 1990. *The arena of masculinity: Sports, homosexuality, and the meaning of sex*. New York: St. Martin's Press

Robertson, S. 2003. "If I let a goal in, I'll get beat up": Contradictions in masculinity, sport and health. *Health Education Research*. 18 (6): 706 - 716

Ryan, C. 1995. *Researching tourist satisfactions: Issues, concepts and problems*. London: Routledge

Sanderson, T. 1999. *How to be a happy homosexual*. London: The Other Way Press

Siegal, S. and Lowe Jr., E. 1995. *Uncharted lives: Understanding the life passages of gay men.* New York: Plume/Penguin.

Skelton, C. 2000. "A Passion for football": Dominant masculinities and primary schooling. *Sport, Education and Society.* 5 (1): 5 - 18.

Smith, J. K., and Deemer, D. K. 2002. The problem of criteria in the age of relativism. N. K. Denzin and Y. S. Lincoln (eds) *Handbook of qualitative research* (2nd ed). Thousand Oaks, CA: Sage Publications. pp. 877 - 896

Walton, M. 2007. *The experience of regular exercise participation for women moving into their middle years: Its nature, meaning and benefits.* PhD. thesis, University of Central Lancashire, Preston.

Wellard, I. 2002. Men, sport, body performance and the maintenance of 'exclusive masculinity'. *Leisure Studies.* 21: 235 - 247

Whitson, D 1990. Sport in the social construction of masculinity. M.A. Messner and D.F. Sabo (eds). *Sport, men, and the gender order: Critical feminist perspectives.* Champaign, Human Kinetics. pp. 19 - 29

Wilkins, D. 2001. Promoting weight loss in men aged 40 - 45: The `Keeping It Up' campaign. N. Davidson and T. Lloyd (eds). *Promoting men's health: A guide for practitioners.* London: Bailliere Tindall. pp. 131 - 138

CHAPTER TEN

WHAT HAVE WE DONE
AND WHERE SHOULD WE GO?

YANIV PORIA AND NEIL CARR

Introduction

This chapter begins with a revision of the book's main contributions to tourism and leisure research. Specifically, some of the commonly taken for granted assumptions made by scholars in tourism research and challenged by the studies presented here, are discussed. Following that an attempt is made to provide a theoretical framework based on the roles sex and sexual desire play in tourism and leisure. Finally the chapter opens up new directions of research (research topics as well as research epistemologies). It is hoped that this chapter will encourage further studies on a component which is essential to the understanding of people's leisure and tourist experiences; namely sex and sexual desire. It is argued that sex and the sexual should play a part in the academic discourse, especially if we wish to describe what is actually happening out there as far as tourism and leisure are concerned.

The book's contribution

Sex and the sexual during people's leisure and tourism experiences contributes to the literature on leisure and tourism in several ways. The first of these stems from the fact that there is now a place where studies centring almost solely on sex and the sensual in tourism and leisure, and not on sex tourism alone, are gathered together. It is surprising that such a meaningful topic, essential to the understanding of contemporary, as well as historic, tourism and leisure as social phenomena, is not yet a part of academic discourse in either the tourism or leisure fields. With almost all introductory books on tourism studies discussing the four S's; namely sun, sand, sea, and sex, the absence of sex from tourism journals and books aiming to contribute to theory development raises fundamental questions on current research in tourism. The fact that the word "sex" is not part of the academic vocabulary in tourism research, while gender is, is highly problematic and should put into question the content validity of tourism studies. One explanation for this could be the desire of scholars to visibly contribute to an existing theory, resulting in scholastic ignorance of issues that are fundamental to the social reality of tourism. Researchers become involved in studies through which they can demonstrate their cultural capital and their multilayered thinking. The investigation of mundane activities (e.g., having sex and eating), however, is not regarded as sophisticated enough. For example, the literature is abundant with studies dealing with sustainable tourism (there is even a journal dedicated to this topic), but very few studies have focused on sea-and-sun vacations. This book argues that sex should play a part in the academic discourse, especially if we wish to describe what is actually happening as far as tourism is concerned. Another possibility (outlined in Ch 1) is that tourism and leisure academics have not touched the issue of sex because they have preferred to focus on the "moral high ground" and looking at "sex" may undermine the academic credibility of leisure and tourism studies (something already viewed as low) – hence looking at something "credible" like sustainability.

The second contribution of this book rests in the attention given to the human body in the studies presented here. Tourism research in general tends to ignore the human body. Some attention has been given to this topic in studies of the representation of women's and men's bodies in the marketing mix of hotels and tourists destinations (e.g., Marshment, 1997; Oppermann, et al., 1998; Pritchard & Morgan, 2000) but such work is limited compared to the importance of the topic. Conversely, almost all the chapters in this book address the human body and highlight its important role in helping to understand the relationship between sex, tourism, and leisure. Someone reading the existing academic literature may falsely deduce that tourists' bodies have only two organs: the mind and the eyes. Tourists merely think and see (and, based on the literature, also search for authentic experiences); they rarely eat, listen, or smell, let alone have sex. The studies reported in this book demonstrate that tourists have other organs in their body, such as breasts, genitalia and buttocks, which are highly important to the understanding of tourism. In addition, *Sex and the sexual during people's leisure and tourism experiences* reveals that the body, not just the mind, constitutes a factor that affects tourism and leisure behaviours. In this book, the body's needs and desires explain tourist and leisure behaviours. The body dictates individual behaviour; no thought or hesitation is described. There is a desire to touch someone else's body, to expose one's body, to feel other people's bodies, to see other naked people's bodies and sex organs, etc.

The third manner in which this book contributes to the study of tourism and leisure stems from the fact that some of the conclusions of the studies presented here are not in line with the political agenda (i.e., Third wave feminism) to which many scholars presently adhere, an agenda that, in turn, affects their research implementation. For example, López and Broeck reported:

> "However, some of the interviewed—especially those who see themselves as gay, often with a higher educational level—did admit to have the possibility of finding a well-paid job, but they preferred and enjoyed offering their sex services, which affords them sexual gratification while allowing them to make 'a lot of money' in little time."

Such a statement, describing male sex workers, rarely appears in the literature on tourism, as it does not regard sexual intercourse strictly as a power relationship. Additionally, López and Broeck and Córdova-Plaza suggest that gay male sex workers often regard their work as involving a fair exchange, with which they even associate a sense of enjoyment (some scholars while acting as referees would undoubtedly refuse to publish such findings). Their approach, while possibly appearing very politically incorrect in general and in the academic arena in particular, is essential to describe "what is actually happening." Córdova-Plaza and Guthrie raise the idea that it is often the locals who take advantage of the tourists. This thought is novel in tourism studies, which often emphasize how the white rich western male tourist uses and abuses the "other" (Ryan & Hall, 2001). In addition, the studies of Córdova-Plaza and Guthrie further reveal that not only are women subject to exploitation by men, but men are also subject to exploitation by women. Furthermore, Córdova-Plaza's study reports that locals prefer sex tourists to local sex customers, portraying the tourists as the "good guys" in comparison to the locals. It has also been common practice in tourism studies to address heterosexual homophobia towards gay men and lesbians. Visser's study, however, identifies a similar pattern among lesbian women in their consumption of leisure spaces and their attitude towards heterosexual men, heterosexual women, gay men with "straight" appearances, feminine gay men, and even certain groups from within the lesbian population.

The fourth contribution of this book relates to the locations of the studies reported within it. Puar (2002) challenges the fact that research is usually conducted where scholars feel comfortable and in spaces they can easily access. Visser (2003), while addressing "gay landscapes," suggests that studies should be conducted in spaces and locations other than North America and the United Kingdom. It is claimed here that his assertion is relevant for studies of sex in tourism and leisure in general. This book addresses "other" landscapes such as Israel, Dominica, South Africa and Mexico. For example, such studies as conducted by López and Broeck and Córdova-Plaza contribute to the understanding of the conceptualization of what is gay and its links with maleness and power, suggesting that not all men having sex with men are gay. They demonstrate that the role one has in the sexual intercourse (i.e., active vs. passive) is essential in understanding men-to-men sex social constructions. These studies demonstrate the importance of studying both the tourists' home environment and the host environment in order to fully capture and understand the tourist experience.

With specific reference to tourism studies, the fifth contribution of *Sex and the sexual during people's leisure and tourism experiences* is that it places an emphasis on sex during tourism (sex in tourism) rather than focusing solely on sex tourism. Most tourism studies centre on sex tourism taking place between rich white men and young girls or boys, or just "regular" prostitution (e.g., Ryan & Hall, 2001). The studies reported here address more standard forms of sex as well. The major contribution of the focus on sex *in* tourism (and not just on sex tourism) may be the possibility that the collection of studies reported in the book could lead to further research, which may bring sex in tourism out of the closet.

Sex and tourism: A form of dark tourist experience

An attempt is made here based on the material presented in the book chapters which originated from varied research areas and rest on different bodies of knowledge to conceptualize the roles sex and the sexual play in tourism and leisure.

The literature on tourism customarily institutionalizes new tourism subcategories, with one of the most recent of these being dark tourism. Dark tourism is usually understood as an act of travel that is focused on or linked to death, atrocities and tragedies (Timothy & Boyd, 1993). In contrast, it is argued here that leisure and tourist attractions are socio-cultural constructions and, as such, their existence should be understood based on visitors' perception and emotions rather than on the attributes of the space or its presentation (McIntosh, 1999). While dark tourism may be linked to death, its core is behaviours and activities in which we cannot be involved in our home environments unless we do so covertly; in the dark. Sex is one such activity, and it plays a central and substantial role in present-day dark tourism experiences.

A conceptualization of a dark tourist and/or leisured experience should be based on the links between the site's attributes and the tourist's characteristics. The definition suggested here for dark tourism and leisure emphasizes the individual's perception of his or her home social environment, the environment at the destination, and the tourist's individuality. Dark tourism is an experience in which individuals wish to visit a site where they are able to see or do things that are perceived as taboo and/or repulsive in their normal place of residence. If such activities were to take place in the visitors' place of residence, they would happen in the dark, as they jeopardize the individual socially (but not necessarily legally) and are associated with a sense of shame and embarrassment.

Such activities can play a role in mass tourism activities such as visiting Amsterdam to look at prostitutes, going to London's Soho to observe gay men and lesbians gathering and kissing in their leisure spaces or visiting sex shops, or walking along a nudist beach to see naked people. Other behaviours that are still considered sexual dark behaviours include going to see sex shows or participating in wet T-shirt competitions. Other more common examples include travelling with the aim of having sex that is socially (rather than legally) unacceptable in the tourist's home environment. This may include having sex in ways and forms that are considered socially unacceptable in one's home environment (e.g., dressing in non-normative ways, etc.). This may also include anal sex or oral sex with one's partner, if this is considered socially unacceptable in one's home environment, or, for same-sex couples, kissing in public. Other less common sexual dark experiences could be going to darkrooms (places where one can have sex but all forms of talk are forbidden), watching BDSM or participating in it, or going to swinger clubs.

To further exemplify the role sex may play in dark tourism experiences a visit to a sex museum is discussed here. It is argued that visiting the museum may constitute cultural tourism (for those who wish to learn about sex and the sexual) or heritage tourism (for those whose group's sexual rituals are presented at the museum). However, for others the visit may constitute a dark tourism experience. The museum allows its visitors to look at pictures of sex organs, see and touch vibrators and dildos, or see sex films in public and in the light, together with other visitors. Moreover, the museum allows its visitors to do so in public and watch other people doing it. To conclude, as sex and fulfilling sexual desire are things people often cannot do freely in their home environments such activities are part of the dark experience that tourism, which takes place within a liminal space, can host.

It is speculated here that the media may affect people's sexual dark experiences, as sex and dark sex in particular can be easily observed. Using the internet, almost everything can be observed in the safety and privacy of one's own home, thwarting the possible social dangers. As indicated by Carr and Taylor in relation to sex shop buying patterns, you can currently purchase sexual dark experiences from your own private home with no social danger. One outcome of the fact that people can watch different forms of sex (including dark sex) is that dark tourism may be based more on touching, smelling, tasting, and feeling. Another issue of importance to the understanding of the place of sex and the sexual in dark tourism or dark leisure is that sex and the sexual are available in geographical proximity; it is everywhere, including the High Street. There is no need to go to a sex shop to buy unique lingerie as it can now be found in some of the most prestigious high street clothing shops. Additionally, sex shops themselves are moving closer to the High Street. The fact that sex can be seen easily via the internet as well as its presence in the high-street means that as sex and the sexual come to light, the roles they play in people's dark experiences may diminish. Travel will continue to be composed of sex, and sex will continue to be a motive for travel, but it may no longer be such a dark experience.

Directions for future research

Sex and the sexual during people's leisure and tourism experiences does not aim to bridge the gap that currently exists in the literature, as "bridging the gap" implies that there are only a few elements missing to complete the picture. Rather, in this book we propose that there is a need to start painting the picture. We have no doubt that sex during leisure and tourism (including sex tourism) and the sexual will all play major roles in tourism and leisure studies in the future and here we wish to offer a few possible directions for future research. We set out to highlight research that can contribute to the understanding of tourism and leisure as social phenomena, and study the significance and impact of people's sexual behaviours during tourism and leisure.

Future studies must examine people who have sexual experiences during their tourist experience (possibly all tourists). Additionally, to determine the importance of sex in tourism, the focus should expand from the sex industry to sex in tourism in general (sex tourism is only one component of sex in tourism). Only such studies could clarify the role and significance of sex and the sexual in people's travel and leisure. Studies that centre on sex in tourism could assist the management of people's leisure and tourists' experiences. For example, such research could assist hotel managers in providing their customers with an atmosphere and environment conducive to their involvement in sexual activities, which may be the central reason for going on vacation.

Studying sex shop websites, as in the chapter by Carr and Taylor, constitutes an important step to understanding these fascinating shopping activities, which have been almost ignored in the marketing literature. However, there is also a need to interview people so as to understand their actual consumption experience as well as their perception of that experience. Note that many more common service encounters and consumption experiences include sexual components in them. Research should explore, for example, the role of sex and the sexual in services in which there is a physical contact with the service provider, such as massage or hair dressing. Additionally, the possibility that sex and the sexual may play a role in more mainstream service activities such as service in restaurants or banking should be clarified.

It is claimed here, and also based on the studies presented in this book, that we know more about commercial sex and sex involving payment than we do about sex that is not part of a financial or quasi-financial transaction. Additionally, a review of the literature suggests that research about sex behaviours focuses more on the gay and lesbian population than on the heterosexual population. This is not to say that researchers should stop studying minority groups or to claim that studies aiming to reveal the power distribution in society and its effects on sex tourism and child abuse are not important socially or theoretically. Nonetheless, there is also a need to study mainstream activities. Consequently, the heterosexual couple should exist as an active research field in the academic arena. The mainstream should be part of the discourse. The concept of the "dirty weekend," coined by Pritchard and Morgan (2006) to describe couples' weekend vacations, should also be studied. It is true that such studies may be regarded among scholars as less sophisticated or less prestigious and are not in line with the feminist research agenda. However, if as scholars we aim to create knowledge, the heterosexual population should not be ignored. Such studies are also highly important for the management of tourism, leisure and hospitality and should be integrated into courses in tourism and hospitality academic programs.

Further research should identify the role of sex as a motivator and highlight its impact on people's travel and leisure experiences. Such research should focus on the phenomenology of tourists' and leisure people's sexual behaviour, clarifying the nexus between social reality and sexual behaviour, linking sex to the actual tourism and leisure experience. Such exploratory research should also identify the effects of sex on people's satisfaction with various forms of travel and leisure. This research is essential for the understanding of today's tourism and leisure experiences. It is also argued that the importance of such research will grow as, due to people's lifestyles, sex will play an increasingly central role in tourists' experiences. However, it should be noted that sex and its presence can also be a barrier to visiting destinations or leisure spaces. For example, the findings arising from Visser's study suggest that the presence of darkrooms sometimes prevented gay women from visiting certain locations. Future studies should examine when and how sex and the sexual acts a motivator or a barrier/constraint for leisure and tourism.

The introductory chapter stated that sex is something individuals are involved in because they enjoy it. Sex has been linked to notions such as "feeling good," "fun," and "pleasure and entertainment" (Gini, 2006). Like many other human behaviours, there is no reason to believe that humans are involved in it only for their enjoyment. Based on some of the studies presented in this book, it can be argued that sex should not be seen only as fun, leisure, and entertainment. The findings show that having sex is also a "must do" activity, in which tourists feel obliged to be involved. Additionally, according to testimonies by Israeli backpackers, having sex with the locals constitutes another way of getting to know the host. Future studies should elaborate on this issue. Is having sex with a local another thing tourists *have* to do while travelling (like seeing famous tourist attractions); does it add to the authenticity of the tourism experience? Such studies could further highlight the nexus between sex, the sexual, and tourism, possibly revealing that sex is not only about desire but also a social obligation or ritual.

The studies in this book almost all centre on the tourism experience or leisure experience themselves. The studies attempt to describe "what is going on." This is a common approach in tourism studies in general, highlighting the actual experiences or the reasons why people are involved in such experiences, but ignoring their influence on the tourist. For example, most studies focus on the reasons for visiting heritage attractions or attempt to quantify the quality of the visit, but almost no studies centre on the impact on the visitor. Future studies should go one step further and study the effects of sexual behaviour during a tourist experience and following that tourist experience. Studies should examine how the sex someone has during his or her travels as a tourist impacts that tourist's life and "self" upon returning to his or her home environment. For example, has the fact that someone has had the opportunity to fulfil aspects of her sexuality that were lacking in her home environment, contributed to her well-being? Has it provided her with a sense of existential authenticity (Wang, 1999), which has in turn empowered her? How does the fact that a woman has had the opportunity to be exposed to new social norms as far as her sex life is concerned affect her perception of herself as a woman and/or individual? How has this woman's sexual experience during travel affected her sex life at home? Does a visit to a sex museum where vibrators and ancient sex toys are presented have an effect on people's sense of legitimacy to use sex toys? The clarification of such research questions may help to capture the significance of tourism in modern-day people's lives, a research area that has been virtually ignored in tourism studies to date.

In their study, Carr and Taylor indicate that sex shops that target women try to market a different experience and atmosphere than do sex shops that target heterosexual males. The assumption is that women's views on sex differ from men's. In their study, while referring to shops such as SH!, they argue that these shops try to appear more romantic and gentle, attempting to provide women with a safe social arena for shopping. Carr and Taylor's findings are not in line with Berdychevsky, et al's study of Israeli women's travel experiences, which indicates that women are also interested (but not strictly) in sex per se, to which no romantic feelings are attached. Specifically, Berdychevsky, et al. claim that women, in their backpacking experiences, use men to fulfil their sexual desires. The interviewees in their study testified to wanting to have sex to which no feelings are attached. Future research should clarify, if possible, whether women have no monolithic desires (which could be true of men as well), but rather context-oriented desires as far as sex is concerned.

Another possible area of research is to identify the factors and elements that cause or prevent people from practicing irresponsible sex, meaning sex activities that could harm their health, or that of other people, during their leisure and/or tourism experiences. Such a line of research, attempting to clarify the reasons or factors that prevent individuals from participating in sexual behaviours that could endanger them (and others) may be important for health policy-making. Studies in health-related journals (e.g., Clift & Forrest, 1999; Clift, et al., 2002; Hawkes & Hart, 1993) indicate that people's sexual behaviours during leisure times, and specifically during their travel, are often dangerous and may account for the spread of sexually-transmitted diseases worldwide. Such studies indicate that tourism is one of the causes behind the spread of the HIV epidemic as well as other sexually-transmitted diseases. Studies that clarify what factors cause tourists to become involved during their leisure time in behaviours that they themselves identify and consider as dangerous to their own health could generate knowledge of importance to securing public health.

People's interactions with gay men and lesbians can serve to minimize and reduce prejudice. Scholars relying on Contact Hypothesis Theory regard tourism and travel as ways of resolving conflicts between groups of people (Reisinger & Turner, 2003). An issue that was not investigated in this book, however, and is of tremendous importance is the impact of visits by homophobic heterosexuals to spaces where they can be exposed to gay men and lesbians touching one another and expressing physical affection. It is argued here that such experiences, based on Contact Hypothesis Theory, may be useful in changing people's attitudes towards gay men and lesbians, allowing homophobic heterosexuals the chance to interact with gay men and lesbians. An example of one such possible study may be the effects of visits to gay and lesbian leisure spaces by parents of gay men and lesbians, whose children recently informed them as to their sexual orientations. This line of research could produce a study that would significantly influence people's quality of life. Nonetheless, there is a need to recognize that such visitation patterns may have major negative effects on gay and lesbian leisure spaces, as the heterosexual gaze could disturb the locals (Hughes, 2006; Skeggs, 1999). However, if managed responsibly, the benefits may outweigh the negative impact of these visits.

Visser's research dealing with lesbian women's leisure spaces and Jones and McCarthy's study about gay male amateur football players suggest that not all gay men and lesbian women are interested in being with people of their sexual orientation. Moreover, some prefer not to be part of the "mainstream" gay and lesbian scenes at all. The same pattern of findings demonstrated in these studies was found in the hotel experiences of gay men and lesbians (Poria, 2006). Future studies should concentrate on the visitation patterns of gay men and lesbians to gay-friendly leisure spaces; however, such studies should also explore who avoids visiting these spaces and the reasons for these behaviours. Moreover, and in line with Visser's study on lesbian women's leisure spaces, research should further clarify whether homophobia, lesbophobia, and hetrophobia are relevant to understanding gay and lesbian people's leisure behaviours.

The study by Visser of white gay women's leisure spaces presents conclusions rarely voiced in literature on leisure and tourism, contradicting most current researchers' political agendas. It is common to highlight the power of heterosexual society and its ways of oppressing gay men and lesbian women. Studies (e.g., Harper & Schneider, 2003) even refer to feelings such as disgust and fear of the "other" when referring to heterosexual oppression of gay men and lesbians. Moreover, this heterosexual oppression is adopted as a rationale for justifying the existence of leisure spaces and accommodation open strictly to gay men and lesbians (discriminating the heterosexual population due to their sexual orientation). However, Visser's study clearly identifies that there is hate and even disgust amongst lesbian women towards the heterosexual population (which they see as weird), heterosexual men (who want to hit on them, join them for threesomes, or have sex with them in order to change their sexual orientation), heterosexual women (who treat them arrogantly), straight-acting gay men (because they feel they could support any leisure space), over-effeminate gay men (who are irritating), and even subgroups of the lesbian population (such as butch lesbians or the dykes who they watch out for). The conclusion of Visser's study is that lesbian women prefer being with people like them. It can be argued based on Visser's findings that during leisure time, if aiming to enjoy ourselves, it is essential for us to feel safe and protected. For this to happen, tourists and leisured people wish to be with people like them, exactly like them. Note that this can be linked to the concept and notion of freedom, which is essential to the understanding of leisure and tourism (Carr 2002; Poria, et al., 2007). Future research should elaborate and clarify whether, when during leisure and really wanting to enjoy ourselves, we become racist and egocentric as these feelings serve our sense of safety and freedom.

The studies presented in this book reveal an often neglected issue; namely the service provider's body. Scholars (in tourism and marketing alike) rarely refer to or study the service provider's physical attributes, even though these may be at the core of the service experience. The importance of the human body has been briefly mentioned in reference to beautyism and in literature dealing mainly with people with disabilities. Córdova-Plaza addresses the size of the genitalia (the bigger the better), the service provider's age (young), and his or her appearance (the more sex workers differ from their customers and resemble the imagined local stereotypes, the better – i.e., the exotic "other"). The issue of the human body's appearance was also found to be of importance to understanding Israeli women's sexual behaviour during their backpacking experiences. They voiced preferences for men that looked different from Israeli men. Future research should elaborate on this matter and further explore preferences for the (service provider's) body in tourism and leisure. Additionally, more attention should be given to the human body as a motivator for travel and leisure desires and experiences. Are the bodies of locals in general (men's and women's alike), and their naked bodies in particular, something that visitors wish to observe, something by which they wish to be touched or to touch, or even something on which they wish to fantasize. For example, studies on massages given for non-health purposes suggest that sex fantasies are part of the service experience (Poria, 2006). Is the different appearance of the locals' part of the present-day tourist experience? Note that such studies could result in the discrimination of employees in organizations that cater to tourists, based on their looks. Thus, scholars should take the implications of their research into account.

Finally, it is claimed here, not apolitically, that in the literature, due to current trends, we almost completely ignore certain types of travel as well as motivations for travel, as they are not seen as sophisticated enough. This ignorance is not confined to sex alone. As scholars, we know more about heritage tourism and green tourism than we do about city breaks or sea-and-sun vacations. We know much about the visitation patterns to the British Museum, but we ignore the fact that it is a must-see attraction where there is no entrance fee and the toilets can be used for free (a very human yet unsophisticated reason to visit a museum). Someone reading the academic literature may get the impression that tourists are not travelling with the aim of "doing nothing." Based on the series of studies presented in this book, we call on scholars to also study less sophisticated travel patterns. In such travel patterns, not only is there no quest for authenticity, the tourists' even attempt to avoid it and this should not be classified in a demeaning way.

Changes in the methodological approach

The studies reported in this book tackle fundamental issues that are linked to the execution of research concerning people's sexual behaviour in tourism and leisure. First, the studies conducted demonstrate that an experientially-based approach should be adopted. To understand sexual behaviour in tourism (as well as sex tourism), one must study the interactions between the tourists' place of residence and the tourist environment. For example, Israel is seen as a place where people are highly familiar with one another, and so, in the search for anonymity and self, one has to travel far away. The studies dealing with Mexico present a different construction of homosexuality and masculinity relative to that commonly adopted in the Western world. A gay man is not a man who has sex with men; rather, one must be penetrated to be considered gay. In light of the above, it is clear that the execution of future research should include attempts to obtain a clear understanding of the local culture as well as the tourist environment, relating to the social construction of sex and the sexual, as these are fundamental to the understanding of the role sex plays in tourism.

It is clear from the collection of studies presented in this book that cross-cultural research is needed for the sake of understanding the mechanisms of sex and the sexual within tourism and leisure. For example, as highlighted in the chapter by Ambrosie those who wish to influence policy-making so as to prevent child prostitution and their exploitation by tourists need to compare the regulations of spaces and power distribution in various locations where child sexual abuse can be found. Such studies could provide knowledge not only on the regulations and the role of power distribution, but also on the evolution and development of sex tourism. In addition, this type of research could assist in understanding how certain locations and tourist destinations become hosts to sex tourism while other destinations do not. Conducting such cross-cultural research would benefit our understanding of why "Canada spends more money investigating stolen cars and credit cards which are already insured, than on investigation of sexual predators" (Ambrosie). Note that such studies may reveal that other Western countries act like Canada. Additionally, Berdychevsky's study is based on Israeli Jewish participants who are living in an environment affected by Judeo-Christian values. Research with participants from Asia who do not follow such values systems may suggest that sex and the sexual play a different role in their tourist experiences (as well as daily life).

There is a need to speak with the "devils" as well. Researchers must integrate the sex tourists (or the "users" or even "sex predators," if researching sexploitations) into their studies and grant them a voice if aiming to undermine the exploitation of the subordinate "other" by the sex industry. Such studies may be problematic and challenging as far as research approval is concerned. Nonetheless, only such studies can lead to a clear and constructive understanding that could aid those who, through their academic work, wish to prevent or minimize sexual abuse in tourism and leisure.

It is common to highlight power relation distributions in society, arguing that international tourists are using and abusing the local population in general and sex workers in particular. This abuse has often been linked with capitalism or masculinity. However, the findings presented in this book, specifically by the studies on sex workers in Mexico, challenge this line of thought. It is argued here that while possibly appearing politically incorrect and contrasting with current conceptualizations of the host-guest relationship, as currently described in the literature, it is essential to describe "what is going on out there." This is especially necessary if researchers and scholars wish to ensure that their body of knowledge will have a beneficial effect on reality.

The studies presented in this book have adopted different research epistemologies, resulting in the adoption of different research strategies. It is argued here that the research strategy to be utilized should depend on the research question. Note that people's sexual behaviour has been studied in the fields of psychology, sociology, anthropology, geography, and health, in many different ways and forms. Nonetheless, when adopting a quantitative research approach, tools such as scales and measures need not be adopted automatically, but only following exploratory research.

Most studies in this book attempt to describe findings that also relate to the visual. The visual is composed of everything that we see, a term not confined to brochures, advertising billboards, TV advertisement, or postcards, which commonly serve as subjects for research in tourism (Burns & Lester, 2005) but are often ignored by the tourists themselves. Moreover, in some of the studies presented in this book the understanding of the visual lies at the core of the study. Studies here relate to issues such as: the human body, gender performativity, and descriptions of leisure spaces. This means that the visual should play an important role in data collection. Additionally, in studies where there is a need to paint a picture for the readers the visual should be incorporated in the findings section as well as the literature review section. In the context of the studies reported in this book, for example, it would have been valuable to provide a picture of a macho man in Mexico or a picture of a gay women's club in South Africa, on which the studies centred, as these images lie at the cores of the studies. Such visual evidence would facilitate the readers' understanding of the social worlds addressed by the studies. Nevertheless, such visual evidence should be carefully selected, and the researcher should explain the reasoning for his selection, as the researcher's positioning could affect the visual evidence presented, which would in turn affect the readers. Moreover, there is also a call to include information about issues of taste, smell, and touch when researching the sexual and sex, as arguably these are vital senses (and not just for sex and the sexual) ones that have hardly been touched upon either by the chapters of this book or any other research on sex in tourism or leisure.

We live in an age of increasing concern about ethical standards and guidelines that is driven at least as much by the desire of institutions to avoid litigation as to ensure the physical and emotional safety of the individual. Yet arguably fear of litigation should not preclude the undertaking of academically justified research. However, at the same time, the creation of academic knowledge cannot be used as justification for the undertaking of research that potentially causes harm to the individual. Furthermore, it is naïve and unfair to expect researchers to undertake research which may open them to litigation. All of these ethical issues are highly relevant within the context of sex and the sexual and the suggested future research areas identified in this chapter. The sensitivity of people and society to open discussions of sex and the sexual necessitates the careful handling of research in this field in a manner that benefits all those involved, both directly and indirectly. This is especially the case with regards to some of the vulnerable groups (i.e., minors, sexual minorities, and prostitutes) that arguably need to be actively involved in the research identified throughout this book. In this context the safety (emotional and physical) of participants and researchers should be the ethical priority. By ensuring this institutional ethical codes/ panels can become conduits for ethical research rather than potential barriers to valid research that should be conducted on sex and the sexual in the tourism and leisure experience.

References

Burns, P., and Lester, J. A. 2005. Using visual evidence: The case of cannibal tours. B. W. Ritchie, P. Burns and C. Palmer (eds). *Tourism research methods: Integrating Theory with practice*. Wallingford: CABI Publishing. pp. 49 - 61

Carr, N. 2002. The tourism-leisure behavioural continuum. *Annals of Tourism Research*. 29 (4): 972 - 986

Clift, S. and Forrest, S. 1999. Factors associated with gay men's sexual orientation and risk holiday. *Aids Care*. 11 (3): 281 - 295

Clift, S., M. Loungo, and Callister, C. 2002. *Gay tourism: Culture, identity and sex*. London: Continuum

Gini, A. 2006. *Why it's hard to be good?* New York: Routledge

Harper, G. W. and Schneider, M. 2003. Oppression and discrimination among lesbians, gay, bisexual and transgendered people and communities: A challenge for community psychology. *American Journal of community Psychology*. 31 (3/4): 243 - 252

Hawkes, S. J. and Hart, G. J. 1993. Travel, migration and HIV. *AIDS Care*. 5 (2): 207 - 214

Hughes, H. L. 2006. *Pink tourism: Holidays of gay men and lesbians*. Oxfordshire: CAB International

McIntosh, A. J. 1999. Into the tourist's mind: Understanding the value of the heritage experience. *Journal of Travel and Tourism Marketing*. 8 (1): 41 - 64

Marshment, M. 1997. Gender takes a holiday: Representation in holiday brochures. M. T. Sinclair (ed). *Gender, work and tourism*. London: Routledge. pp. 16 – 34

Oppermann, M., McKinley, S. and Chon, K-S. 1998. Marketing sex and tourism destinations. M. Oppermann (ed). *Sex tourism and prostitution: Aspects of leisure, recreation, and work*. New York: Cognizant Communication Corporation. pp. 20 – 29

Poria, Y. 2006. Assessing gay men and lesbian women's hotel experiences: An exploratory study of sexual orientation in the travel industry. *Journal of Travel Research*. 44 (3): 328 - 334

Poria, Y. R. Butler., and Airey, D. 2007. Understanding tourism – Memorable moments in a complex timeframe. *Asian Journal of Tourism and Hospitality Research*. 1 (1): 25 - 38

Pritchard, A. and Morgan., N. J. 2000. Privileging the male gaze: Gendered tourism landscape. *Annals of Tourism Research*. 27 (4): 889 - 905

Pritchard, A. and Morgan, N. J. 2006. Hotel Babylon? Exploring hotels as liminal sites of transition and transgression. *Tourism Management*. 27 (5): 762-772.

Puar, J. 2002. A translational feminist critique of queer tourism. *Antipode*. 35 (5): 935 - 946

Reisinger, Y. and Turner, L. W. 2003. *Cross-cultural behaviour in tourism: Concepts and analysis*. Oxford: Butterworth-Heinemann

Ryan, C. and Hall, C. M. 2001. *Sex tourism: Marginal people and liminalities*. London: Routledge

Skeggs, B. 1999. Matter out of place: Visibility and sexuality in leisure spaces. *Leisure Studies*. 18 (3): 213 - 232

Timothy, D. and Boyd. S. 2003. *Heritage tourism*. Harlow: Prentice Hall

Visser, G. 2003. Gay men, tourism and urban spaces: Reflections on Africa's gay capital. *Tourism Geographies*. 5 (2): 168 - 189

Wang, N. 1999. Rethinking authenticity in tourism experience. *Annals of Tourism Research*. 41: 348 - 354

CONTRIBUTORS

Linda Ambrosie is a Certified General Accountant and PhD Candidate in accounting at the Haskayne School of Business, University of Calgary, Canada with a special interest in tourism policy, public finance and sustainability measures. Her dissertation reviews tourism, taxation and sustainability in Mexico to propose full-cost measures of genuine progress. Email: lambrosi@ucalgary.ca

Liza Berdychevsky is a Ph.D. student in the Department of Tourism, Recreation and Sport Management at the University of Florida. Her research interests are located at the intersection of gender and tourism, focusing on female tourist experience, motivations and constraints, liminoid effect, existential authenticity and sexual behaviour in tourism. Email: liza@hhp.ufl.edu

Anne Marie Van Broeck (PhD Social and Cultural Anthropology) teaches Tourism and Culture at the Master in Tourism Program of the Consortium Catholic University, Leuven, Belgium. She has conducted several research projects on tourism, particularly from an anthropological perspective, with a strong professional interest in Latin America. Her key interests are sex and tourism, literature and film tourism, cruise tourism and tourism and conflict (including armed conflict). She is also an independent researcher and consultant. Email: amvanbroeck@skynet.be

Neil Carr is an Associate Professor in the Tourism Department at the University of Otago, New Zealand. His research focuses on aspects of leisure and tourism behaviour including sex and alcohol consumption. In particular, Neil's research is focused on young people, university students, children, families, and non-humans (particularly dogs) and their owners. Neil has published over 35 peer-reviewed papers in a variety of academic journals and edited books and supervised over 20 PhD students. Email: neil.carr@otago.ac.nz

Deirdre Guthrie teaches International Studies, Gender, and Anthropology at the University of Illinois, Chicago. Other examples of her ethnographic work have been published in the *Chicago Reader, Village Voice, Z,* and *Mother Jones* magazines. Email: vamosnina@aol.com

Louisa Jones is a Senior Lecturer in the School of Sport, Tourism and The Outdoors at the University of Central Lancashire, UK. In 2005, she instigated a longitudinal research study exploring the growth and development of amateur gay football clubs in the UK. Louisa serves as an adviser to The Football Association and the European Gay and Lesbian Sports Federation on their strategies for tackling homophobia in football and is a member of the steering group establishing The National Lesbian, Gay, Bi-sexual and Transgender Sports Network. Email: LMJones@uclan.ac.uk

Álvaro López López has a PhD in Geography from the Universidad Nacional Autónoma de México (UNAM) and was a postdoctoral fellow in Tourism and Environment at the University of Waterloo, Canada. He is a researcher at the Instituto de Geografía, UNAM. His research focuses on spatial analysis of tourism: coastal, urban, natural protected areas, and male sex tourism in Mexico. He is currently president of the Academia Mexicana de Investigación Turística (Mexican Academy of Tourism Research: http://www.amiturismo.org/). Email: lopuslopez@yahoo.com.mx

Mac McCarthy is a senior lecturer at the University of Central Lancashire and an Associate Lecturer with the Open University. Mac is currently examining the responses of premier division football clubs to the FA strategy on homophobia and perspectives on the gay holocaust. Mac has worked as an independent management consultant, with a client base in the public and private sector throughout Western and Eastern Europe, as well as in Canada and Thailand. Email: mmccarthy1@uclan.ac.uk

Rosío Córdova Plaza is a Research Fellow at the Institute for Socio-Historical Research at the Universidad Veracruzana, México. Her research interest deals with gender, sexuality, male prostitution, family and migration, focusing on societies in central Veracruz. She has received the Mexican Senate Special Award for the best essay on the Independence War, and the "Helen I. Safa" award from the Latin American Studies Association. Her book *Migración internacional, crisis agrícola y transformaciones culturales en la región central de Veracruz* received the honorific mention of the Bernardino de Sahagún award for the best anthropological research of 2009. Email: rosiocordova@hotmail.com

Yaniv Poria is an Associate Professor at the Department of Hotel and Tourism Management, Guilford Glazer School of Business and Management, Ben-Gurion University of the Negev, Israel. His main research interest is people experience at heritage settings as well as the conceptualization of heritage tourism. Additionally, he studies groups usually ignored in the tourism literature, among them the gay and lesbian population and people with disabilities. Email: YPoria@som.bgu.ac.il

Steve Taylor is a PhD candidate at the University of Otago, New Zealand. His research interests focus on adventure recreation, exploring issues such as motivation, risk versus thrill, and factors influencing destination decision-making. His research has been presented to the *Leisure Studies Association* and published in *Annals of Leisure Research*. Email: steve.taylor@otago.ac.nz

Natan Uriely is an Associate Professor at the Department of Hotel and Tourism Management at Ben-Gurion University, Israel. He specializes in the sociology of tourism and his work spreads across various topics, such as the tourist experience, backpacking, deviance and tourism, risk and terror in tourism and guest-host contact. Uriely´s studies are published in leading tourism journals, including Annals of Tourism Research, Journal of Travel Research and Tourism Management. Email: urielyn@som.bgu.ac.il

Gustav Visser is Professor of Human Geography at the University of the Free State, South Africa. His key research interests relate to the tourism and development nexus, as well as the role of gay leisure space consumption in urban morphological change. In the recent past he has co-edited (with Christian M. Rogerson) two collections of essays focused on tourism development in the developing south. His latest co-edited book (in collaboration with Lochner Marais) is titled *Spatialities of Urban Change*. Email: visserge@ufs.ac.za